THE KING STRANG STORY

Best wishes from the author of this unique history of Strang's vanished kingdom —

Doyle C Fitzpatrick

The King Strang Story offers proof that most of the derogatory statements written about James J. Strang and his stormy career on Beaver Island, will not bear critical scrutiny.

"Come away to the floods and the fields, the flower banks and the forest — out HERE, in open space and free air, where sea and earth and sky mingle in mutual embraces, like the greeting of youthful lovers! Listen to the pine-songs which are chants of praise, and the wind-warbles which are hymns of hallelujah! Look up yonder on the fire-dance of innumerable rolling worlds, and then answer me before the sun and all the stars — "Is there no God?"

James J. Strang

From the Gospel Herald
April 26, 1849

FROM COLLECTION OF THE AUTHOR

JAMES JESSE STRANG

As he appeared on Beaver Island between the years 1854-1856.

The portrait on glass from which this was reproduced may have been presented by Strang to his third polygamous wife, Sarah Adelia Wright Strang, in 1855, perhaps as a wedding gift.

To
James Jesse Strang

Preface

It has been said that all men are historians. Human historical endeavor, honestly recorded, should serve as a basis for factual research. It should, therefore, be true history, a combined recording of events and personal biography. Doing both honestly and accurately is a major accomplishment, indeed.

There is no guarantee this accomplishment will benefit posterity. The result is sifted by public opinion. "Truth shall prevail" is wishful thinking in recorded history. If the public doesn't like the truth they often write their own history. Beaver Island historical events of mid and late 19th century are impressive examples.

A great amount of unfavorable public opinion about the Beaver Island Mormons was moulded by 19th century feature writers from semi-truths and fabrications gleaned from completely biased Gentiles who hated them. They colored their mock research toward one goal: selling their literary works. Tabloid editors bred this type of writer to guarantee active circulation. Facts merely complicated the whole operation of making money.

Perhaps the prime Michigan victim of 19th century character assassination, brought about through the unwholesome mass of inaccurate writings, was James Jesse Strang. To this day, careless research and biased reporting continue to create warped documentation of Strang and his 1847-1856 Beaver Island Mormon Kingdom of God.

Interest in local and personal Michigan history has never been greater than it is today. Pioneers apparently began taking a serious interest more than a hundred years ago. During the past decade, a marked increase has presented itself. Prior to 1850, wilderness pioneers in Michigan worked long and hard to insure a decent existence. While conscious of their future and aware of Michigan's great natural resources, the real concern within family groups had to be food, clothing and shelter.

James Strang left a quantity of manuscripts and correspondence worthy of research. However, this historical accumulation has been shamefully neglected for many years, resulting in a warped interpretation of his life and time. The present writer hopes to disturb historians and the public toward recognizing the good qualities of this remarkable man, one of the most unique personalities of 19th century America.

"The King Strang Story" is devoted to the vindication of Strang as a man and a sincere public servant. His early contributions to the State of Michigan have long been unrecognized. Lack of recognition today is due to 120 years of disrespect by a misinformed public. Historically, the name of James Jesse Strang represents a mistrusted tyrant. There is every proof that he was not, that he actually was morally excellent, honorable in principle and a dedicated servant concerned with our national human welfare and a genuine concern for his Saintly flock on Beaver Island.

Prior to the "The King Strang Story," no individual outside the church itself, has deliberately and publicly championed Strang as a man of good quality.

Strang loved books and freedom. As early as 1834, the following notation appeared in his diary:

Preface

> "Today for once I shed tears! Aye, tears of distress: of deep heart felt distress. The halls of the British Parliament with their Libraries and their documents, sacred to the freedom and the greatness of our ancestors, are burnt to ashes.
>
> "All the works of man are destined to decay. Monuments of greatness and creations of luxury; memorials of antiquity and structures of today: palaces of Princes, Halls of Legislatures and cells of Prisoners, all the works of art and alike, the systems of intellect, fall before the tooth of time. Even the soul-inspiring poetry must die with the language in which it is written. And fame, fame alone, of all the productions of man's folly may survive."

Had the writer championed the public and private life of James Strang by writing a novel about him, perhaps less literary difficulties may have been encountered. Instead, a portion of this work includes reviews of previous publications. This places the writer in a rather uncomfortable position as "critic," but does not indicate skill in judging the literary merits of others.

The primary purpose of this narrative is to set the record straight.

This subject may also have been more entertaining as a novel. The decision to write a historical fault-finder was not easy, and the method may be somewhat unique. To successfully point a critical finger at faulty, erroneous, fabled, untrue and imaginary statements about James Strang demanded thorough reviews of all known important publications written about him.

"The King Strang Story" represents a clearing house for overhauling the 120 year accumulation of historical deception about James Jesse Strang, the Mormon "King."

Strang was a giant of human compassion on this fascinating Lake Michigan paradise known as "Beaver Island."

DOYLE C. FITZPATRICK
SAINT JAMES
BEAVER ISLAND, MICHIGAN

CORONATION DAY
JULY 8, 1970

Table of Contents

Preface	ix
List of Illustrations	xv
Acknowledgment	xvii
Introduction	xix

	PART I	1
Chapter		
I	The Strang Ancestry	3
II	James Strang Formative Years and Introduction to Mormonism	23
III	God and James Strang	29

	PART II	41
Chapter		
IV	A Brief Geographical, Cultural and Economic History of Beaver Island	43
V	Strang Surveys Beaver Island	51
VI	Voree and City of James	65
VII	Beaver Island — 1850	73

TABLE OF CONTENTS, CONT'D.

Chapter			
	VIII	Beaver Island — 1851	81
	IX	Beaver Island — 1852-1853	99
	X	Beaver Island — 1854-1856	109

Epilogue
    The Five Wives and Fourteen Children of James Strang 117

MISCELLANY 135

A Sampling of Strangite Impostures
    George J. Adams and *John C. Bennett*   137
A Sampling of Strangite Defenders
    Bishop George Miller   159
    Wingfield Watson   177
Rescue of a Strang Portrait   189
Strang's Beaver Islanders   191

REVIEWS 197

The King of Beaver Island   199
A History of the Grand Traverse Region   202
Beaver Island and Its Mormon Kingdom   215
A Moses of the Mormons   222
Assassination of the King   227
A Child of the Sea; and Life Among the Mormons   232
The Kingdom of Saint James   252
Crown of Glory   253
The Diary of James J. Strang   257
The Saga of Beaver Island   267
The City of the Saints   276

INDEX 281

List of Illustrations

James Jesse Strang . . . . *(Frontispiece)*	iv
James Strang and Joseph Smith, Jr.	xxi
Joseph Smith's Famous 'Letter of Appointment'	xxv
John Strang Manuscript	13
Clement and Abigail Strang	20
Holy Bible, Book of Mormon, Book of the Law	25
The Voree Heralds	31
The Voree Plates	35
Christopher Latham Sholes	36
Mitchell Map of Michigan (1835)	46
Elvira Field Strang	77
Idyllic Life on Beaver Island	83
The Strang 'Castle' at Saint James	83
Strang's Printshop on Beaver Island	91

Ancient and Modern Michilimackinac	103
The Steamer Michigan	112
Home of Strang's Parents (Voree)	119
Marker on Strang's Grave (Burlington)	119
Bronze Map of Mormon Settlement (Voree)	119
John Baker and Elvira Field Baker	123
Evangeline, Abigail and Gabriel Strang	124
Phineas and Amanda Wright	126
Sarah Wright as Mrs. Strang and Mrs. Wing	129
Four Generations of Sarah Strang Family	129
James Phineas Strang and Eugenia Jesse	130
Hazel Strang McCardell and William H. McCardell	133
Wright Genealogy Chart	134
The Star in the East	154
Mother of George Miller Jr. and Bishop Miller	165
Five Generations of the Miller Family	171
Lorenzo Dow Hickey and Wingfield Watson	179
The Wingfield Watson Pamphlets	186
Daily Northern Islander	209
Holograph Letter of Strang	217
Charles, Clement and James Strang, Jr.	221
James Jesse Strang (portrait used by Legler)	223
American Weekly Sunday Supplement	243
Typical Page from the Diary of James Strang	259
Mark A. Strang and Wife Gertrude	261

Acknowledgment

An author can cite authorities fully and carefully; can originate a theme; can implement new material; and, as in this book, hopefully combine historical accuracy with insight. Beyond these attributes, however, an author needs help.

Grateful *appreciation* must first be accorded Hazel Strang McCardell, granddaughter of James Strang and Sarah Wright, for material, counsel, and suggestions. Her belief in the writer never faltered, always maintaining that "no one could present a more just analysis, be less prejudiced, or write of good and evil with more understanding and clarity, using only the *facts*."

Grateful *appreciation* must also be accorded to Phyllis Fitzpatrick for typing and proofing the manuscript for seven years, while her husband was mentally traveling through the soul of James Strang; and to Marion Hunt, for reading and correcting the typescript and galley proofs every step of the way. Both reached back toward old frontiers. Both knew — as did the writer — there would be little glory in vindicating James Strang, and little pity in failing.

Encouragement and *friendly cooperation* has been very generous. First, sincere thanks to Archibald Hanna, Curator of the

Western Americana Collection of the Beinecke Rare Book and Manuscript Library, Yale University, for assistance in filming, for the first time, a complete record of the largest collection of Strang manuscripts known; to Michigan's Governor, William G. Milliken, for reading the typescript; to Chester Ellison, past President of the Michigan Historical Commission, for supplying original material; to John Cumming, Director of the Clarke Historical Library for material assistance; to Peter Amann, author of "Prophet in Zion: The Saga of George J. Adams"; to Rose and Patrick Bonner of Beaver Island; to Geneva Wiskemann and Donald Chaput of the State Archives, Michigan Historical Commission.

To James C. Totten, Editor, Continuing Education Service, and Madison Kuhn, Professor of History, Michigan State University; to William B. O'Neil, Chairman of the Division of Architectural History, University of Virginia; to Ernest J. Wessen, Antiquarian, former collector-dealer, Mansfield, Ohio; to George L. Egbert, journalist and conservationist; to A. J. Roy, untiring Director of the Beaver Island Museum; to Stanley L. Johnston, staunch supporter in the beliefs of James Strang, after years of agitated controversy; to Anna Strang Bevan and Gail Strang Palmer, grandchildren of Strang; to Charles A. Strange, Vice President of the Bankers Trust Company in New York, whose current genealogical research on the ancestors of James Strang is thorough and documented; to Barbara Drew, granddaughter of Wingfield Watson; to Philip Stirdivant, Don Kuehle, Howard Dekker, John Stephenson, Charles Leneweaver, Rajee Tobia and Ford Ceasar, for indispensable help toward producing a book that honors the literature it perpetuates.

Wright Howes, compiler of rare Americana, may sometime say that *The King Strang Story* is a reservoir of worthy information, to which the writer must add: none of which is the responsibility of those listed in the Acknowledgment.

Introduction

On the "Hill of Cumorah" near Palmyra, New York, began the most controversial period in American religious communal living, now commonly called Mormonism.

A direct quote from the Book of Mormon reveals:

> "The period covered by Book of Mormon annals extended from B.C. 600 to A.D. 421. In or about the latter year, Moroni, the last of the Nephite historians, sealed the sacred record, and hid it up unto the Lord, to be brought forth in the latter days, as predicted by the voice of God through his ancient prophets. In A.D. 1827, this same Moroni, then a resurrected personage, delivered the engraved plates to Joseph Smith."

The publicly disputed birth of Mormonism must not be compared with the high status and heavenly reputation of the present Mormon church factions. Good often emerges from public interpretation of evil. In this respect, the writer fully agrees with the feelings of Franklin Roosevelt, when he wrote the following to Winston Churchill on New Years Day, 1944: "I have a very high opinion of the Mormons, for they are excellent citizens." Adding a line further, he jokingly gave them credit for originating the Good Neighbor Policy.

It must be emphasized that "The King Strang Story" is not concerned with the merits or demerits of Mormonism. Nor is there any desire, whatsoever, toward the slightest religious controversy. This is not meant to be more than a corrective and informative book about the human side of historically important James Jesse Strang, Mormon.

The origin of the Mormon Church appears to have been little more than a semi-religious group of six men, the minimum number to obtain a New York charter, described more accurately, a secret society. The Church reputedly built up its initial membership by encouraging enlistment of hard-working farmers, who preferred being looked after, spiritually, in those troubled times by these six organizers.

In the 1830's, it is probable that many who felt Mormonism born of incredulity also felt it developed into fiction from the visionary parents of Joseph Smith. It was no secret that his father had visions, his seventh when Joseph was 14. Both parents had religious doubts to the point all creeds were considered false. Joseph, not yet 15, claimed he prayed to God for an answer to this question about a true religion. According to him, two heavenly messengers appeared, telling him every religion in the world was corrupt and abominable.

It is very easy to conjecture that young Joseph was greatly impressed by his parents' visions. Young people are susceptible to images during adolescence.

About this same time, Joseph had earthly enemies who felt him to be "unruly and good-for-nothing," according to his mother. She revealed that one of them tried to kill him — that he fired a gun at Joseph, the ball missing him and lodging in a cow's neck.

Most early Mormons were Masons. It should be noted that the Masonic order was not particularly proud of members who treated their teachings so lightly. The American Masonic order also left much to be desired during this period in Masonic history.

JAMES JESSE STRANG — JOSEPH SMITH, JR.

Founder of The Church of Jesus Christ of Latter-day Saints (STRANGITE)

Founder of The Church of Jesus Christ of Latter Day Saints (MORMON)

The Reorganized Church uses the large 'D' with a hyphen, thus: Reorganized Church of Jesus Christ of Latter-Day Saints.

There are infinite numbers of informative books on Mormon history. Readers interested in researching the origin of the Church must choose authors carefully. Church publications are obviously not good sources. Early anti-Mormon books, written purely for the notoriety of the authors, also are poor sources. These narrators, more often than not, ridiculed Joseph Smith personally and attempted to expose his claims as fraudulent.

Very few authors have appreciated the significance of James Strang in Mormon history. William A. Linn wrote an excellent book, "The Story of the Mormons from the Date of Their Origin to the Year 1901." It may possibly be the best general account. However, there is almost a total disregard of the Strangites. Either the source of material was not known to him or he failed to appreciate its significance.

That Joseph Smith, Jr., the projector of Mormonism, was considered by many who knew him as a youth, to be a lazy, careless and insolent person does not, in any way, detract from his being chosen by the power of God to be His earthly Prophet in the flesh. This was true of a few Bible Prophets, as well.

If Joseph Smith, as a youth, was a "money digger," as many who knew him claimed, he had plenty of company. Along the banks of the Hudson River, hope of discovering treasure buried by Captain William Kidd about 1698 made explorers of many. Even to this day, the Hudson banks, the shores of Long Island Sound and Gardiner's Island still beckon a few to find the gold, silver and precious stones entombed by the fabled pirate captain.

John Hyde, an apostate Mormon, claimed, along with many, that Joseph Smith composed the Book of Mormon by expanding the stolen "Manuscript Found," an amateur narrative written by a Rev. Solomon Spalding. This claim has been considered a hoax for many years but must remain, for some, a fascinating mystery for eternity.

From its charter date of April 6, 1830, in the town of Fay-

Introduction

ette, Seneca County, New York, to the infamous assassination day of June 27, 1844, Joseph Smith was the one and only Prophet of God this Mormon group had. Nor have they had one since. James Strang professed succession through his claimed "Letter of Appointment" from Smith and by his claimed revelation from God by angelic messenger. These were ruled fraudulent by Brigham Young. In the end, Young was able, through systematic elimination, to emerge as head of the ruling body of the Mormon Church.

Many important officers of the Nauvoo Church believed Strang to be the rightful successor to the so-called martyred Joseph Smith. John E. Page, one of the Council of Twelve, along with chief Patriarch, William Smith, brother of Joseph, were advocates of Strang. Even President William Marks of the Nauvoo stake subscribed. Of greater interest to those about to examine "The King Strang Story" may be the knowledge that the entire Smith family, except one, subscribed to the claims of Strang. Lucy Smith, mother of the founder, accepted Strang though Emma Hale, whom he called "Daughter of God," did not. Smith married Emma on January 18, 1827. Later she apostatised and married a Gentile.

Perhaps the writer should explain "so-called martyred Joseph Smith." If a religious martyr is one who voluntarily suffers death as the penalty for refusing to renounce his beliefs, then Joseph Smith was not a martyr.

The first Christian to become a martyr was Stephen. He was stoned to death for blasphemy, and was considered a true martyr. Smith, however, though he may have had the "courage of his convictions and did all that mortal man could do to prove to the world that he knew his teachings were true," did not die for them. One of Harper's editors felt that "Joseph Smith was arrested as any culprit might be, and died as any criminal might, and certainly as much against his own will or intention as ever did a felon of greater or less degree at the rash hands of an outraged community."

Brigham Young eventually moved his Saints West to the Valley of the Great Salt Lake. In Utah, for the first time in their history, they were safe. Up to this time, the Mormons were continually harrassed wherever they went. In Utah, they were protected from howling mobs by high mountains and distance. This protection may be the very reason the Mormon Church exists in strength today. To this period, their success had been achieved in spite of violence and persecution. No American religious group ever suffered more hardships and privations and survived in strength. Most of the early violence was apparently brought on by their own behavior, however. Many leaders considered persecution as a blessing in disguise.

It is the studied opinion of this writer that Brigham Young Mormonism owed its dramatic ascendancy, primarily, to isolation. Enemies could not reach them in Utah, as they did in Ohio, Missouri and Illinois. Nor did they have reason to. They removed themselves from Gentile competition, for one thing — Gentile meaning any person other than a Mormon. Such a sweeping over-simplified statement may be considered unfair to those who feel survival due to religious destiny.

It is a further studied belief that the eventual downfall of Strangite Mormonism on Beaver Island was caused principally by their vulnerability. Had founder James Strang taken his saintly flock to a more remote area comparable to the Valley of the Great Salt Lake, rivalry between the factions might well have been very significant.

Had Brigham Young not succeeded in his trek to the Great Valley, Beaver Island may have become the gathering place of the main Mormon body, and the island, today, a great metropolis, welcoming tourists from all over the world to view a magnificent Mormon Temple. Its members would then have followed the doctrines of Joseph Smith and James Strang.

Utah Mormons have a vigorous rival in the present Reor-

> Nauvoo June 18th 1844
>
> My dear son Your epistle of may 24th proposing the planting a stake of zion in wisconsin and the gathering the saints there was duly received & I with most of the brethren whose advise I called in were of opinion that you was deceived by a spirit not of this world great but not good. brother Hyrum however thought otherwise and favored the project not doubting it was of God I however determined to return you an unfavourable answer for the present but oh the littleness of man in his best earthly state not so the will of the Almighty, God hath ruled it otherwise and a message from the throne of grace directed me as it hath inspired you and the faith which thou hast in the shepherd the stone of Israel hath been repaid to thee a thousand fold and thou shalt be like unto him but the flock shall find rest with thee and God shall reveal to thee his will concerning them. I have long felt that my present work was almost done and that I should soon be called to rule a mighty host but something whispers me it will be in the land of spirits where the wicked cease from troubling and the bands of the prisoner fall off my heart yearns for my little ones but I know God will be a father to

COURTESY OF YALE UNIVERSITY LIBRARY

THE FAMOUS 'LETTER OF APPOINTMENT'

Claimed to have been received by Strang at the Burlington, Wisconsin post office after being sent by Joseph Smith from Nauvoo on June 9, 1844.

Section above represents part of first page and section below the final paragraph of the third and final page.

> so spake the Almighty God o, heaven thy duty is made plain and if thou lackest wisdom ask of God in whose hands I trust thee & he will give thee unsparingly for if evil befall me thou shalt lead the flock to pleasant pastures God sustain thee
>
> Joseph Smith.
>
> James J Strang
>
> PS Write me soon & keep me advised of your progress from time to time

" ... *so spake the Almighty God of heaven thy duty is made plain and if thou lackest wisdom ask of God in whose hands I trust thee unsparingly for if evil befall me thou shall lead the flock to pleasant pastures.*"

ganized Church of Jesus Christ of Latter-Day Saints. The Reorganized group claims to being the true religious body of the original chartered organization. In some instances, their claims have been substantiated by the U. S. Courts when it became necessary to deliver legal decisions.

It is not generally known that the originating group of the present Reorganized Church included members from the Mormon colony on Beaver Island. The three men largely responsible for the reorganization were Zenas H. Gurley, Henry H. Deam and Jason W. Briggs. All were important followers of Strang. All repudiated the doctrine of polygamy and eventually founded the Reorganized Church.

Those inclined to check history books will find remarkably little about Strang. The Mormon hierarchy after 1844 deemed it wise, following the murder of Smith, to eliminate certain influential members from their recorded history, who either claimed prophetic succession or resented the usurpation by Brigham Young and the Council of Twelve. Strang was one of them.

However, it is important, historically, to place James Strang in his proper and peculiar niche in early Morman history. This does not mean he was successful. He was, as Riegel accurately states in "Crown of Glory," a man whose failure was magnificent.

After eliminating the opposition one by one, by pitting one claimant against another, Brigham Young saw to it, through cunning maneuvers, that Strang be classed as a fraud and proceeded to cut him off from the Church as quickly as possible.

Strang was never a pronounced success in his lifetime. Nor was he a very happy man, though he more than once claimed to be. He once wrote: "Of all the men on earth, God has made me the most happy." He may have had his good days, but in general, his life was filled with sorrow and frustration.

In one letter, written in reply to an unknown female who believed him to be the Prophet of God, Strang disclosed his great burden. In this reply, written May 23, 1846, Strang wrote:

Introduction

"The ministry to which I have been called I neither sought, desired or expected, and when you learn how much I have been opposed and how little I have been seconded you will see that I have had no desirable situation."

This "Story" includes a discussion of polygamy on Beaver Island. It may be prudent to soften the blow for readers who think polygamy "shocking" by informing, rather disappointingly, perhaps, that Strang was a good and true husband. "At least, he legalized all of his wives and children," so writes an admiring granddaughter, Hazel Strang McCardell, to the writer, September, 1965.

Strang wrote the following to an unidentified woman, who was seeking his love, though she herself was married:

"Love your husband. Give him your whole heart. If it cannot be, never-never-never dream of another till by the law of God you are separated from him."

The draft of this letter is in the Coe Collection at Yale University Library. In it, Strang actually scolded her, saying flatly that he "could not rob another man of what belongs to him," nor would he "desecrate the ministry God has given him in such manner." Strang also returned her letter for destruction.

There has been no desire on the part of the writer to minimize the faults of James Strang. Nor has there been a desire to exaggerate the faults of the Gentiles, who let it be known they were his sworn enemies. Every attempt toward accuracy has been the real intent of "The King Strang Story."

Near the end of the Strang diary, written entirely while a young man, is this rather interesting entry of December 6, 1835:

"O! the curse! to have done nothing for posterity."

Strang was only 22 years of age when this line was written. Twenty-one years later, in the ears of the Gentile world, these same words could have been repeated on his deathbed at Voree.

But the Gentiles were wrong. Any sincere, unbiased study of his nine years at Beaver Island will clearly show James Strang to be a good man. There is no question that he was one of the least appreciated public officials during Michigan's 19th century. Perhaps "The King Strang Story" will justify a re-evaluation by historians and may end the injustice done to his memory.

Destiny may have placed James Jesse Strang on this beautiful, isolated island far out into Lake Michigan. Beaver Island, because of him, has a richer heritage than most citizens of Michigan comprehend, more, certainly, than the present island inhabitants are aware of.

DOYLE C. FITZPATRICK

PART I

CHAPTER I
The Strang Ancestry

While 'The Strang Ancestry' is the first chapter in this story about James Strang it is the last to be written.

Had an attempt been made to compile factual information toward completion of this chapter first, a revision would have been necessary. Only in the past few years have researchers been aware of public records revealing seventeenth century French ancestors of James Strang. The results are currently being published in the New York Genealogical and Biographical Record.

While this chapter is being researched and compiled, the writer is looking upon the village of Saint James, from his home built entirely since 1963 — the year of decision — the year the idea was born that *someone* should write the *true* story about James Strang.

At this moment also, the writer is thinking about the terrible expulsion of the Mormon saints from Saint James more than a century ago, reminiscent of the story of Evangeline and the expulsion of the Acadians from Nova Scotia.

Here, behind the battered sand dunes of Beaver Island's Lake Michigan shore, it is important to contemplate the events leading up to James Jesse Strang's becoming a Michigan pioneer; to contemplate the explorers who were here as early as the seventeenth century, and before them the Indians of Algonquian stock. Mound builders were on Beaver even before the Algonquins. After them, during the Colonial period, Beaver Island was in possession of the Chippewas and the Ottawas.

The American pioneers of "The King Strang Story" came from France, and called themselves 'Streing.' They came as the result of religious persecution. Seventeenth century immigration to America was almost wholly theological or political, the eighteenth, primarily economic.

Great numbers of Huguenot-French Protestants, mostly Walloons, settled in America during the seventeenth century. They divided themselves into two classes, the first coming by choice and all before 1664, and those coming after the English captured New Amsterdam (New York) because they were desperate for life and livelihood. The Streings came because of persecution, in the year 1688.

Persecution of the Protestants began when Louis XIV revoked the Edict of Nantes, thus depriving them of civil rights, including free exercise of their religion. By this act, a half million eventually surrendered their properties and fled France, among them Daniel Streing and his wife Charlotte.

Daniel Streing was one of the promoters of the Huguenot settlement at New Rochelle, New York. His name, prominently identified with the history of New Rochelle during the Colonial period, appears on the bronze tablet on the wall of the Huguenot Monument.

Authentic data from Streing family documents thoroughly researched by a member of the Strang family, Charles A. Strange of Milford, Connecticut, challenge several statements made by John Strang in the genealogy owned by the writer and reproduced below in its entirety. While this manuscript is an authentic source of lore, there are two additional versions, apparently. One of them is in script form at the Huguenot Museum and Library in New Rochelle. A second is preserved by the New

The Strang Ancestry 5

York Historical Society inscribed to Jerusha Strang Dillingham. Most of the vital statistics in these two have been updated to about 1805.

Regardless of discrepancies in the John Strang manuscript, it is offered for reader interest, though suspecting it to have been originally written as early as 1750 and copied by John Strang for his niece, Sarah, in 1819. Since it draws on reminiscences and may perpetuate a number of errors, it behooves the writer to include these five documented corrections compiled by Charles Strange:

1. Wrong identification of the family name in France as L'Estrange. (Streing)
2. Wrong identification of Charlotte's maiden name as Hubert (Le Maistre)
3. Wrong birth place and birth years for both Daniel and Charlotte.
4. Garbled names and birth places for two of their children (Ason for Louison and Penelope for Clorinda)
5. Story concerning an infant left with Paris Guard may be suspect.

Daniel Streing died in Rye, New York, leaving a will dated December 16, 1706, which was proved February 11, 1707. Charlotte also died in Rye, leaving a will dated October 20, 1722, which was proved January 31, 1723.

Charles A. Strange, a Vice President of the Bankers Trust Company in New York, is continuing his documentation of *'The Strangs of Westchester.'* Over fifty pages have so far been published in the New York Genealogical and Biographical Record, a quarterly. In the October 1967 issue, the following is of particular interest:

> "In the France of the early 1680's the families of Daniel Streing and his wife Charlotte Le Maistre had common interests — provincial, business, and religious. Members of both families had taken up residence in Paris while retaining ties

with their native town of Gien in the Loire valley; members of both families listed themselves as "marchands de vins," an occupation comparable to a present day wholesaler of wines; and both families were of the Protestant faith.

"The occurrence of their signatures on various Paris documents mentioned below, as well as the text of the later family manuscript, leads one to suppose that Daniel and his brother Jacques were sent to Paris by their father, Henry, to learn the wholesale wine trade in the cellars of Michel and Guillaume Hubert, Michel being the maternal uncle by marriage of Charlotte Le Maistre. Other "marchands de vins" in Charlotte's family were her late father, her brother-in-law, Blaise Thibou (Bibliothèque Nationale, Paris, Manuscrits Français, F 7051 f⁰ 341), her brother Samuel *(Ibid.* f⁰ 345), and at least one member of her mother's family, the Mariettes (Bull. Soc. de L'Hist. du Prot. Fran., Tom XXX p. 89). A genealogy of the Le Maistre family in the Bibliothèque Nationale shows it to have produced merchants in and around the Loire valley for eight generations prior to Charlotte.

"On the marriage contract, dated 3 August 1680, Daniel's parents are listed as residents of Gien, near Orleans. Eight years earlier, on 29 July 1672, Daniel had signed the roster of students at the Protestant Academy of Geneva, Switzerland, as coming from Orleans (Académie de Genève, 1672, p. 175-188, at Bibliothèque Publique et Universitaire, Genève). Baird, who identified Daniel's signature on this roster with only the New Rochelle autographs for comparison, is to be commended on his sleuthing. This document, incidentally, provides the best clue presently available to Daniel's date of birth. As an out-of-town student, the newly matriculating Frenchman would, in the opinion of a local researcher (Anne-Marie Pfister, Conservateur des Manuscrits, Geneva Public Library), be one or two years older than the sixteen-year-old day students, and thus have been born between 1654 and 1656.

"There is reason to hypothesize that the union of Daniel Streing and Charlotte Le Maistre began as a *mariage de con-*

The Strang Ancestry 7

venance. On 16 May 1680 Charlotte, her mother, Charlotte (Mariette) Le Maistre, her sister Louise Thibou, and Louise's husband Blaise signed a contract (Arch. de France, Etude XLIV 1. 71) for Charlotte's marriage to Pierre Pittan, merchant of Paris. On the same day, Blaise and Louise Thibou recorded an *inter vivos* gift to Charlotte of £500 cash and several income-producing properties in Gien which had come down from their father Jean and grandfather, Samuel Le Maistre, this in view of the expected marriage with Pierre Pittan *(Ibid.* Etude XLIV, Notarie M. Baglan, f⁰ 182). Yet less than three months later, she married Daniel Streing. What could have shattered these plans and led Charlotte to marry the fledgling wine merchant from her home town? One is tempted to accuse Pierre of weakness in his Protestant belief. People took their religion seriously in those days, and most of our cast were shortly to forfeit their not inconsiderable properties and flee the homeland. At that time, five years later, Pierre Pittan, merchant, and his wife Marie (Durand) officially renounced the Protestant faith (Bibliothèque Nationale, Manuscrits Français, F 7055, f⁰ 315, 25 November 1685). They were not the only ones.

"When, on 18 October 1685, Louis XIV revoked the Edict of Nantes, the first of what was to number half a million Frenchmen forsook his properties and left the realm. Listed officially as refugees before the year was out were Daniel Streing and Blaise Thibou *(Ibid.* F 7051, f⁰ 341), Samuel Le Maistre *(Ibid.* f⁰ 345), Guillaume and Michel Hubert *(Ibid.* f⁰ 342, 344, 1685). Because one had been a practicing Protestant he did not necessarily have to flee for his life. All that was required was to sign the Act of Abjuration and Reunion with the Catholic Church. Having done this, one was classified as "bien disposé," and it is amusing to identify members of the family who so behaved and then hurried to grasp the possessions of their Huguenot relatives. Daniel's brother Jacques appears to have signed up on 14 December 1685 *(Ibid.* F 7050, f⁰ 147), and, according to the archivist, Maggy Carof, Pierre Le Maistre, who was either Charlotte's brother or her cousin, immediately seized several of the Mariette properties in Paris. For more than a hundred years afterward the names Pierre and Jacques were not conferred upon the Streing progeny."

The following memorandum of the Strang genealogy is from the writer's holograph copy written by John Strang in 1819:

FOR MISS SARAH ANN STRANG
June 9th, 1819
By her Uncle John d'Estrange — otherwise called John Strang

A Memorandum of the family of Daniel d'Estrange and of Charlotte his wife who escaped from France in the year of 1685 in the persecution under Louis XIV and came to America in the year 1688 and settled at New Rochelle in the County of Westchester, then Province of New York.

"It has by some been understood that the name is Le'Estrange, by others d'Estrange. Of the former there are many instances in England and there are recent instances of the name of d'Estrange in France; the French pronunciation of both in the English are so very similar that it is rather uncertain which it be; the English is Strang — in the French, Straing's the pronunciation. The French frequently designate a family by the name of their residence as LeStraing of the residence d'estraing the place of their residence. There are of both names in the French and English Naval and Military Calendars.

"Daniel d'Estrange was born about the year of 1650 in the City of Paris in France and educated for the mercantile line of business, into which he commenced at about the age of 22 years and about that time married to Charlotte Hubert, a daughter of Francis Hubert and Levina his wife citizens of (   ) in France, and soon after entered into business in the mercantile line in company with Gabriel Hubert, a brother of Mrs. d'Estrange, his wife. Mr. d'Estrange and his wife had been educated in their religious tenets in the Episcopal faith.

"The Protestants in France had for near a century under the Edict of Henry IV continued to exercise their religion freely but in the year 1685 Lewis (Louis) XIV, the King of France instigated through his enthusiasm in the Roman Catholick faith was induced to revoke the Edict of Henry IV which

The Strang Ancestry

had confirmed the Protestants in the full exercise of their religious tenets and continued ever since that time. This measure in the revocal of this edict which had secured ever since the time of Henry IV the Protestants in France in the full exercise of their religion, was allowed and considered at once very arbitrary and extremely impolitic, since scarcely any inconveniency had arisen in this time, nearly a century from the privileges enjoyed by the Protestants under it.

"It had been considered irrevocable; therefore, the greatest obstinancy of these religionists, as is usual now, arose in proportion to the severity with which they were persecuted and threatened. Previous to this Edict of Henry IV which was passed in 1598 and called the Edict of France; great had been the sufferings of the Protestants; for in 1572 in one night at St. Bartholomews 30,000 was massacred; among whom was Admiral Coligni — The Prince of Condi was at the head of the Protestants — The Duke of Guise of the Catholicks; that in about a century 1,000,000 suffered.

"In the course of the persecution which ensued, the revocal of this Edict by which the liberty of conscience and the full exercise of their religion was denied to the Protestants, about 500,000 persons were forced to seek refuge in different parts of Europe who preferred their liberty of conscience to their Country. About 50,000 of whom sought their safety and liberty of conscience in Great Britain upon such revocal where they were received by James II the King of England who openly aided them with money and protected them as Protestant refugees with his power admitting of them without any expen(c)e to the privileges of English Subjects.

"Mr. d'Estrange and his wife with Mr. Gabriel Hubert with others, their neighbours, Citizens and acquaintances were amongst those who were noxious to the Roman Catholicks and Jessuits from their great and rigid adherence to their Protestant religious tenets; and therefore amongst those who were constrained to seek safety and take refuge in England from the cruelties practiced in the persecution by death, tortures, exclusion from sleep confiscation etc., etc., etc.

"Mr. d'Estrange and Mr. Hubert in the having sought their safety and relief retired to the City of London in England where were some of their mercantile correspondents to whom they introduced themselves, and Mr. d'Estrange procured for himself a Lieutenancy in the Guards of King James II, and Mr. Hubert resided in the City and went into business in the mercantile line.

"Mr. d'Estrange and Mr. Hubert in having so escaped had left all of their property in France and Mr. d'Estrange had also left his wife Mrs. d'Estrange with one child, Ason, of about one year old exposed to the prevailing fury of the times and the rage and fury of the Roman Catholicks and Jessuits.

"The property of Mr. d'Estrange and Mr. Hubert was confiscated and Mrs. d'Estrange being thereby divested of it, she soon became destitute in a great measure of all support and subsistence and nearly suffering through the malice of the Catholicks and Jessuits. Under these circumstances Mrs. d'Estrange was constrained in the course of a year to attempt her escape also, and to seek her husband and brother through the extreme sufferings to which she was exposed too for subsistance and necessarys of life. This she effected after many and repeated attempts by applications made to the Guards of the City for a permission to go out of the same into the suburbs of the City with a view of procuring of such necessaries as those of meat-bread-wood-water etc., etc., etc., the latter of which was frequently refused of which she very often experienced the greatest want.

"This liberty being refused to her upon several and repeated solicitations and applications made in the most submissive terms, backed with the most pressing urgency painted, she finally urged by necessity and with hunger etc., etc., etc., which not only now, but generally proves the parent of all inventions, was induced again to attempt a repetition of her applications to the Guards with all of the most feeling urgency and to propose to deposit her child Ason of about two years old with the Guards as a pledge for her return, as the escape of the Protestants was most narrowly watched and prevented under the most strict, rigid and attentive orders. This proposition was at length listened too by the officer of the Guard, upon such her most ardent and pressing entreaty, and accepted and embraced when she was permitted upon her so depositing of her child to the custody of the Officer of the Guard to pass through the gate and so she effected her purpose under the pretence of passing only into the suburbs of the City for the assigned purposes. She having by this means effected her escape did immediately proceed to England in the persuit of her husband and brother; and having come to the City of London, and entering the City was passing through the street when she was observed by some gentlemen from an upper story of a dwelling house and being recognized as a French woman and supposed to be a refugee they addressed her by an enquirry from *where she was — her business — her name — her wishes* etc., etc., etc. when they learned that she was a French refugee, and that she was in the search of her husband and brother and who they were etc., etc., she was then and thereupon invited to come into the house when she was soon made acquainted with the gentlemen and that they were acquainted with her husband and brother and that she should be conducted to them; and that her husband was in the Guards of the King; that her brother was in the city. Hereupon these gentlemen conducted her to her husband.

"Mr. d'Estrange shortly after, was from the extended benevolence and bounty of the English government, enabled to settle himself in the City of London where he resided and remained some time; he continuing in the Guards until about the year 1688 when he, having disposed of his commission was enabled thereby to, and did embark with a number of other Protestants — refugees, his associates, many of whom was his acquaintances, for America; and arriving there landed at the City of New York in the course of the year 1688 with his wife and one son and one or two daughters with a large number of those, his associates, French refugees.

"Mr. d'Estrange now in company with many of his associates, the French refugees and acquaintances, proceeded to New Rochelle in the County of Westchester where they, making of a settlement, did settle themselves in their different and respective professions and callings of life, some as merchants — Physicians — farmers — mechanicks etc., etc.

"Mr. d'Estrange, having procured for his use a farm of new lands and a lot in the village (as now) commenced a grazier and farmer. Among those of Mr. d'Estrangs intimate friends and associates and who accompanied each other to New York and from thence to New Rochelle was the family of the LeBesley known by the name of Bayly (the English Doctor) — Allair — Guion — LeHommideu etc., etc., and with the descendants of some of these families there have been much of a familiar intercourse, and Mr. d'Estrange, about the beginning of the Revolution in America.

"Mr. d'Estrange and his associates having made the settlement of New Rochelle where the village is, he settled down on his lott in the settlement and had his farm about one mile out of the settlement and near where Shute, Esquire, has since resided. Here he commenced the grazing occupation, but his want of a competent knowledge of the business was such as exposed him to many loses and much and great embarrassments and inconveniences so that he did not from the newness of the Country succed to his expectations and wishes. This induced him to relinquish this occupation and to turn his mind to some new course of dependence and of embarking in the mercantile line. This he did in the village, paying an attention to his farming business also. In this way he continued, residing in the village a few years, in this occupation.

"Having resided thus a few years, he determined to make a settlement at the town of Rye in the County of Westchester, where was a settlement then progressing. Accordingly he moved to Rye and settled himself down with his family in the mercantile — Inn keeper and farming business; he having procured a lott in the town (now) and situate upon the East side of the Blind-Brook and including the lands East thereof and where the Park family have since possessed. He had likewise a farm lying north of the town plot and near to the line of Harrison's purchase, including of the lands since possessed by Jesse Hunt, Esquire. He was likewise a proprietor in the pattent of White Plains where he had a farm situate South of the Court-house (now) and where Bartholomew Gedney has possessed and has descended in the family of the Gedneys.

"Mr. d'Estrange resided in Rye several years in the respective business of a farmer — Inn keeper and merchant and until his death which was about the year 1710, as near as can be ascertained, and was buried at the Episcopal Church at which he was an attendant and of which he was a member, it is said. His great antipathy to the Catholicks and Jesuits is said to have been very warm and almost unbounded so that

have been much of a familiar intercourse, and Mr d,s thage
about the beginning of the revolution in America——

   Mr d, strange and his associates having made this settlement of new Rochelle where the village is; he settled down
on his lott in the settlement and had his farm about one
mile out of the settlement o[n which?] Mr
Esquire has since resided —
occupation, but his want of
business was such as expose[d him to losses?]
and great embarrassments
did not from the newness
-tations and wishes; this
occupation and to turn
dependencies and of emb[arrassment?]
he did in the village, pay[ing attention to?]
business also. In this [way he continued in the?]
village a few years in th[e ...]

   Having resided th[ere ... determined to?]
make a settlement at [Rye in the County of?]
Westchester, where was a settlement then p[rogressing?]

   Accordingly he moved to Rye and settled himself
down with his family in the mercantile — Innkeeper and
farming business; he having procured a lott in the
town (now) and situate upon the East side of the Blind-
                                                        Brook.

For
Miss Sarah Ann
Strang June 9th 1819

By her Uncle John d,estrange — otherwise
called Jno Strang

FROM AUTHOR'S COLLECTION

THE JOHN STRANG MANUSCRIPT

often it occurred that upon the very mentioning of them, and upon his recounting and calling to his mind and memory the sufferings — cruelties and hardships which he had himself experienced and which he had seen practiced upon the Protestants in France he would be most frequently elated to almost a fury and frensy and scarcely able to resist his passion and to govern and retain himself of which some instances are related.

"Mrs. d'Estrang survived him with three sons — Daniel — Henry and Gabriel, and four daughters — Charlotte — Mary — Penelope — and Lucey.

"Lewis (Louis) the XIV the King of France in his lifetime or the Duke of Orleans the Regent, after the death of Lewis (Louis) XIV in or about the year 1720 by a proclamation, notified all such of the Protestant refugees who had made their escape leaving of their estates and property in France to return and that upon their personal, or upon the application of their representatives that their several estates and property should be restored, returned and repossessed by them. Whereupon Mr. d'Estrange being dead then, Mrs. d'Estrange embraced the opportunity so offered by the proclamation for an application thereunder for that of her husband Mr. d'Estrange, and being aided by a Mr. Simpson, a merchant (a Jew) in the City of New York, an acquaintance of Mr. d'Estrange in his lifetime, prepared her youngest son Gabriel, who was so patronized by Mr. Simpson to go to France in the name of her husband Mr. d'Estrange deceased, and in pursuance of the proclamation to solicit the restoration of his estate in France which had been left there by him when he made his escape. Having accomplished his preparation, she sent him to New York where he embarked for England under the patronage of Mr. Simpson, her friend, in his way to France, counting for the aid of his Uncle Hubert and friends in England.

"He arrived in London, and from thence proceeded toFrance and arrived in the City of Paris where, under the aid of Mr. Simpson, he made his application in persuance of the proclamation for the restoration of the estate of his late father. What aid was afforded to him by Mr. Hubert, his uncle, or his friends cannot be ascertained. He was successful in some measure as report at that time passed as he acquired a considerable sum but not to the full amount of the estate, and to what amount or sum remains very uncertain.

"After having accomplished his business, he returned to England to his uncle Hubert in the City of London, and from there forwarded to his mother and the family a sum, and but trifling in comparison with what the estate was esteemed worth, and was expected to be had as report then passed, and settled himself there with his uncle Hubert. He only enabled his mother by his remittances to settle her two sons and four daughters in a decent way. The eldest son, Daniel, at the White Plains upon the farm of land acquired by her husband Mr. d'Estrange as one of the proprietors in the Pattent of the White Plains, and where the Gedneys have possessed about South of the Court-house. Henry, her other son in the village of Rye on or near the homestead. Her daughters were married into the family of Budd-Purdy-Park of the County of Westchester, except the youngest who married to one Davie, a merchant or a planter from one of the West-India Islands where she went with him to reside. Some of her descendants have but a few years ago resided in the City of Philidelphia and very opulent. Charlotte married to _____ Park, Mary to John Budd of Rye Neck, Penelope to Samuel Purdy, Esquire.

"Her son Gabriel remaining in England after he had returned from France, and his remittance to his mother of a part as was said of his obtainings from France, with his Uncle Hubert, he married a wife and settled himself in London by whom he had one child (a son) if no more. Report says that he was opulent and in the mercantile line but his filial duty and attention to his mother and the family was much wanting as he very seldom corresponded with them in the lifetime of his mother and less so with the family after her death. He lost his wife and was said to have afterwards married to a second.

"Mrs. d'Estrange died in the town of Rye and about the year of 1722, an aged woman as near as can be ascertained from information and she was buried in the Churchyard of the Episcopal Church, having lived to see all of her children settled from her.

"This information has been acquired, and the narrator is indebted for it, to a very respectable old lady in the City of

New York by the name of Mary Gilliot, a widow — who was a child of a respectable family of the French refugees who escaped from France also, with Mr. d'Estrange and his wife in the persecution, to England, intimate acquaintants of theirs, and whose parents, having died in England, Mr. and Mrs. d'Estrange patronized and adopted her when a child into their family, and brought her to America with them, and with whom she remained, and with Mrs. d'Estrange also after the time of Mr. d'Estrange's death. She married from the village of New Rochelle and from there moved to New York where she lost her husband and was residing when the narrator acquired this information from her on what was called Golding-hill in 1772. Her attachment and respect for the family of Mr. d'Estrange was very strong and warm and which her advanced age served to heighten, and contribute to more, so that when she met with the narrator and found him to be a descendant of the family of d'Estrange she seemed most happy and to be elated with joy.

"To another most respectable and antient lady, Mrs. Phebe Lee (of the Purdy family) the narrator is likewise indebted for a confirmation of most of the circumstances related as she had heard them related by Mr. and Mrs. d'Estrange freequently and of which and of whom she retained the most and a very perfect recollection.

"Gabriel having settled in London and there married, had by his first wife a son named William. In the year, or about that of 1754, William came to America and while here made several visits to his relations and spent much time with them. He was a Lieutenant in the British Navy and upon his station at New York where he remained for nearly two years. He had had a liberal education and was esteemed, and said to be a young man of good abilities but was much inclined to, and had a great propensity for, liquor. For this reason his father, whose intentions were and who had designed him for the Clergy and Gown, was constrained to relinquish such his aim, and to procure a commission for him as a Lieutenant in the Navy. While he was upon the American Station he keept upon a regular correspondence with the families here and also after his return to England (some of his letters are yet to be seen in the possession of Jarod Strang) when he left the Station of New York he was

The Strang Ancestry

from England, stationed in the East India from whence there is the last direct intelligence of him. His father married a second wife but there is no correct information of any family he had by her or whether any, nor of the Hubert family, tho there are of the names in Europe as appears from the Military and Navy Calanders in England.

"Not much distant of the year 1740, there came to America a person who called himself d'Estrange from Paris in France as he represented, and called upon the family in the County of Westchester and particularly upon Mr. Daniel d'Estrange who was then residing upon the Manor of Cortlandt, and claimed that he was the son of Mr. Daniel d'Estrange and Charlotte d'Estrange who was left in France with the Guards by Mrs. d'Estrange in the city of Paris when she made her escape in the time of the persecution of the Protestants and said that he had been brought up in the City of Paris by a person, and who he said was an acquaintance of Mr. and Mrs. d'Estrange, but whose name cannot be called to mind by the informant who saw him. He urged many reasons to induce the family in America to accept of him as a descendant of Mr. and Mrs. d'Estrange upon which he founded his claim to be the same person who was so left when a child and was entrusted to the charge of the Guards.

"Mrs. Phebe Knapp, the widow of Mr. David Knapp, deceased, is the informant and recollects the seeing of him, and her memory serves her as to all the circumstances and the occasion of his visit as he said. She was the daughter of an intimate neighbour of the family and says that it was by many persons supposed that it was very probable that he was the same person whom he claimed himself to be. However, that the family had so much, their doubts in their minds, that they refused to extend to him the hand of connection, and as a branch or descendant of the family and that he left them and proposed to return to France and endeavour to procure the necessary and authentic evidences of his claim. That his vissage and Countenance were considered favourable to his claim and that many of the circumstances by him related, greatly corresponded with those related by Mr. and Mrs. d'Estrange in their lifetimes. However, he was not known to ever return to America afterwards.

"In coroboration of this circumstance of his coming to America and presenting of himself as and for the child which was deposited to the care of the Guards by Mrs. d'Estrange when she made her escape, there are now at this day several persons of great respectability and v(a)racity whose memories serve them to have heard it related by their ancestors and others and by some of the family, and must greatly serve to do away all doubts of that circumstance."

Narrator

Daniel d'Estrange and Charlotte Hubert had children

Viz Daniel — In England
    Penelope — In England
    Mary — In New Rochelle
    Charlotte — In New Rochelle
    Henry — at Rye
    Gabriel — at Rye
    Lucey — at Rye
    Ason — born in France, does not appear in this 1819 compilation.

Daniel — married to Phebe Purdy, a daughter of _____ Purdy of Rye — Settled at the White Plains (near the Court House) Moved from there about the year 1744 to Cortlandt's Manor in the now town of Yorktown — There procured three farms, viz:

One on which he set himself down, now known by the name of **Rye Hoff farm** — including the farm where Doctor Elias Inger(?) lives called the Saw Mill farm.

One on the Ridge North of his dwelling house and where Benjamin Field has since possessed.

And the other in what is called **Stony Street** now, since possessed by Caleb Morgan and now in part only.

The two first he possessed as a tenant as follows —

He deposited in the hand of the proprietor one hundred pounds for each of them — for the interest of which he was to possess the farms. The one mentioned as settled upon himself, he died in the possession of. The Saw Mill farm he

The Strang Ancestry

gave to his oldest son Daniel. The Field farm he gave to his son Francis. The one in Stony Street to his son Gabriel — but this son died before he was settled thereon. He had children, viz:

Daniel — who was married to Elizabeth Galpin, a daughter of Joseph Galpin of Kingstreet on the line of the now state of Connecticut and settled upon his farm.

Francis — who married to Elizabeth Hyatt, a daughter of John Hyatt, Esquire of the Manor of Cortlandt and settled upon his farm.

Joseph — who married (Irmina?) Budd, a daughter of Joseph Budd, Esquire of the Manor of Cortlandt, and who soon after he was married — went into the Provincial Service as a Lieutenant in 1757 where he served in the Campaigns made against the Indian on the Northern frontiers, his father having deceased he had no provided farm, only his share in the estate.

John — who died while in college at Newark, New Jersey about the year 1749 and buried at what is called Lanes Burying Ground — where was his father also.

Gabriel — who married Hannah Clements, a daughter of Johannes Clements (a Dutch family) of the Manor of Cortlandt — he at the same time with Joseph went as a Lieutenant into the Provincial Service, and at the end of the Campaign came home and died (being sick when he returned). His father having died before he had married he had not settled on his farm.

Phebe — who married Abraham Purdy of the Manor of Cortlandt

Elizabeth — who married to Joseph Sackett a son of Reverend Mr. Samuel Sackett the Presbyterian Minister of the Church at what is called Yorktown.

Henry — who married to Margaret Hazard, a daughter of

COURTESY OF STANLEY L. JOHNSTON

MOTHER AND FATHER OF JAMES STRANG

The Strang Ancestry

Daniel Hazard of the City of New York (merchant) and his father having died when he was young — had no assigned settlement made for him.

It is obvious that this John Strang memorandum has not been updated, as have the Huguenot and New York copies, as previously noted.

Gabriel, the issue of Daniel and Phebe, and the great grandfather of James Strang, was born about 1728 in White Plains. About 1750, he married Hannah Clements, daughter of Johannes Clements. Of two children born to Gabriel and Hannah, one was named Gabriel, the grandfather of James Strang. He was born on June 14, 1755. His marriage to Catherine Chichester produced seven children. Marriage to Deborah Seeley after the death of Catherine produced four additional issues.

Of the seven children born to Catherine, the sixth was the father of James Strang. His name was Clement, and he was born on September 22, 1788 in Stillwater, Saratoga County, New York.

The marriage of Clement to Abigail James, the daughter of Jesse James, produced three children: David, born June 9, 1811; Jesse James, born March 21, 1813, and Myraette, born April 24, 1818.

When James Jesse Strang was born at Scipio, Cayuga County, New York, he was given the name of Jesse James Strang. During his youth he wrote a diary covering the years 1831-1836. In 1831, he used the name "Jesse J. Strang" exclusively when recording it at the top of his diary pages. In 1832 and 1833, both variations were used. After 1833, only the name "James Jesse Strang" was recorded.

James Strang was survived by six sons, five of whom carried on the family name. Two were born after his death. The last of his sons became a Grier by adoption. One son died an infant on Beaver Island in 1854, the year of his birth. Strang left six daughters, two of these were born after his death. One daughter, his first child, died in infancy in 1838.

CHAPTER II

James Strang Formative Years and Introduction to Mormonism

It is reasonable to place Strang as an infant and youngster in the class of "genius," though most friends of the family, even his teachers, thought him deficient in ordinary mental powers. Genius was apparently difficult for them to recognize, especially being aware of his frail physical condition. Adult questions, asked when he was little more than an infant, created attention. There were raised eyebrows. Strang recorded in his personal Diary the memory of those unanswered questions, adding further:

> "My mind wandered over fields that old men shrink from, seeking rest and finding none till darkness gathered thick around and I burst into tears and cried aloud, and with a voice scarcely able to articulate told my mother that my head ached."

Strang's mental retention through life included the memory of nursing his mother's breasts! In Strang's own words, he recalled his mother:

> "Carrying me in her arms, nursing me, and conversing with her sister about me."

In "The Kingdom of Saint James," Quaife pointed out that before Strang was a year and a half old:

"His parents moved to another community, yet so distinctly did he remember the place of his birth that after an absence of twenty years he was able to recognize the location when riding through the place."

From 1816 to 1836, Strang lived a normal, somewhat frontier type of existence at Hanover, Chataqua County, New York. Knowledge of his attitudes and thoughts, many never meant for prying eyes, may be gleaned from his Diary, written between May 29, 1831, and May 29, 1836. Previous to 1831, a rural-type education was added to his own invaluable self-education, affording a great advantage over other less ambitious opponents.

At the age of 23, Strang was admitted to the bar as a competent lawyer after half-heartedly deciding a few years earlier to study law instead of becoming a speculator, fur trader, military man or one of many other considered careers. Strang also proposed marriage at this time to Mary Perce, daughter of a Baptist clergyman.

His marriage to Mary in 1836 represents Strang's first close tie with Mormonism. Her brother, Benjamin C. Perce, one year before, had migrated to southern Wisconsin with a sincere Mormon by the name of Moses Smith, their brother-in-law. Each marked a claim for land — Smith the site of modern Burlington and Perce the site of now non-existent Voree, destined to be the future Strang "Garden of Peace."

In 1843, Strang and his family left Ellington, New York, where he had practiced law, served as postmaster and edited the Randolph Herald during his first seven years of marriage. Their destination was Burlington, Wisconsin. From the time of his arrival, it was evident that Mormonism and Strang would influence each other for the 13 years he was destined to remain alive. It was here Mormonism was taken seriously for the first time.

Strang's formative years as a youth were unhappy ones. A desperate thirst for knowledge evidenced by his own personal

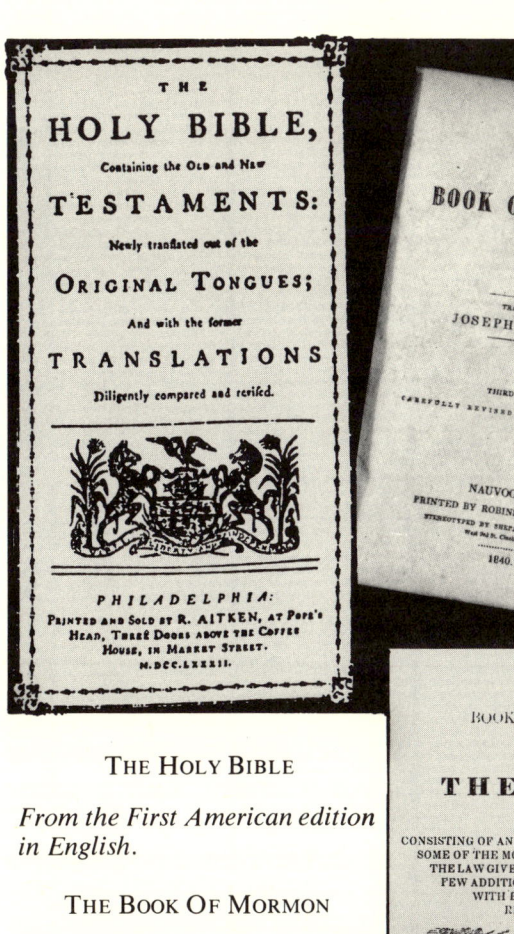

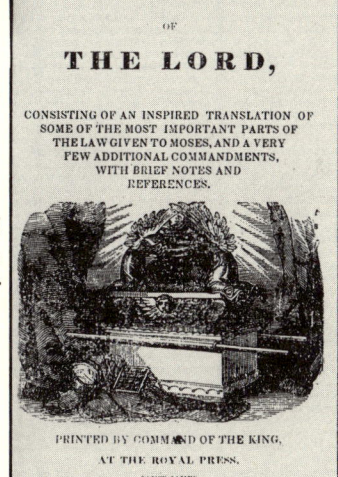

THE HOLY BIBLE

From the First American edition in English.

THE BOOK OF MORMON

The author's copy of the third edition... first with Nauvoo imprint, only one year after founding of city.

THE
BOOK OF THE LAW
OF THE LORD

Rare first edition in Coe Collection at the Yale University Library.

diary replaced an unhappy childhood to some extent. Therefore, books were a tremendous influence during his short life.

James Strang and Abraham Lincoln were influenced in their early adult years by a great French writer, Constatine Francis Chassebeuf de Volney. In many ways, Strang and Lincoln imitated Volney. Both were years ahead of their time, especially in respect to their concern for the happiness of the common man in a social state. Volney's influential book was titled, "Ruins."

Apparently, the Mormon movement was used primarily by Strang as a vehicle to promote his own ideas about the betterment of individual virtues considered by Volney of great importance in the improvement of the human race.

Volney projected five virtues needing elevation:

Science	- prudence and wisdom
Temperance	- sobriety and chastity
Courage	- body and mind
Activity	- love of labor
Cleanliness	- body, dress, habitation

Broadly speaking, Strang and Volney devoted their lives to search after truth in all things. Devotion by Strang may appear in opposition to the uncomplimentary references directed toward him a few years later by the Gentiles at Mackinac and Beaver Island.

Strang and Volney were persuasive men, accurate and candid. They led lives of personal ambition, specifically: to be of service to mankind. Each hoped to make his mark in the world for posterity. How well each succeeded is a matter of personal opinion.

An important first line in the James Strang Diary, recorded at the age of 18, reads:

(1831)

"(May) 29th. Today I read seven hours in Volney's Ruins, reading more than 360 pages. It is an admirable work and well executed."

Formative Years and Introduction To Mormonism 27

Volney narrated his unusual observations of existing human mass enslavement in Egypt and Syria after extensive traveling in those countries. Worldwide fame assured him a seat as deputy in the Assembly of France in 1789, at the age of 32. He was born at Craon, France, on February 3, 1757.

Traveling also inspired a devoted interest in agriculture. As a result, he bought a farm on the island of Corsica. This highly successful farming venture brought an appointment as Director of Agriculture on Corsica.

While Strang may have considered Volney's claim to fame the volume called "Ruins," perhaps the chief claim was his ability as a lecturer on history. At least, it was a literary glory. Because of this and other honors, it was said that Volney was "one of the very few whose memory shall never die." This statement was made after his death in Paris, April 25, 1820.

"Ruins" was undoubtedly packed with his worldly goods when Strang and his family headed west to Burlington, Wisconsin, in 1843. His thought of establishing a law practice, but not working very hard at it, materialized, giving the Strangs a livelihood. The Mormon influence of his brother-in-law, Benjamin, and highly respected Moses Smith became the real turning point of his life, resulting in a trip to Nauvoo to see Prophet Joseph Smith. In February, 1844, only a few months before the murder of the claimed God-appointed Prophet, James Jesse Strang became a Mormon. He was personally baptized by Smith.

It is not difficult to understand why the appearance of Strang in the Mormon hierarchy meant a great deal to Smith. Strang was a brilliant orator. He was primarily a self-educated man. His talents were numerous and convincing, especially his thorough knowledge of the law and of geography.

Strang was baptized at Nauvoo, Illinois, then the headquarters of the Mormon Church. However, he never resided there. Instead, he asked to "plant a stake" at Voree, west of Burlington. Permission was granted. Voree, now called Spring Prairie, was founded on faith and built with the hands of very poor Saints. While the Saints had precious little money, they had great faith in leader Strang and his communal ideas, and were delighted to follow the teachings of Mormonism as interpreted by him.

Although the name Voree meant "Garden of Peace," it was soon far from that, not because of resentful Gentile neighbors, as at Kirtland, Zion and Nauvoo. This time they fought verbally with each other.

It is not surprising that there was dissension at Voree. After the murder of Joseph Smith, many influential followers fought for control of the Church. Former pillars of the Council of Twelve, having been cut off from the Church previous to the murder or soon after, fought for control against Brigham Young. Some chose to join Strang at Voree. A few of these were scoundrels. This created dissension at Voree and the expediency of welcoming this questionable strength to his own Stake caused continuous trouble for Strang.

The murder of Smith caused a permanent break, within a year, between the Voree Mormons and the main body of the Mormon Church. The Nauvoo Saints soon consolidated under the ruthless, but talented, organizer, Brigham Young. Strang made a bold attempt to head the Church, but failed.

Strang was branded a liar when he displayed his "Letter of Appointment" to the prophetic office, purported to have been sent to him by Smith a short time before the Prophet's murder. If genuine, it meant that Strang was to be the new Prophet in the event of Smith's death.

Brigham Young won his fight against Strang, and thereby disposed of his last and most feared contender.

CHAPTER III
God and James Strang

James Strang believed in God and considered himself divinely called of God to continue the prophetic work of Joseph Smith.

In one effective paragraph, a grandson, Mark A. Strang, appraised his grandfather's beliefs by effectively including within it, a quote from The Book of the Law of the Lord:

> "He was a determined monotheist and taught a joyous religion of love and logic wherein, without benefit of any intermediary, each individual works out his own salvation by conforming to the character of God by *preferring good to evil, not from the fear of punishment which evil deeds entail, but on account of the innate loveliness of undefiled goodness; of pure unalloyed holiness.*
>
> "The source of his power for good was his conviction of the reality of things not seen."

It was a privilege to have corresponded with Mark Strang before his death on July 27, 1965. Additional excerpts and letters from the pen of this fine gentleman, eulogizing the memory of his grandfather, are included in this volume.

On October 19, 1848, James Strang published one of a series of letters in the Gospel Herald, informing subscribers of his inner thoughts about God and the Universe:

"I affirm that there is a God, and that there be no doubt as to the true intent of this affirmation. I add by way of explanation that by the name God I signify a PERSON possessed of INTELLIGENCE, MOTIVE and WILL, who is Lord of the UNIVERSE.

"The conclusions to which I have come on the subject of the existence of God are not the result of other men's reasonings, but of my own. My reasons were not derived from any book, publication or discourse whatever. I have read one hundred volumes of different authors on the existence of God and the divine authority of the Christian religion without finding one argument that I deemed conclusive. Since seeing you (Edwin Burgess of Racine, Wisconsin) I have read the first argument of real force that I ever had the pleasure of reading to prove that there is a God. This is a re-print in the Wisconsin Argus from the Democratic Review. And this is but a repetition, dressed up in better and more scientific language than I am able to use, of part of the arguments used by me in private conversations in Pittsburgh, New York and Boston two years since, and repeated in successive public lectures in Voree last winter and spring.

"Believing this credence (simple human testimony that universal material objects exist) of mankind well founded, I appeal to similar evidence to prove a God. HE HAS BEEN SEEN OF MEN. In this the testimony of all mankind concurs. I shall not attempt to give the evidence in detail. It would require a re-writing of the history of the earth. Every nation under the whole heavens furnishes its quota of that mass of evidence which, if written out, would crowd libraries — the testimony of man that they have seen God. From the earliest times of which we have written records to the present, there never was one nation which did not give its share to this testimony. Neither savage tribe or civilized people has refused its contribution.

"Among the savage nations of America, Africa, Asia and the islands of the Indian and Pacific Oceans not one people is found where similar testimony is not furnished from generation to generation. And though this testimony is often only of the seeing of some of the inferior spirits, and not of God himself, yet I doubt not it is equally in point. For

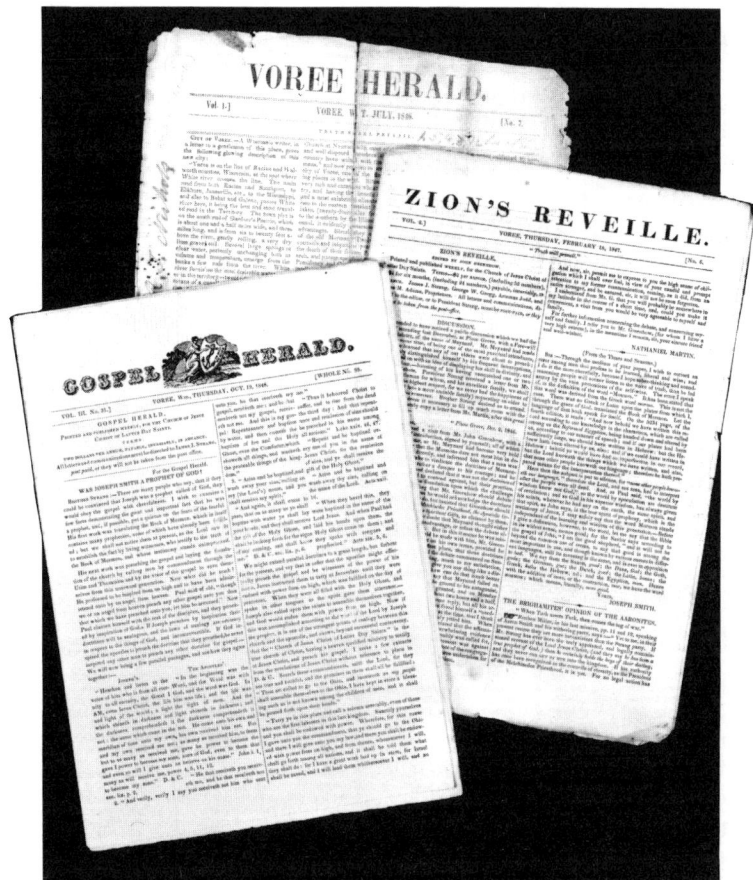

FROM THE COLLECTION OF THE WRITER

THE VOREE HERALDS

Official organ of the Strangite movement prior to the establishment of the Kingdom of God on Beaver Island.

No complete file of the "Herald" exists. The Clements Library, University of Michigan, has the most comprehensive file and the Strangite archive at Burlington, Wisconsin has a confidential run of numbers. Others include, in order of completeness: The New York Public Library, Wisconsin State Historical Society, New York State Library, Fitzpatrick collection, and the Coe collection in the Yale University Library.

if I made good the existence of a world of spirits, I think you will have no difficulty in acknowledging one superior, a Lord of the Universe. Even should you take issue on that point, showing a world of supernatural beings, lays a good foundation for showing that one is supreme, that is God.

"CAN IT BE FALSE? Have men in all the ancient nations from China to the Pillars of Hercules, and of all ranks from the king to the beggar, and of all characters from the philosopher to the dunce, with all their national divisions and animosities, conspired together to impose a lie on their fellow men? — And have men of every faith, and of every nation, and of every age, from Abraham till myself, made their whole lives one living lie for the purpose of palming off such an imposition on our brothers, our sisters, our wives and our children?

"In all else the united testimony of those who have studied the facts is deemed sufficient and satisfactory proof. The facts of geology, the facts of astronomy, the facts of chemistry, the facts of botany, the facts of zoology, are all proved by testimony like this in kind, less in accumulation.

"It is not necessary to give samples where masses are at hand. No man in his senses will deny that the existence of God, the Lord of the universe, a being of intelligence, motive and will, is proved by more testimony than that of Julius Caesar. And a world of spirits is proved by more living witnesses, and has been in every generation of man, than can or ever could be adduced to prove the existence of one half the species of living animals on the earth.

"The world is now a vast crowd of living witnesses of the supernatural, shamed down to silence by the Atheistical doctrines of modern chemistry. This truth is a spring that can never be dried up. A generation shall yet arise who, taking facts as they find them, will make religion a science, studied by as exact rules as mathematics. Then will these facts be sought for as are new discoveries in geology and astronomy. Facts well attested will be generalized, rules be drawn from them. Man's prejudices will cease to minister to his blindness. The mouth of the seer will be opened, and the whole earth enlightened."

Three weeks after these thoughts were published, the Herald

God and James Strang

of November 9 included this excerpt, commenting upon Strang's 35 years of poor health and the merit of his religious cause:

> "I possess no one advantage over the common mass of my countrymen, except the intrinsic merit of the cause I have espoused.
>
> "Born of poor parentage, raised on the very borders of civilization, suffering with debilitating disease from infancy, I had a most indifferent opportunity of obtaining even a common school education. I have neither had the benefit of a private tutor, nor attended school one week since I was fifteen years of age.
>
> "I have never known one day of health since I was born; and at the age of thirty-five find the weakness of youth and the decrepitude of old age meeting in me. Yet in this cause I feel myself able to endure all things, and the thought of failure never enters my heart. I seek the encounter, knowing that among my friends the most flattering success is but hardly what they would expect of any one, and will bring with it no honor; and that the slightest failure would bring with it the most overwhelming disgrace."

On December 28, 1848, James Strang inserted his conviction that God is an intelligent being.

> "It is inevitable that intellectual force is the cause of all physical motion, and that SOME INTELLIGENT BEING GIVES MOTION TO THE MATERIAL UNIVERSE. This BEING, possessed of intelligence, acting from motive, and by his will, and GOVERNING THE UNIVERSE, IS WHOM WE CALL GOD. Call him natural or supernatural, I care not. Say it is one being or many, I care not. Say it is several equals, or a superior and inferiors, I care not.
>
> "The intelligent power that gives motion to suns and planets, as well as to mites and molecules, is GOD."

The claim by Strang that he acquired and translated metallic plates by divine intervention may deter many believing him a sincere man of God. However, he did claim two distinct sets delivered to him by the power of God and therefore it is necessary to contemplate their credibility. The first set was unearthed at Voree, Wisconsin and was called "Voree plates" or "plates of Manchou." A few years after the Voree plates were unearthed, Strang announced the miraculous reception of a second set called the "plates of Laban." These became the basis of his Book of the Law of the Lord.

The Voree plates were dug up on September 13, 1845, near the White River, which flowed through the eastern part of Walworth County, Wisconsin. They were removed with great difficulty from three feet under a one foot-thick oak tree in view of Aaron Smith, Jirah B. Wheelan, James M. VanNostrand and Edward Whitcomb. Most of these witnesses eventually repudiated their testimonial as did those witnessing the plates of Joseph Smith, which were also claimed to have been acquired by "divine intervention" from the hill of Cumorah.

The Voree plates, unlike the plates of Mormon, were viewed by thousands. There were three of them. They were made of brass, each about one and one-half by two and three-fourths inches with engravings on all six sides. On one side was engraved a view of the hills from which the plates were taken. A man with a crown holding a scepter was on another. With him were engraved: an eye, Sun and Moon surrounded by 12 stars; 12 larger stars from which three pillars extend, surrounded by seventy tiny stars. On the remaining four sides were hieroglyphics Strang claimed to have deciphered by viewing them through Urim and Thummim, two miraculous stones used also by Joseph Smith.

Many visitors stopped at Voree after the dramatic excavation of the purported ancient records became known. According to Strang, Voree was "filled with the fame of the occurence" and thousands of people made a concerted examination of the ground. One visitor, L. D. Graham, wrote his impressions to the Gospel Herald. The writing is remarkable for its content and brevity, projecting an excellent word picture of Strang and his environment:

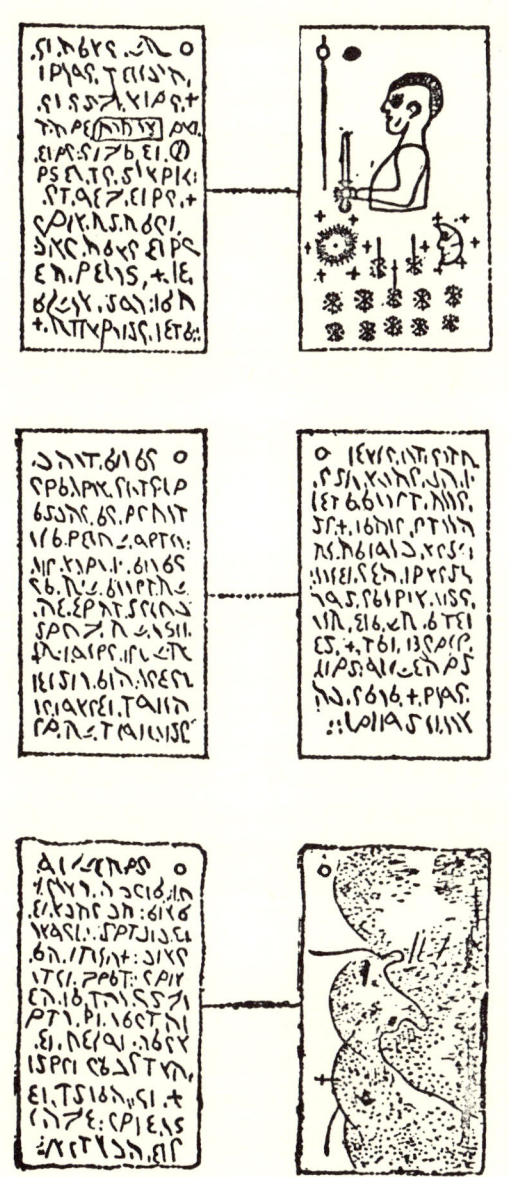

THE VOREE PLATES

Reproduced from a Wingfield Watson pamphlet, two-thirds actual size, and showing all sides of the three plates.

CHRISTOPHER LATHAM SHOLES

Christopher Latham Sholes received a patent for the first practical typewriter less than a quarter century after his investigation of the unearthing of the famous Voree plates. One of his admirers was Thomas Edison.

In September, 1845, an investigation of the unearthing of the plates by C. Latham Sholes, while a youthful editor of a Southport (Kenosha), Wisconsin country paper, revealed this personal observation:

"The prophet appears to us a very intelligent man, devoid of anything like enthusiasm; and, so far as we could judge, honest and earnest in all he said. The men who subscribe the statement (concerning the finding of the plates) are said to be the most honest and intelligent in the neighborhood; and, taking it all together, it is something to stagger ordinary credulity.

"The popular opinion will doubtless call it humbug. So should we from the natural impulse of our mind. But when the testimony appears in opposition to such impulse, we are content to have no opinion about it."

God and James Strang

> "The prophet Strang is a man truly displaying many admirable qualifications, among which is a depth of thought seldom reached by man; a rapid speaker, eloquent and powerful in argument, and although I may not concede to the fact of his being a divinely inspired prophet, yet he is certainly a gentleman."
>
> "A brief description of his residence may not be out of place. He lives in a rudely made log house, about ten feet by fourteen, one story high, containing a chest or two, two beds, common low post bedsteads, a small stove, three or four chairs, and a very intelligent and agreeable companion. (Mary Perce)
>
> "The Voree plates, the wonder of many, I saw them and the place from whence they were taken. They are about one inch and a half by two and three-fourths, thickly covered with ancient characters of curious workmanship."

Under the illustration of the Voree plates in "The Kingdom of Saint James" is a line reading, "The plates have long since been lost." For the benefit of the faithful, history should record the possibility of their return to a heavenly depository, as were Urim and Thummim through which the plates were claimed to have been read.

Dr. Quaife had this comment about the Voree plates, in addition to his observation that Strang's second divine revelation was given to his Saints "with a view to encouraging his followers in their ministry":

> "It is quite conceivable that Strang's angelic visitations may have had only a subjective existence in the brain of the man who reported them. But the metallic plates possessed a very material objective reality; and we can hardly escape the conclusion either that Strang knowingly fabricated and "planted" them for the purpose of duping his credulous followers, or that they were what they purport to have been, ancient records divinely preserved, in the discovery and translation of which Strang was divinely guided. If the former alternative be accepted, it follows that Strang's prophetic career was a false and impudent imposture; if the latter be the true one, we are confronted by the sad fact that of all the people now on earth only a few score at most have comprehended it."

Four eventful years elapsed before James Strang informed his second in command, George J. Adams, that he had divinely received the plates of Laban, the ancient pre-Babylonian record once kept in the Ark of the Covenant. These were soon to become the Strangite bible, "The Book of the Law of the Lord." Partial translation was dramatically read to the Saints on Beaver Island informing them on that memorable day, July 8, 1850, that God had commanded him to re-establish His kingdom on earth.

Except in the mind of Strang, knowledge of this second divine intervention was apparently not revealed until Adams was informed in early 1849. There is no chronicle comparable to finding the Voree plates and no indication the "plates of Laban" were physically transferred to Beaver Island from another location. It is known they were seen by a chosen few at the April conference at Beaver in 1851, about a year after reading part of the translation to the Saints during the coronation ceremonies.

The "plates of Laban," were also made of brass, 18 in all, measuring nine inches by seven and three-eighths. All who witnessed them, according to their historian, Warren Post:

> "handled them and saw the engravings thereon, and were satisfied that they were of ancient workmanship; and the real plates of brass mentioned in the Book of Mormon which, according to God's promise should in his own time come forth."

Translation was given to Beaver Island Saints in 1851 in the form of an 84-page guide to religious worship. Also included was a guide for the establishment of a theocratic government for the colony. Early in 1856, after much delay, a revised and enlarged translation appeared in the church paper, the *Northern Islander*. A few months later, a 350-page edition reached the binding stage, printed from the same type, just prior to the assassination of Strang.

The Book of the Law of the Lord and the Book of Mormon are accepted as sacred writings by respective church bodies, each supplementing the Holy Bible. Both projectors considered themselves prophet, seer, revelator and translator of the new gospel which they chose to call "dispensation of the fulness of times." Both planned to rule over their respective kingdoms of God on earth.

Doctrines in the Mormon church have changed over the years. For nearly half a century, they swore "eternal enmity" toward the United States to avenge the death of Smith. The church leaders were belligerent and powerful during the Brigham Young presidency, to the point that Young proclaimed he would "dictate who would be elected President of the United States before 12 years."

The Book of Mormon has been printed in many editions in America and England and translated into many foreign languages. It was first published in New York State in 1830. In this edition, Joseph Smith, Jr. claimed authorship, although subsequent editions recognized him more appropriately as translator. His claim of translation was accomplished by looking through the biblical stones, Urim and Thummim.

Urim and Thummim were two mysterious stones used to "inquire of the Lord." They were divinely supplied, according to Smith and Strang, as the only means by which the hieroglyphics on the divine plates could be read. With them, ancient records could be translated into understandable "light and truth." The first reference to them in the Bible occurs in Ex. 28:30, but they may have been known to the Jews prior to that time.

During their brief acquaintance, Smith and Strang admired the abilities of each other. Smith appointed Strang an elder in the Mormon Church at their first meeting. Later, Smith requested an educated survey for removal of the Saints west. In addition, Strang was given authority to establish a Stake at Voree. Strang believed Smith to be a true latter-day prophet of God. Though Strang founded what could have been a very successful schism of his own, there is evidence he continued his admiration and belief in Smith to the end of his life. Four years after the death of Smith, the following complimentary eulogy to his prophetic predecessor was inserted in the Gospel herald:

> "Joseph Smith was a very illiterate boy, as uncouth in manner and expression as one could well be, and, in fact, profoundly ignorant on all subjects without exception (unless he was taught of God), laid the foundation of a church, became its first preacher; declared and defended its doctrine, having more than this usual advantage in every point of faith; and its preachers selected among those like himself, having universally prevailed everywhere."

James Strang could very well have become successor to the prophetic office in the Mormon church had Joseph Smith lived another year. But for Brigham Young he may have succeeded after the death of Smith. Instead, for more than 100 years, Mormon history has chosen to ignore him. American history continues to record him as a ruthless, conniving demagogue, though facts prove otherwise.

While Strang may have attempted to build his own Church of Jesus Christ of Latter-day Saints on the current vogue of Mormonistic chicanery, he did so harming no one and benefitting many. Though he failed, and many people doubted his claims as they did those of Smith, it may be of some importance to understand that he neither "sought it, desired it nor expected it."

PART II

CHAPTER IV

A Brief Geographical, Cultural and Economic History of Beaver Island

The Beaver archipelago consists of 12 islands varying 21 to 40 miles northwest of Charlevoix, Michigan, in Lake Michigan.

In this group is one called Beaver. "The King Strang Story" is primarily concerned with what has been said about the one great personality who made history on that island, James Jesse Strang.

Beaver also is the largest island in Lake Michigan. All of its 58 square miles is similar to the mainland "cover," rising gradually from its shores to varying heights of 50 to 80 feet. One captured sand dune about 200 feet in height was given the biblical name "Mount Pisgah" by the Mormons.

Looking at a "cover map," conservationally speaking, Beaver today has one-fourth second and third growth hardwoods, one-half pine, a small amount of cedar, spruce and balsam and the remainder fields, grasses and the beaches. The island was depleted of virgin timber about 1939.

A cover map also reveals eight lakes of varying sizes. The larger one was biblically named by the Mormons, "Lake Gennesareth." Most of this mile-square lake has a firm sandy bottom and at the south end a hard sandy beach. A "River Jordan," also named by the Mormons, runs from the east center of Lake Gennesareth into Lake Michigan. Contemporary maps locate this river about eight miles north, but these are in error. Today it is merely a trickle. The Bay, now called "Beaver Harbor," is one of the finest on the Great Lakes. Before the Mormons arrived, it was known as "Paradise Bay."

Five members of the Voree, Wisconsin, Strangite Mormon Church — Strang and four of his Saints — first investigated Beaver Island in 1847. Two hundred years before this, French explorers briefly occupied cleared fertile areas on the island. It is possible that Spanish explorers experienced life here a half century earlier than the French.

A mapping of the area, as shown in the Jesuit Relations, took place about 1672 as a result of the Marquette explorations. Father Joliet and Father Allouez also contributed greatly as Jesuit explorers. Geographical research took place during the first decade after 1665. At this time, Lake Michigan got its name, although it was still known as Illinois for many years.

Beaver Island was without a name until 1744. It was first called Isle du Castor. Bellin's map in Charlevoix's History of New France recorded this as "I, du Castor." The first map using the name "Beaver" appeared in 1755. This appeared on the John Mitchell map as "Beaver I." Also, in 1755, atlas maker Thomas Kitchin called it "Castor's Island." Nearly 100 years passed before the area was accurately surveyed by John Farmer for the first time, being published by him in 1853.

An excellent map was drawn by James M. Greig in 1852 and presented to the skipper of the *Troy*. The legend on the map reads:

> "This map of Beaver Island is respectfully presented by James M. Greig to Captain Dobins of the Propeller *Troy* as a small token of *Public* Esteem for his uniform kindness and attention to his passengers without distinction for their religious faith by his humble friends and admirers."
>
> James M. Greig, draftsman
> Troy, Beaver Island, July 24, 1852

(Greig, Sr. a former minister, joined the Saints on Beaver in

Geographical, Cultural and Economic History   45

1849, was later elected County Judge at Saint James, holding Court also at Mackinac)

The end papers of this volume are reproductions of this map, courtesy of the State Archives, Michigan Historical Commission. For additional maps and more detailed information, see Karpinski's monumental "Bibliography of the Printed Maps of Michigan," published by the Commission in 1931.

The name "Beaver" was apparently given to the main island in the archipelago because of its shape, not as shown on the 1852 J. M. Greig map, but a beaver stretched flat on its stomach as it appeared on earlier maps, such as the S. Augustus Mitchell map illustrated in this section.

There were no beaver on the island during the Strang era, nor were there beaver on other islands in the group. Three pair were brought here in 1932 by R. W. Bunday, accounting for the present beaver colony.

Established fur traders at Mackinac, now modern Mackinaw City on the south side of the Straits, and at Old Mackinac on the north side, bought many kinds of fur. Black and silver fox were the most valuable. These were scarce on Beaver Island and, for this reason, most of the valuable skins acquired from the Ojibway and Ottawa Indians were first trapped elsewhere and brought to Beaver where the North-West Company had a trading post.

The biggest fur trader in Michilimackinac was John Jacob Astor of New York. He had a multi-million dollar business, having organized the American Fur Company in 1809 to compete with the British-owned Mackinaw Company organized in 1808. In 1811, he bought out the Mackinaw Company and from it organized the American Company in 1815-16. Astor became one of the wealthiest men in America, as the fur trade reached its peak about 1830. He continued until he sold the business in 1848, the period Beaver Island was becoming important economically in the marketing of fish as a replacement for the declining fur market.

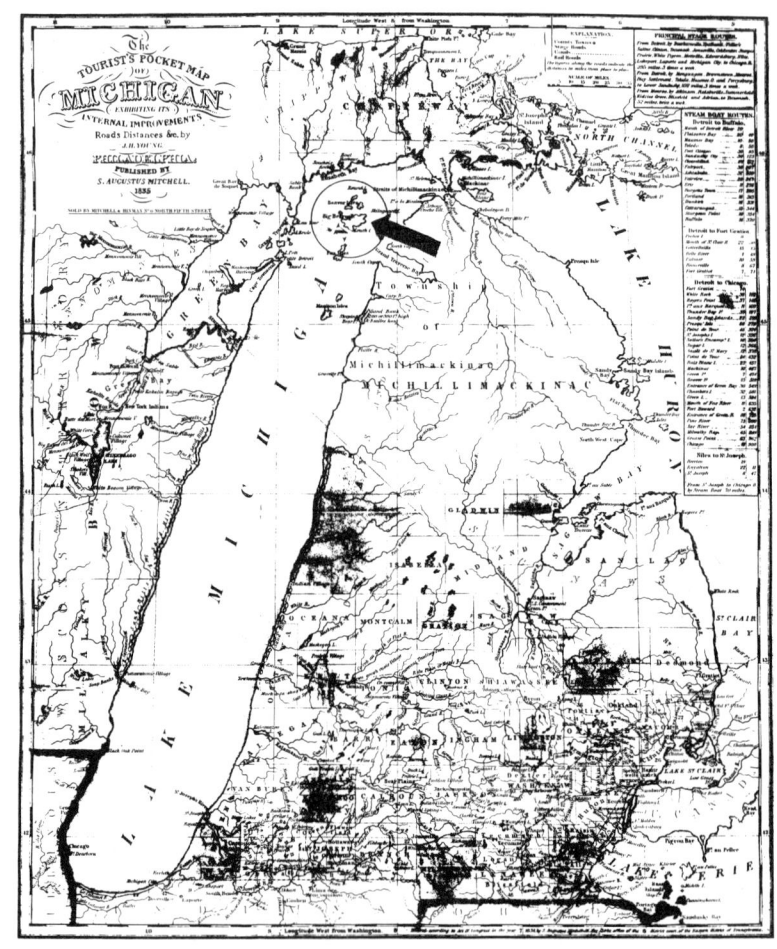

MITCHELL MAP OF MICHIGAN (1835)

Geographical, Cultural and Economic History

The trading post of the North-West Company on Beaver Island continued its ruthless business methods trading for fish as it did for furs, cheating the Indians. Anyone now wishing to rationalize may say this was a very common practice in meeting competition in the early pioneer days. Immoral is a better word. It is well known that many Michigan Indians were shamefully cheated and mistreated by early traders, not merely by individuals and established companies, but by a few dishonest government agents as well. Beaver Island Indians were no exception in this exploitation.

The American Indian, in general, learned many of his evil ways through contacts with white men.

In 1847, Beaver Island Indians, who wished, had a friend in James Strang. His arrival that year was the beginning of any consistent decency shown to them and the first genuine interest in their economic welfare.

Cheating the Indians on Beaver, as elsewhere, involved the manufacture of a special liquor called "Indian Whiskey," a concoction used as barter for furs and fish. When Mormons first arrived at the island, furs, fish and firewood were the three most profitable products. It was soon apparent that some traders found it very lucrative to manufacture a poor quality whiskey for about $1.75 a barrel by combining two gallons of whiskey with 30 gallons of water. The dilution was then strengthened by adding tobacco and cayenne pepper. This potent mixture made the Indians very drunk. The addition of cayenne achieved an effective "fire water" potency at little cost, a dubious Gentile achievement. A barrel of "Indian Whiskey" sold in exchange for $16.00, amounting to three-fourths of any single trade. The Indians were induced to intoxication first to assure success of the barter.

Another version of Gentile whiskey known to the Utah Mormons included the addition of nitric acid. This was appropriately called "Tangle-leg." If a man could walk more than 400 yards from the demijohn, the concoction lacked a sufficient quantity of one ingredient.

One independent trader who had purchased Cable's Trading Post at Whiskey Point was Peter McKinley, reputed to have been a cousin of yet-to-be President of the United States, William McKinley. He was later Assistant Postmaster on the island, a member of the Michigan Legislature and one of the island's lighthouse keepers.

A few years after Prophet Strang made his first inspection trip to Beaver and the island boasted a Mormon population of about 600, with a voting power of 165, he was easily elected to the Michigan State Legislature. "King" Strang, as he was called after 1850, was the moving force in getting the legislature to enact laws restricting the sale and barter of intoxicating liquor to Indians. Although this restriction again indicated evidence of Strang's desire to serve his fellow men throughout life, it is ironic the law was eventually a major underlying cause of the "Battle of Pine River."

Culture in respect to knowledge and society also arrived at Beaver Island with the coming of the Mormons. Strang was their leader spiritually and intellectually. He took a great deal more to Beaver than he has been given credit for. According to Gentiles he took only his wickedness. Strangites were given little credit for goodness and sincerity. Unlike many of the original Mormon Saints, only a very few sowed seeds of dissension. Unfortunately, all reaped the harvest of abuse.

The murder of Strang in 1856 and the shameful expulsion of all the Strangite Mormons from Beaver Island reversed the cultural and economic progress all Saints had worked so hard to gain. The economy never returned to equal that of the industrious Mormon era under James Strang.

Economic growth had begun to move noticeably after the Saints emigrated to Beaver in greater numbers in 1849. For seven years, these hard-working people, though continually harassed by the Gentiles, were able to support themselves and continually raise their standard of living. Economic progress reached its peak in 1856.

Pistol shots ended the life of James Jesse Strang, one of the

Geographical, Cultural and Economic History

greatest, but unrecognized, personalities in Michigan history and the Mormon world.

With Strang died the culture of Beaver Island . . . until the charming and industrious Irish arrived from Ireland to start life on their new Emerald Isle.

The Beaver Islands
Information Compiled from U.S. Lake Survey

Island	Square Miles	Acres	Shore Line in Miles
*Beaver	58.4	37,385.6	41.6
Garden	7.8	4,914.6	20.7
Gull	0.4	270.1	3.4
Hat	0.025	16.0	0.6
High	5.8	3,692.8	12.5
Hog	3.9	2,530.0	16.0
Pismire	0.004	2.5	0.3
Shoe	0.005	3.2	0.3
Squaw	0.1	75.5	1.6
Trout	0.2	115.2	1.8
Whiskey	0.2	129.2	2.0

*Beaver Island in 1744 was first known as "Isle du Castor." It may be the first island in Lake Michigan to be recorded.

CHAPTER V
Strang Surveys Beaver Island

Although James Strang first set foot on Beaver Island on May 11, 1847, it must be assumed he saw it from passing ships on occasions more than a year before.

His restlessness at Voree, caused by conflict within the Church, set the stage for his first claimed revelation involving the Beaver Islands. Strang claimed a message from God had described a "land amidst wide waters and covered with large timber, with a deep, broad bay on one side of it." The claimed revelation took place on the Monongahela River at Elizabeth, Wisconsin on August 25, 1846.

When Strang surveyed Beaver in the Spring of 1847 he had four Saints with him, four very poor saints, and with them one very poor Prophet. Milo Quaife narrated:

> "So destitute of means were the Saints that they sold their blankets to pay their steamer passage, and on reaching Big Beaver they went ashore with less than two days' supply of provisions and without a cent of money. Building themselves a shelter of hemlock boughs, they began a survey of the island, scantily clad and still more scantily fed."

Quaife stated further:

> "One of them recorded that the Prophet took off and mended his only pair of trousers, after which they plunged into the forest. They camped for the night under the stars, without dinner, supper, or fire."

The first notice in the Voree Herald that such a survey was contemplated appeared on March 11, 1847, under the title, "Indian Mission." The two-fold purpose included, first, to give the Indians the arts of civilization and, second, to get lands at a price that a farm could be supplied to every man according to his need, however poor he might be.

On the following July 8 the Herald published a full report of this survey. Not only is the report an economic justification for "gathering the Saints" on Big Beaver, it is a beautifully written description of the island. It is reprinted here in full as it appeared in the Herald. To the Clements Library at the University of Michigan, the writer is indebted for the following, published in Zion's Reveille at Voree. Strang was the author.

BEAVER ISLANDS

> "This group of islands is situated in the northern part of lake Michigan, and consists of Big Beaver, about equal to two townships, Little Beaver, Garden and High Islands, each about equal to one township; Bull, Trout or Turtle, Squaw, Virgin and Hat Islands, each containing from fifty to five hundred acres, and a considerable number of islets, rocks and keyes. With this group the two Manitou and the two Fox Islands are sometimes reckoned as being equal to two or three townships more.
>
> "Big Beaver lies in the centre of the group, and is 13½ miles long and 6½ broad in its extreme measure. At the northeast corner, and about six miles from the usual track of the Chicago steamboats, is the best harbor on the lakes — consisting of a broad, deep bay, running up into the island some two miles. The channel between the reefs at the entrance of the bay is a mile in width. Inside of that is a straight ninety rods wide, between

headlands connecting the outer with the inner harbor. The inner harbor is about ¾ of a mile by one mile — is perfectly land locked, so that in the severest storms its waters are scarcely disturbed, and has usually from six to eighteen fathoms water; and thus making good anchorage and a harbor of the largest class, easy of access and perfectly safe in all winds and at all seasons.

"The west coast of the island consists of a range of steep broken hills, covered with a very heavy growth of valuable timber. The entire east coast is in like manner bordered by an almost impassable barrier of pine, cedar and black ash jungle, which connects at each end of the island (by means of two lakes within) with the range of hills upon the west coast; thus surrounding the entire central part of the island by a barrier which will forever break off the winds from all directions, and which is hardly passable by man.

"At the harbor (and one or two other places) dry land is found immediately on the shore. That at the harbor amounts to almost one thousand acres — is elevated almost 25 feet above lake Michigan, and though indifferent for cultivation is a most beautiful location for a town. The entire centre of the island is a most beautiful table land, elevated from forty to seventy feet above lake Michigan, covered with a heavy growth of sugar maple and beech timber of the finest quality. The soil of this table land is a rich loam, with a large proportion of decomposed limestone and sand intermixed; thus producing a rich, mellow and inexhaustible soil. The island is well watered by means of six lakes enclosed within it, and by numerous springs and brooks. These lakes vary in size from forty to six hundred acres — have generally deep pure water and clean beaches. In their waters are found abundance of trout and other fish. The outlet of one of them affords a valuable water power.

"There is found on the island an abundant supply of beech, maple, white and yellow pine, yellow oak, white and red cedar, fir and black and white ash timber, in size and quality no where surpassed. Many other kinds of timber are more or less abundant. Beech, maple, elm, ironwood and ash are the principal growth of the land naturally destined for tillage, and when cut into steamboat wood finds a constant cash market at the harbor, at $1.50 per cord.

"The pine, fir, cedar, &c., occupy principally the borders of the island, and are naturally destined to remain in perpetual forest, and must ever be of great value to the inhabitants.

"On Big Beaver are several old Indian clearings of considerable extent, only one of which is now occupied by them. A few wood choppers, temporarily resident there, have also made small clearings, on which they get excellent crops. Some hundred fishermen resort to the island during a considerable part of the year, as well as to the other islands of this group, and the main lands near by.

"Garden island lies to the north of Big Beaver, separated from it by a strait two miles wide. The soil of this island is believed to be seldom equaled. Besides large fields now cultivated to corn and various other crops by the Indians, it has several hundred acres of land cleared and partially cleared, and entirely unoccupied. It has also extensive sugar camps, no where surpassed in quality or productiveness.

"A short distance to the east of this lies Little Beaver, a very beautiful island, formerly the principal resort of the Indians, and containing 2,000 or 3,000 acres of excellent meadow and pasture. It is doubtless inferior to either Garden island or Big Beaver for the production of grain but no where excelled in the richness of its grazing.

"High Island lies four or five miles west of Big Beaver; — is quite hilly — contains a large extent of valuable pineries, and several thousand acres of land of excellent quality for cultivation.

"The other islands named are high, dry and well timbered, with a soil sufficiently rich, but quite too stony for cultivation; but at the same time furnishing excellent stations for the fishermen employed among them.

"The Indians have raised considerable quantities of corn on the islands every year from time immemorial, as they have of various kinds of roots and vegetables. The finer grains have but recently been introduced by occasional traders who have temporarily resided there, but have universally succeeded. The proximity of the lake precludes the possibility of unseasonable frosts, and thus gives a reasonable warrant that fruit will succeed there.

"Fishing is the most extensive business heretofore engaged in. — The fisheries extend north fifty miles, south forty and east and west the width of lake Michigan. We are not able to say how many persons are employed in the fisheries, but about one hundred fishermens' cabins are found on Big Beaver. They are equally numerous in other locations, and several small sail craft are constantly employed in transporting fish and fishermen's stores. The principal fishing season is from the beginning of June till the setting in of winter. Many persons, however, pursue it throughout the year. Many kinds of fish are taken; but the most abundant and celebrated are Mackinaw trout, white fish and herring. Necessarily growing out of this is an extensive business in coopering, boat building &c.

"A very considerable business has been done for many years in Indian trade, especially in fish, furs and sugar. This business is very profitable and can be indefinitely extended.

"Supplying steamboats with wood is a business but recently begun here, but offers a wide field for enterprise. It is well known that the shores of lake Michigan furnish wood suitable for this purpose at very few accessible points, and only in limited quantities. — The Beaver Islands have over fifty thousand acres of wood of the superior quality for steamboats, in the immediate vicinity of the best harbor in the lakes; easily accessible at all times and in all weathers to the steamboats passing both ways, daily from Buffalo to Chicago. The demand is equal to 100 cords per day, or 20,000 cords per year, and is annually increasing; and the price never less than $1.50 per cord. Choppers get fifty cents per cord for cutting.

"The soil and climate justify the opinion that general agricultural employments would succeed well here, even with less favorable markets. The unlimited demand for milk, eggs, poultry, fresh meat, potatoes, and every variety of culinary vegetables, to supply the fishers and the many hundreds of persons daily passing on the steamboats, who can get these articles from no other place within hundreds of miles, must make the furnishing of these things a source of unlimited wealth. To a certain extent this trade depends on the vigorous prosecution of the wooding business. But it is hardly possible that it should be overdone, even with the present demand.

"As the seat of the Indian mission, these islands present advantages found no where else. Situated on the border of the Indian settlements, from which, in all probability, they never will be driven, it will make a permanent establishment where they can be frequently personally present to receive instructions in everything pertaining to their salvation, and become acquainted with the entire order of the church. By means of the numerous routes radiating from Beaver as a common centre to every part of the Indian country, constantly traversed by them in bark canoes, a continual intercourse can easily and constantly be kept up with the most distant tribes, both elders and traders, at an expense merely nominal. By its extentless fisheries and various other natural resources, many thousands of Indians can sustain themselves according to their accustomed habits when attending conferences, or stopping for other purposes, without any expense of their benefactors. By its superior facilities for agriculture and the arts of civilized life, the civilization and elevation of the Indian can there be accomplished without exposure to the contaminating vices and infidelity of an unconverted world. At the same time its easy and rapid access to the principal cities of the United States, and the numerous towns on the lakes, secure the highest advantages of society, trade and the arts.

"These islands are all included within the bounds of Michigan. — The United States have purchased the Indian Title, and Big Beaver island has been surveyed and is now subject to preemption, but is not offered for sale. The other islands have not been surveyed, but are open

Strang Surveys Beaver Island

to settlers who wish to locate there. The Indians remaining in this region have declined emigrating beyond the Mississippi, but purchase lands of the United States, as they come into market, as other persons do.

"The policy which has been adopted in regard to the gathering on Beaver islands, is that the entire islands be purchased by the church, and divided among the saints who wish to make it their home, AS THEY SHALL SEVERALLY NEED. Saints who have the means, and who believe in living by every word that proceedeth out of the mouth of God, offer to give the money to purchase the land as it comes into market. Until then we are entitled to hold it by preemption. On this point we have the written assurance of the Commissioners of the General Land Office, and several distinguished officers of the National Government."

S.

A somewhat detailed description of the harbor appeared in the May 24, 1849, issue of the Gospel Herald, also sent back to Voree by Strang. This excerpt was taken from a long report narrating difficulties experienced in getting to Beaver, including being forced to pay for occupying part of an open dock while waiting for a lake steamer part of one night.

"At one o'clock we made the pier of E. J. Moore, at the west side of Paradise Bay. By the way, this name is new to you, as it is also to me, but I understand that this harbor has always been so called by the sailors, and for reasons which none can appreciate more than they.

"The outer bay indents between broad points more than a mile into the east shore of Big Beaver. Here it is a strait, ninety rods wide, and from forty to one hundred and fifty feet deep, running up into the harbor, which is about one mile across in either direction, and throughout one half of its extent, varying in depth from twenty-five to one hundred and fifty feet, and throughout the other half from nine to sixteen feet. On two sides the water shoals out several rods, and then drops off into deep water, but about half the distance around the deep water comes up very near the water's edge, and in some parts so close that passengers can be landed from a steamboat without a wharf."

The following letter, published in the Gospel Herald on December 13, 1848, reveals the type of soft pressure put upon the Saints toward a successful gathering on Big Beaver. Strang personally wrote this to a Saint, requesting information to assist him in his decision to "gather," either at Voree or Beaver Island.

> "Brother _____ brought to me a letter from you (when he came to Conference) in which, among other things, you requested me to write to you, and gave me also a dollar to pay me for my time. This was well; for my time is nearly all occupied in serving my bretheren; and with all their kindness my family are sometimes neglected. But as I read your letter, and pocketed the dollar, I said, "the poor have the gospel preached to them."
>
> "Recollecting the vast amount of requests and inquiries accumulated before me, I could not have it in my heart to change the order of answering. Many of the saints cannot send the dollar, but they have the same need of spiritual aid. It will be a glorious time when there are no more poor among the saints of God; when he shall make them all rich together, in a common possession sufficient for the wants of all.
>
> "Sometimes I get somewhat discouraged at the prospects before us, fearing that the day of our deliverance is far off, and that the Lord delayeth his coming. But his coming shall be as that of the flood, when men think not. Few he will find having faith. Many will be destroyed, for he will make the earth empty, and there will be few men left.
>
> "You speak as though there was a vacuum, a something wanting in your mind. I doubt not nearly all the saints can say the same. Once the shepherds have been careless of the flocks committed to their charge. Now the flocks are careless of the shepherds whom God has set over them. The spiritual leaders are not sustained with the prayers, the faith or the confidence of the saints. We are not a flock in a fold, but a flock scattered, and act

like strangers and enemies to one another. We come together in little companies, glance our scorning eyes at one another; a few leaders butt; the lambs are trampled on, trodden under foot and forgotten. It is no wonder we are so poor, diminished and scrawny a flock. No wonder the shepherds have so much trouble with the flock, and with all their troubles do it so little good.

"I truly believe more efforts have been made and more pains taken to get members out of the church than to bring members in for the last three years. More to wound and break afresh old wounds than to heal and strengthen. No man can do a good deed but it is attributed to an ill motive.

"There are very few that calumny does not pursue. However ridiculous a story is put afloat on any one, the man that doubts it is suspected of being PARTICIPIS CRIMINIS. The man that admonishes an offender is deemed contaminated by his association. If he hopes for reform, the vicious will themselves cry down as the apologist of iniquity.

"I know of but one way to flee from these evils, and that has been recommended so often IN VAIN that I have hardly face to repeat it. A little external pressure — persecution from without — would go far to unite us in bonds of brotherhood. It would prevent much apostacy. But these are not the days to try us in patience, but in faith.

"There are in my acquaintance many saints possessed of an abundance in farms, houses, etc., who are not in the least anxious about gathering. Nothing but persecution will drive them to the places God has appointed for them. Two or three such would put the saints in Voree on a footing of competence and abundance for all time to come. The Order of Enoch have here land enough for one or two thousand — they need a little help NOW in paying for it and building on it. By and by they will not need it, or it will be too late.

"Three thousand dollars judiciously laid out at Beaver gives us the undisputed control and exclusive occupation of the Beaver Islands (sufficient for a small county) for all time to come.

"Who cares for the kingdom of God as much as for his farm? This lethargy is too deep to rouse men from it on the promises of God.

"If it was necessary that a saint should sacrifice houses and land for the sake of the kingdom of God, we might encourage them with the promise of an hundred fold, with persecution also, and in the world to come life everlasting. But one could do that and not sacrifice one cent. Not one in a hundred of the saints but can leave his present residence, making such disposition of his property as circumstances admit of at all times, and come up to one or the other place of gathering and improve his condition.

"If some great sacrifice was required, possibly some would come. They have only to believe, obey and live. It is too easy. Few will do it. I sometimes almost pray for persecution. It would make the saints love one another.

"But God governs, and he will accomplish his purposes in wisdom and righteousness. He has long since tried many of us in severe sufferings and persecution, and many stood them whose faith has since failed.

"There is something of pride in the perilous hour that nerves us for the struggle, but it is a strong faith that, with much goods and no outward peril, can say, "I know that my Redeemer liveth."

"When all the flock hear the shepherd, we shall live."

Sincerely, James J. Strang

The Gospel Herald of May 17, 1849, includes a most informative letter describing conditions and needs on Beaver Island. Here is an excellent companion description to the Strang survey, written by Brother James Blakeslee to Brother Cooper.

"I write to inform you that I am still on the Island. I arrived last Saturday, (April 21, 1849) in company with President Strang, and some thirty odd others. The brethren on the Island received us gladly, and we were soon provided with places to stop among them until houses can be built.

"During my stop here we have explored part of the Island, and find it as good or better than it has been represented. There is plenty of sugar maple and beech timber on this Island, and as handsome as I ever saw. The land is also good for farming purposes, except immediately at or about the harbor and the shores of the Island, which are sandy and rocky. There is also plenty of cedar for posts and rails for fences and other purposes, and as handsome as grows in any part of the world. There is also some balsam or fir, very fine, and some white and Norway pine, of a good quality, and some oak.

"I have visited many of the brethren and friends here, and find them all well pleased with the location. Wood sells at $1.50 per cord to the boats which stop at this port on their way up and down the lakes, and the wood business makes employment for a good number of hands now, and it will increase yearly. Wood choppers get fifty cents per cord, cash, for chopping wood, and the timber is about the right size to make it a good business. Any smart boy, of a dozen or thirteen years of age, can chop a cord of steamboat wood in a day, and do it easy. They cut the wood a little short of four feet, and do not split it very fine.

"The fishing business employs a good many hands, and is a good business also. If the business of growing potatoes here was entered into with more energy and far more extensively, it would still be a profitable business. I have eaten potatoes grown on the Island, which were kept in a pit or hole out of doors, covered first with hemlock boughs and then with dirt, and was informed that not one of the potatoes was found to be affected with rot or any disease whatever, and I have not eaten as good since I left the Isle of Man in 1841. I ate as good there, but no better. And better maple sugar cannot be made or manufactured in any country than is manufactured on this and the adjoining Islands, both by the whites and also by the Lamanites.

"Last Monday I passed through a Lamanite sugar works, and had expected or anticipated a pleasant visit with them. But, Oh! what was my disappointment when passing through their bush for some fifty or sixty rods, and observing on either side of the foot path, as far as the eye could reach, the birch bark vessels full of sugar water and running over; and on arriving at a wigwam, instead of finding the Lamanite men, women and children capable of conversing with us on any matter of moment to them or ourselves, we found the most of them had learned, not only how to make sugar from maple trees, but had learned how to exchange their sugar for fire water, and had been trafficking with the whites and obtained a sufficiency of the "critter," not only to put a full stop to their work, but to put some of them to sleep and others to fighting and quarreling. And finding our Lamanite brethren in that situation, we felt to mourn for them, and also to remember in our prayers those who had done so wickedly as to sell poison to them, when we should learn who they were.

"There are two stores at the harbor, which are pretty well supplied with all things necessary. All with whom I have conversed say that they have wanted for nothing since coming to the Island, and no industrious person need want for any of the comforts of life on this land. Indeed it is just the place for the saints to gather to, and it would be well for the brethren who have capital to come on immediately with as little delay as possible, and come prepared to put up a good steam saw mill at the harbor; it will be good property here, and is greatly needed. And it would be well for the brethren who come to the Island to settle, to prepare to furnish a good assortment of goods, such as are wanted on the islands, and make their calculations to sell as cheap as any establishment in the State, and a good business can be done in that line. A word to the wise is, or should be, sufficient.

"We want a good chair maker here. That will be a good business in this place. And mechanics of nearly all kinds would do well here. A good boot and shoe maker is wanted here. Come, then, my brethren who are scattered abroad, gather up your families and property and come up to the places that God has appointed for the saints to gather to, and take an active part in preparing places of safety against the day when the wrath of God is poured out upon the wicked.

"I expect to leave here in a day or two for Louisburg,

Ohio, by way of Detroit, where I expect to tarry until our Conference on the Island in July next, when I expect to be here, and then build a house for my family, and move them on this season. The Island is organized into a township, with the town officers and a post office appointed here, called the Beaver Island post office, and a side mail weekly from Mackinac will run to and from the Island, so that letters and papers can be directed to Beaver now, via. Mackinac, Michigan.

"We learned by Capt. Snow, of the schooner Telegraph, last evening, that a company of the brethren from Chicago of about fifteen families would start for the Island in a few days. Capt. Snow came in night before last, and is still here wind bound. Bro. Samuel Graham, Nathan Foster and myself will start together I expect, and it may be we shall go with Capt. Snow to Detroit. The brethren who came with us are pleased with the Island, and are all at work preparing to build houses."

Truly and sincerely,
JAMES BLAKESLEE

In the same issue of the Herald appeared the following written at Beaver Island April 28, 1849. Nathan Foster appealed to Saints throughout the world to gather for freedom and equal rights.

"To the Brethren in Koskonong and Porter:

"Having stopped several days on Beaver on my way east, I thought I would write you my views of the importance of gathering up to the places appointed for the salvation of God's people.

"I am much pleased with this land, much better than I anticipated. The brethren here are industrious and united in the cause of Zion, and must prevail, for the Lord has spoken it. I have explored the centre of the Island. The timber is very beautiful. The hard timbered land, which is about two-thirds of the Island, is very good for farming. The remainder is timbered with pine and cedar of the best quality.

"This is a good place for the rich and the poor, the widow and fatherless, freedom and equal rights to all the saints throughout the world, and no deaths from starvation. Thanks be to God.

"Now, brethren, you that can gather up with me when I return from the east for my family, which will be in the course of two months, I should be glad of your company."

NATHAN FOSTER

CHAPTER VI
Voree and City of James

Of the seven men chosen at Voree to establish a "Stake" on Beaver Island, more than half never had the opportunity. Perhaps they cared little for the opportunity and resented their choice. Four of them were soon removed from the roster for crimes against the Church, though recently praised in the January 14, 1847, "Zion's Reveille" as "tried, substantial and faithful men, servants of the Most High God, in whom the Church may repose the most implicit confidence."

There were plenty of troubles along the White River at Voree during the years prior to the establishment of the Kingdom.

No family migration took place to Beaver until late July, 1847. A few Saints met at the North-West Company trading post during July, under the leadership of Ebenezer Page. The Indians were very friendly. "A noble and intellectual race of men," according to letters written back to Saints at Voree. The Zion's Reveille, as it was renamed from the previous Voree Herald, continually carried accounts of the Saints' progress. The following year, issues of the Gospel Herald for April and May informed members that during the past fortunately mild winter, four families had experienced the rigors of the new Mormon Stake.

A fortunate situation developed when these four families desired to raise potatoes on land needing to be cleared. Because of the constant need for firewood by lake steamers, men were able to cut up wood from all clearings and make a profit. This gave them funds to construct a dock on the west side of Paradise Bay. Even then, the wood supply was critical because of a labor shortage. According to one letter from Beaver Island, during October, 1848, more than 60 steamers purchased fuel the previous season.

Two years after Strang first investigated the island, 12 families were braving its rugged life. Marvin Aldrich, President of the Stake, had much to say in his letters to Prophet Strang at Voree, including the hysterical state of a few Saints. In one letter, published in the Gospel Herald April, 1849, Aldrich wrote:

> "There are many spirits here and some very strange ones, too. Rebellion is as the sin of witchcraft. Witchcraft is sectarianism and every rebel organization that ever sprung out of Mormonism is simply that and nothing more."

President Aldrich referred to a situation on Beaver Island that flared up involving two disturbed Saints, Levi Parmeter and Samuel Shaw. Parmeter wanted to be "the lion to come out of the thicket and destroy the Gentiles." Shaw, himself, thought the Indians were about to "go from house to house in the dead of night and butcher people." Gurdon Brown, another Saint, broke out in revelations. Strang cut all three from the Church roster for such a mental display of instability. It was caused, he thought, by "too much brooding over religion."

At Voree, progress continued at a snail's pace. Saints still arriving there with more than ordinary means resented a policy of sharing each other's earthly possessions in communal living. To this, the writer heartily agrees. American free society is not based on communistic leanings. It kills incentive and it killed it at Voree. The year 1849 was about to be a mighty significant one for the Church.

It is interesting to note that this communistic policy was

Voree and City of James

abandoned at Beaver for one-tenth tithing, although the claimed revelation of January 17, 1849, expressed establishment of it as a God-given commandment.

It is difficult to recall early Mormons without remembering hatred of them by Gentiles. However, the Saints at Voree suffered less Gentile hatred than most earlier Mormon groups experienced. Perhaps they were too busy quarrelling with each other. Lack of provocation may indeed have resulted from restraint on the part of Strangite Mormons. Joseph Smith Mormons were notoriously violent at Kirtland, Zion and Nauvoo, acquiring reputations far from what normally might be expected of God-fearing people.

One great bewilderment toward Gentile understanding of Mormonism was constant name-calling between Mormon members. Name-calling was especially vicious after a member had just been banned from the Church. Even Saints recently held in high esteem meant little if a member was suddenly turned over to the "buffetings of Satan" by the Church.

Gentile hatred was about to be reckoned with again, however, as migration from Voree began to arrive at Beaver in greater numbers. The economic prize primarily was firewood for lake steamers. It was strangely important to Mackinac Island economy to supply wood from Beaver with Mackinac labor. It also was important to continue the use of the costly facilities built up during the once booming fur trade at Mackinac by centering the fish trade there, but commercial steamers preferred to use Paradise Bay at Beaver Island to pick up their wood supply. Mackinac and Beaver Gentiles began to bristle over the energy of the new labor competition.

Economic disadvantage was not the only concern expressed by the Gentiles. It was not difficult to realize that Mormons were about to claim lands having recently extinguished Indian titles. Gentiles had merely used the land in the past. They felt their use of it had been long enough to claim it by pre-emption. They were also concerned because they believed the land around the harbor might soon become valuable.

Land on Beaver was not yet open for homesteading, although 20 or more families lived on the island. There were quite a few Indians and also many trappers who stopped to trade.

In 1848, the Government opened up the islands for entry. The following year found approximately 50 Mormon families on the "land amidst wide waters." Most of these Mormon families were poor. Their industrious nature, however, was more than enough to find them laboriously building a road to the interior, constructing a schooner of their own and setting up a steam saw-mill. The road became the King's Highway, very much in use today and retaining the same name, fortunately.

The City of James hosted the initial Conference of the Saints on the shores of Paradise Bay in 1849. Important decisions made at the conference included the expediency of an Eastern Mission by a dozen elders to secure fifty converts by Spring.

A second conference in the Autumn sent Prophet Strang and Prime Minister George J. Adams to Boston, New York, Philadelphia, and Baltimore for additional converts. In Washington, they sought Governmental assistance. They were interested primarily in securing land concessions from the U.S. Government.

Strang also realized a need for improving the reputation of the Church. Obviously, no trip was considered successful without adding converts to the saintly flock, especially since withdrawal continued from it. This rate of decline lessened, however, as poverty was overcome.

One weapon devised to secure legal concessions from the Government was a plea written at Buffalo, New York, on April 16, 1850. It is known as the "Memorial" and was written during the second eastern invasion by Strang. The "Memorial" asked the U.S. Government to set aside all unoccupied lands of the Beaver Island archipelago as restitution for past material losses. A simple reply from the Committee on Public Lands merely stated the U. S. Government did not own the islands.

The Buffalo letter requesting the islands was written in desperation and was, perhaps, an unfortunate request. It concentrated further attention on the troubled situation at Beaver, not

Voree and City of James 69

only by the Government but by the public. The Mackinac Gentiles became more belligerent than ever toward the Saints.

The return of Strang to Beaver in the Spring of 1850 found the friction between the Saints and Gentiles bristling. The Gentiles knew they had to make a choice: compete economically or drive out the Mormons who were becoming thoroughly entrenched and powerful.

It is important to point out that commercial fishermen located at Mackinac Island were in desperate financial difficulties in the 1850's. This led to economic friction. Most of the resulting violence was based on this friction, but the origin of the violence must be blamed primarily on the Gentiles themselves, though contrary to sensational newspaper reports at the time.

Between 1850 and 1856, it was a common belief that Beaver Island was crime-ridden. After all, had not crime existed at Kirtland, Zion and Nauvoo? Contrary to public belief, crime did not exist on Beaver Island, unless Gentile sponsored. Resistance, yes, but human beings with any backbone would have resisted the type of cruelty administered to the Saints by many Gentiles.

Resistance at Beaver increased as the number of converts increased. After three years of augmented persecution, the Saints began a period of meeting violence with violence. The Gentiles became even bolder, striking fear into the hearts of the women and children as an added measure of their true character.

Strang now viewed the situation of his Saints with greater concern. Nothing short of a dramatic revelation would weld his flock into a fighting religious colony capable of suppressing the growing opposition of lawless Gentiles. Up to this time, Strang fully appreciated a certain amount of Mormon persecution, almost to the point of praying for it. Matters had worsened, however. The fate of his colony was in unfavorable balance and threatened with increased Mackinac injustice.

A dramatic revelation was announced at a conference of the Church on Beaver Island on July 8, 1850. At this meeting, Strang read aloud, for the first time, a part of his Book of the

Law of the Lord, purported to have been translated from a long-promised record of ancient divine origin, which he claimed to be the "plates of Laban." At this conference, Strang was also crowned "King." These plates supplied about one-third of the Book of the Law. Two-thirds represented the progressive thoughts and ideas of James Strang. The plates are mentioned in the Book of Mormon, I Nephi, chap. 1, verses 20-49, but may be considered of different origin.

Simply stated, the hieroglyphics on the metallic record, read by the aid of the identical stones used by Joseph Smith, Urim and Thummim, proclaimed the re-establishment of God's Kingdom on earth. Their divine translator, James Strang, was designated to occupy the throne.

In "The Kingdom of Saint James," Milo Quaife made this observation:

> "If Strang's pretentions be valid this should be the most interesting book ever published in America, if not, indeed, in the world.
>
> "Other religions have their sacred writings, and the Saints themselves the Book of Mormon. But these are mere chronicles of past events: the Book of Mormon, for example, is the history of an ancient race; the Bible, in addition to this, is a literary miscellany, the product of many writers over a long period of time. But the Book of the Law of the Lord is God's own framework of government for his people on earth in the present and all future time. It was the capstone of Strang's prophetic career, the climax toward which all his labors tended. In theory, if not in actual fact, it made him supreme ruler over all the earth.
>
> "Ironically enough, his Kingdom had vanished into thin air before the completion of publication of the book on which it was based."

To those who question the possible existence of the "Voree plates" and the "plates of Laban," it may be surmised that they were returned from whence they came in the manner of delivery, by divine messenger. The plates of the Book of Mormon are claimed to have been divinely returned after sufficient years in the possession of Joseph Smith.

This rather humorous comment about the "plates of Laban" was sent to the writer by Hazel Strang McCardell, granddaughter of James Strang:

> "I remember once asking my grandmother (Sarah Strang) the question, 'Was grandfather Strang a smart and well-educated man?' She replied with some impatience, 'Of course your grandpa was smart and well-educated, otherwise how could he have written those plates?' "

CHAPTER VII
Beaver Island—1850

Perhaps this chapter should be called "Polygamy — 1850." It is the year Prophet Strang publicly embraced polygamy and the spiritual wife doctrine, and by so doing created friction in the colony.

Polygamy was simply a plural marriage for "time and eternity." Any legal marriage outside the Church was for "time" only. Mormons believe that Elders in the Bible had plural wives. Joseph Smith declared marriage the only assurance women had of going to heaven. Since wars left a great many women without an opportunity for marriage, polygamy became necessary, according to Smith. A spiritual marriage was for "eternity" only. This allowed a man to marry a woman who was not even a Mormon, if she was deceased. He could also marry a former love if she was deceased and could marry any deceased unmarried woman just to get her into heaven.

It is necessary to have some knowledge about the teachings of Strang to appreciate his pronouncement of this doctrine. To those unfamiliar with his earlier beliefs, this may not appear unusual. After all, was it not Brigham Young who predetermined polygamy and the spiritual wife doctrine as his cornerstone? And was it not Joseph Smith's highest leaders who secretly practiced polygamy? Joseph Smith left six widows, all of whom became, by inheritance, wives of Brigham Young. The Young household eventually reached a total of 27 wives and a countable 56 children, 49 of whom were still living when he died.

To appreciate Strang's claimed message from Heaven concerning polygamy, it is necessary to examine his beliefs before the revelation on plurality and return to the summer of 1846. At that time, Strang opposed Brighamite polygamy as "abominations." However, plural infection had spread into Voree by the addition of former Smith followers. Because of it, many Saints were "cut off from the Church" as soon as it became known they embraced plurality and practiced it. Strang was not yet convinced it should be practiced.

There were many instances prior to 1850 when the doctrine of polygamy was condemned by Strang. To prove this emphatically, here is an interesting quote from the printed Herald communication of John E. Page, editor and one of the Presidents of the Voree stake:

> "We have talked hours, yea, even days with President Strang, and we find to our utmost satisfaction that he does not believe in or cherish the doctrine of polygamy in any manner, shape, or form imaginable whatever."

In the issue of the Voree Herald for August 12, 1847, Strang signed the following statement, leaving no doubt in the minds of Saints as to just where he stood on spiritual wifery.

> "I am only astonished that it should be necessary to state them at all. Within three years I have, in the work of the ministry, travelled over 16,000 miles, visited all the states north of the Carolinas but three, most of them several times, preached to large congregations in all the principal cities and in most of the large branches in the country, and I have uniformly and distinctly discarded and declared heretical the so-called "spiritual wife system" and everything connected therewith... I now say distinctly, and I defy contradiction, that the man or woman does not exist on earth, or under the earth who ever heard me say one word, or saw me do one act, savoring the least of SPIR-

ITUAL WIFERY, or any of the attending abominations. My opinions on this subject are unchanged, and I regard them as unchangeable. They are established on a full consideration of all the scriptures, both ancient and modern, and the discipline of the Church shall conform thereto."

Strang was a master at expressing his feelings on any subject. His sentiments could not have been substantiated better than the above confirmation given the Saints.

However, his apparently firm opposition to polygamy as well, took an abrupt reversal a year later when it became known he himself had become a convert. The full name of the charming young lady who may have influenced his claimed revelation was Elvira Eliza Field. Elvira was the first and most notorious of his four polygamous wives. In the section entitled "The Five Wives and Fourteen Children of James Strang" will be found a brief review of her life. Also included are reviews of the three who followed, and the only legal wife who preceded them all.

An unconvincing explanation of Strang's reversal was given to Milo Quaife by Charles J. Strang, eldest son of Elvira and Prophet Strang. According to Quaife, son Charles "advanced the theory that the change was made when Strang became convinced that Joseph Smith, before his death, had become a proponent of polygamy." The fallacy of this thought can be clearly nullified by a letter George J. Adams wrote to Strang, dated June 20, 1846. In speaking of Smith, Adams said:

"If he had taken my council and laid aside the cursed Spiritual Wife doctrine, the Military Spirit, the Presidential Campaign and several other operations (that I will tell you when I see you) he would have been a living man until this day."

Another, and more convincing, theory was spoken by Wingfield Watson to Quaife when he made the stout-hearted observation that Strang "was a man of powerful sexual impulses." Quaife continued in this earthy vein that the only solution to possession of the "clever and charming young woman" was through polygamy. This writer is inclined to agree with Watson. However, it does not reflect on the character of Strang simply because his personal magnetism included strong sexual powers.

In using the word "clever," Quaife brings to mind that Elvira was a designing woman out to "get her man." There was no intention on his part to paint such a picture. Elvira Field was a cultured young woman. Her father, a Mormon even before Strang, raised this talented girl with a father's interest at heart.

More will be said about Elvira Field in another section. Since this chapter concerns polygamy, however, it serves a genuine purpose to include here a few brief comments tying her life to that of Strang.

It is important to note that Elvira went to the conference at Voree in April, 1848, and there saw Strang for the first time. Several months later, it was announced by George Adams, the Prime Minister, that Prophet Strang had received a heavenly message to institute polygamy. Elvira was then only 17. On July 13, 1849, she attended another conference, this one on Beaver Island. Soon after, Strang and Elvira were secretly married in the Church. This Mormon marriage was not a marriage in the legal sense, although Strang certainly would have married her legally if he could have, and the additional three polygamous wives, for that matter.

In "The Kingdom of Saint James," Quaife has given us his opinion of the Elvira Field-Prophet Strang eastern mission, during which Elvira travelled as his "male" secretary. Elvira was shorn of her long hair and dressed in male attire.

While nearly all of the "Kingdom" is written in an unbiased manner and is a remarkable narrative, the writer does not fully agree with Quaife when he writes of this important and admittedly fascinating episode.

> "Returning from the realm of surmise to that of demonstrable fact, let us take note of a performance of Strang in connection with his eastern mission of 1849 which is difficult to reconcile with the accepted standards either of common morality or of common sense."

ELVIRA FIELD STRANG
(AS CHARLIE DOUGLASS)

First polygamous wife of James Strang, dressed in male attire as his "secretary" in 1849.

Quaife continued, after an explanation of what transpired in 1848 between George J. Adams, Elvira Field and James J. Strang to culminate this acquaintance:

> "It affords a striking example of the limits of human credulity that Elvira accepted this offer in all sincerity, and vanishing from the ken of parents and loved ones, blindly staked her entire future upon her faith in the Prophet and in his lecherous Prime Minister, George J. Adams."

George J. Adams was a "lecherous" Prime Minister, as indicated without reservation in "A Sampling of Strangite Impostures." That the Elvira Field-Prophet Strang trip east was immoral, this writer does not agree.

Were they not married according to Mormon law? The marriage took place on July 13, 1849, just prior to the eastern mission. Strang wished to avoid verbal spankings by his Saints in the east and, because of it, kept the marriage a secret by the imposture. However, Strang claimed the union was God-sanctioned through a revelation establishing polygamy. Secrecy was very difficult, but the imposture was never admitted during the trip, in spite of unceasing gossip.

Elvira traveled as "Charlie Douglass." Her first son, "Charles" Strang, later a Lansing printer, was actually given her temporary name. Elvira used it with obvious difficulty.

Some historians, and a few Strang descendants, have considered polygamy Strang's most serious blunder. It is difficult to think otherwise. But how can anyone judge? Assuming it was a blunder is saying that God blundered, speaking from the Prophet's point of view. Was it not part of the laws of governance sent by angelic messenger? James Strang and Joseph Smith said it was.

Polygamy was a real source of conflict within the Mormon Church body to the year 1890. Congress then suppressed it with drastic laws. Brigham Young, of course, was its biggest supporter. Strang, at one time, was one of its most vigorous suppressors.

Even Martin Luther ruled polygamy permissible within his church. It was not practiced to any extent. Going back further to ancient Britons, men formed societies with equal numbers of women, all marrying each other. The children belonged to them all! In England, the Church handled all matters of matrimony to the time of James I. Later, it became a concern of the State.

The Territory of Utah finally abandoned polygamy in 1890 by a Constitutional Amendment. This gave impetus to their admission to the Union as a state in 1896. Though they no longer practiced polygamy openly, there were many instances of "crypto-polygamous unions."

This chapter on Polygamy must include the name of another prominent Strangite Mormon. His name will be mentioned several times in "The King Strang Story." An incident involving his Mormon wife and himself indicates that all was not well at Saint James after the announcement of the plural marriage revelation. The name of this Strangite Mormon was Lorenzo Dow Hickey.

This influential Saint was recruiting in the East when news reached him about the Strang revelation establishing polygamy. Mrs. Hickey, the chief fomenter, sent the news from Beaver Island. The letter infuriated her husband, especially the lines about Elvira Field. Hickey was profoundly disturbed that the ugliness of polygamy and spiritual wifery had now been approved as a doctrine of the Strangite Church.

During a meeting in New York City a short time after the letter arrived, his mind having dwelled on his hatred so much, Hickey dared speak accusedly directly in the face of Prophet Strang himself. Traveling with the Prophet was his secretary, "Charlie Douglass," the feminine Elvira Field dressed in male attire. This added fire to the meeting, though it was not "positive" his secretary was a woman. No one dared suggest an obvious solution to find out.

Hickey delivered his barrage of accusations at the meeting for all to hear. He accused Strang of "adultery, fornication, spiritual wifery and all the abominations that were practiced at Nauvoo."

This display of temper and fault-finding brought on his suspension from the Church. Even so, Strang considered the bold actions of Hickey due in part to a temporarily unbalanced mental condition. Actually, Strang was right.

As vicious as Hickey appeared at the New York meeting and as boldly outspoken as he was toward the evils of plural marriage, he, himself, practiced polygamy later, taking two plural wives. Prior to ultimate acceptance, he had confessed his faults and was reinstated into the good graces of the Strangite Church.

CHAPTER VIII
Beaver Island—1851

How was polygamy received on Beaver Island? Surprisingly calm, except for the few already discontented members. The number one proponent was Strang. He was a great leader and naturally had a great deal of influence with the Saints. Otherwise, the 700 already there by 1851 would not have been on the island at all. Because of polygamy, three important members cancelled their membership, eventually founding the Reorganized Church. They were Jason W. Briggs, Henry H. Deam and Zenas H. Gurley, Sr.

Strang, himself, had four polygamous wives: Elvira Field, Betsy McNutt, Sarah Wright and Phoebe Wright, the latter two being cousins. A brief narration about these four begins on page 118.

It may seem strange that the Saints of Beaver Island lived in comparative harmony in contrast to the bickering at Voree. There were enemies on Beaver and enemies to be, but in the main, life was beginning to mean something more than trying to eke out a living hand-to-mouth. The big trouble brewing on the island was outside the Saintly group, the Gentile faction opposing the move of the Saints from the "Garden of Peace".

Within this Saintly group in 1851, there was at least a semblance of peace. Some were still confused and a few disillusioned over the revelation sanctioning polygamy. Even so, little trouble in the Strang family, itself, developed. The legal wife of Strang, Mary Perce, was more than mildly disturbed, but remained passive until her departure by request. Her opposition to many Church policies resulted in a strained relationship with the Prophet.

Mary lived with her Prophet-husband many months after the first plural marriage was consummated. She left Beaver in May, 1851. As late as October 11, 1855, Strang wrote in his newspaper, *The Northern Islander,* that Mary had not separated from him. He went so far as to reveal that she spent one winter with him in Lansing, when he was a member of the State Legislature.

This "Story" has continued without emphasis that Strang was now "King." It is right he be called "King," because of the stature he enjoyed with his Saints. In all activities involving their lives since that coronation day of July 8, 1850, he was "King" to his Saintly Mormons, but never of Beaver Island as many writers seem to enjoy believing.

Strang was "King" in his household as well. Although his word was law, he was a gentle person. Friction did not exist in the home, as might be expected. A letter from Sarah, the third polygamous wife, to Milo Quaife in 1920 is an observation most Strang students may be unfamiliar with, and perhaps its contents are difficult to imagine.

> "You ask if we all lived in the same house. We did, but we had separate rooms and all met in prayer and ate at the same table. He (Strang) was a very mild-spoken kind man to his family, although his word was law. We were all honest in our religion and made things as pleasant as possible. There were four of us living in the same house."

It may be of interest that a door from the Strang home is in possession of the present writer. This was removed from the home in 1857 and built into the John Bonner home on the island. Contrary to most accepted accounts, the destruction of Strang's house in 1892 was intentional. Confusion that fire destroyed the build-

COURTESY, HENRY FORD MUSEUM

IDYLLIC LIFE ON BEAVER ISLAND

Unknown artist's misconception of Strang's family life and surroundings.

THE STRANG 'CASTLE' AT SAINT JAMES

Two log cabins at the rear included covered connectors to this very modest home.

ing may be due to the fact a home, built on the same site, burned and then was rebuilt. The door is now in the writer's home located on the identical property on which Strang built his own modest so-called "castle."

An observation concerning polygamy in the home, written in a letter from Eugenia Strang, daughter of Strang and Phoebe Wright, to Hazel Strang McCardell, granddaughter of Strang and Sarah Wright, is this most interesting personal comment. Written on June 6, 1936, the letter reads in part:

> "Mother had lived with father only eight months when he died, but even then she had begun to feel dissatisfied with polygamy, though she loved him devotedly all her life."

Phoebe never remarried, indicating, perhaps, her complete devotion.

There is an understandable error in the Quaife article, "Polygamy at Beaver Island," published in Michigan History Magazine, July-October, 1921. In speaking about the two Wright cousins who married Strang, Quaife states: "To Sarah was born a daughter, Eugenia," etc. This should be "To Phoebe," as Quaife has correctly stated a few lines later when he wrote: "The mother, Phoebe, lived in Minnesota for a number of years."

Sarah Adelia Wright, her full name before she married Strang, was a very remarkable woman. She married against the wishes of her father, at the age of 19. Her father, Phineas Wright, was important in the high council of the Church and considered by many the right-hand man of Strang. Phoebe Wright, a cousin of Sarah, married the "King" only a few months later. She was 18 years old and fourth in a family of 13, two of them born on Beaver Island. Sarah was one of eight children, four from a first marriage and four from a second. Betsy McNutt was the second polygamous wife. These four are introduced more fully in the Epilogue, "The Five Wives and Fourteen Children of James Strang."

Both young cousins accepted plural marriage to Strang an

honor. Betsy McNutt, admittedly on her way to becoming an old maid, surprisingly suggested marriage herself while at a dance. She was being teased about having no husband. In no uncertain terms she let her tormentors know only one man could interest her, the "King" himself.

Wingfield Watson, on the island from 1852 to 1856, indicated about 20 families were polygamous. Strang had four polygamous wives; Lorenzo Dow Hickey, two; George Miller, two; the others had one. Each had one legal wife. Since there were about 500 families in all, this percentage may be considered small.

The low percentage of plural marriages among the Saints on Beaver Island does not indicate a lack of Saintly interest. Specific instructions demanded ability to support a second wife. Most of them were poor. None of them, including Strang, were much more than comfortable. They were dedicated, proud people, happy to earn their own way.

The estimated 25 polygamous wives was two less than Brigham Young had in Salt Lake City.

The first year of polygamy at Beaver Island created violent reactions from the Gentile world. Center of this reaction, of course, was Mackinac, where plenty of dissatisfaction already existed. The Gentiles were even more furious with the second revelation announced on historic July 8, 1850, the establishment of the Kingdom of God.

The Saints had mighty few complimentary things said about them in the 1850's. "King" Strang was persecuted unmercifully in Sunday supplements, all bellowing lies and accusations bearing no resemblance to truth. Accusations of murder, counterfeiting and lust were spread with regularity. None was true, as proved later in U. S. Courts. People believed them, in spite of acquittal. During the nine year occupation by the Saints, only one fatal shooting ever took place on Beaver Island directly responsible to Mormon guns. There have been accounts as high as seven murders blamed on the Saints. Not one was committed.

The one unfortunate fatal shooting involved brothers Thomas and Samuel Bennett. This story has been misinterpreted for a century. Sensational falsehoods were born from this single incident. Factual details may be found in this volume in the review, "A History of the Grand Traverse Region."

One fuel that kept the Beaver Gentile mob a constant threat was liquor. Whiskey Point, where the lighthouse and life-saving station are today, was the filling station. Here, the rough Gentiles, mainly Irish, gathered to drink and harass the Saints. They beat them up at the least provocation. Whiskey Point also was the location of the Post Office. When it was time for Saints to pick up mail, the ruffians often met them with abusive language and physical violence. The Saints were not even allowed tea or coffee, yet they were forced to protect themselves from ruthless drunken enemies without proper legal recourse.

In the *Northern Islander* for April 13, 1851, Strang made this statement:

> "No fact can be more certain than that throughout the United States there is no legal protection to a Mormon."

The early history of the Mormon Church is one of persecution. While it was not true of Strang, himself, it is true that much of the early Mormon persecution was instigated by the Mormons, themselves, because of their unpopular way of life. This does not mean Strang was totally innocent. A great many of his problems were caused by his eventual "eye for an eye and tooth for a tooth" policy. Strang should have abandoned his non-resistance policy much earlier, before it became necessary to retaliate so intensely, thus bringing upon his already burdened life the additional heavy burden of unpopular public opinion.

His paramount Church problem resulted from periodic punishment of a few unruly Mormons, regardless of their high status as a Mormon. His efforts were toward honesty and human decency. Credit should be given to him for such corrective measures.

One unruly Mormon was George J. Adams. He was an unpopular pillar in the Church for four years and the one who physically placed the crown of metal on Strang's head when he was pronounced "King." Strang catered to Adams, while many Saints distrusted him. Adams had originally been one of the leaders in the Mormon Church under Joseph Smith.

The Saints were right in not trusting Adams. Publicity about him in the Press was most uncomplimentary and much of it was true. Adams, a lover of showmanship, had been an actor of sorts on the stage. The robe used at the Coronation of Strang was, in fact, one of his "props."

While in the east, Adams spent much of his time recruiting, and preaching the virtues of Strangite Mormonism. At one such Boston meeting Adams met a woman of questionable character. According to the *Northern Islander* of December 12, 1850, this woman was being introduced to associates in Baltimore as a "wealthy widow from Charleston, South Carolina." Real trouble began when she was brought to Beaver Island. Here she was introduced as his wife. According to Adams, the former Mrs. Adams had died.

Soon after learning that Mrs. Adams, who had been very ill in New Jersey, was very much alive, Strang deprived Adams of any voice in the First Presidency.

It is doubtful this "affair," alone, caused the dismissal of Adams, but it was the last straw, so to speak, that moved Strang to eliminate the authority Adams had. The Saints were pleased. The newspapers also were pleased, and they made the most of it.

Only a few months earlier, as shown in the Minutes of a pre-Coronation Conference, Adams was so shaken about the mob violence on Beaver Island that he was prepared to sanction a "generous letting of Gentile blood." Strang also was in a bitter mood at this time, considering a death sentence proper punishment for certain leaders of the Gentile mob. It may seem strange to say he was justified in feeling this way, but facts prove he had the right. Proper legal protection was denied the Saints on Beaver.

The removal of Adams caused him to join the opposition based at Mackinac. He first secured a writ for the arrest of Strang. The writ was eventually served on him at Mackinac because he eluded them at Beaver. It accused Strang of threatening the life of the "second Mrs. Adams." Authorities at Mackinac welcomed this chance for prosecution, although the charge was ridiculous. Some of the trial displayed legal ignorance on the part of the prosecutor. Strang won, as usual.

The primary concern here is not the trial nor the ridiculous accusations made against Strang. It is merely to point out that this is the type of sensationalism the nation's press used to persecute the Saints by exaggeration and highly colored reporting. Adam's turnabout caused great injury to the Beaver Island Kingdom of God, especially since it was becoming important politically as the membership increased.

In 1851, as incredible as it may seem, the Whig Party was very conscious that the 1852 Presidential Convention at Baltimore would include a great interest in how the Mormons of Beaver Island might cast their votes in the forthcoming election.

This situation presented itself only a few years after the first Mormon Prophet, Joseph Smith, made a move to gain the nomination for himself in an earlier presidential election. Death cancelled this ambitious possibility. Bishop George Miller attended the meeting at which his nomination was discussed. (see Miscellany)

The reason Strang became an important factor to both prolitical parties, the Whigs and the Democrats, is very simple. His decision might result in either candidate becoming President of the United States!

The two parties were considered equal in Michigan. This meant the Mormons on Beaver Island could sway the election in the state either way. Strang controlled this vote. The Whigs, under President Fillmore, controlled the administration. Fillmore was anxious to get the nomination at Baltimore to win an elected term in office after having completed President Taylor's unexpired term. Taylor had died suddenly on July 9, 1850 creating much confusion in the party.

Concurrent with the political situation of 1851 was the Bennett shooting on Beaver. One serious result of this particular incident was the building up of imaginary Mormon brutality in the mind of George C. Bates, then United States District Attorney in Detroit. Bates was too eager to use the shooting as an excuse to bring Gentile wrath of justice down on the Saints of Beaver Island. He especially wanted to "get" Strang. Bates, however, could not act without federal approval. President Fillmore was not about to antagonize Strang, because he needed the Michigan vote in the coming national election. Michigan's Democratic Governor Bingham had already decided on the same strategy. He, therefore, passed the buck back to the President for the identical reason. Secretary of State Daniel Webster, playing cautious politics, agreed it really was a Democratic problem and strictly one for Michigan's Governor Bingham.

At this point, Democratic Senator Stephen A. Douglas was requested to strengthen the administration position by announcing his stand on resistance to constitutional authority. This meant that the arrest of Strang was inevitable. Through proper federal channels, the "King" and his brothers-in-crime were taken to Detroit and tried for "treason, robbery of the mails, counterfeiting and trespassing upon United States lands."

Few men have been subjected to more arrests for such an array of crimes, avoiding conviction consistently. The acquittal verdicts were just verdicts. The arrests merely emphasized the extent to which authorities went to degrade Strang publicly. The legal farce in Detroit was only one of numerous court battles in the life of James Strang.

"The King Strang Story" is not meant to be a history of the Saints. For this reason there is no point in giving details about the trial in Detroit. The trial involved about 100 men and women, lasted over six weeks and included some of the most serious accusations with which one can be charged. Only one guilt was proved against the Saints — they were Mormons. Still, an aroused public believed the worst, in spite of complete acquittal. Strang successfully acted as counsel for his Saints, as well as defending himself.

Detroit's Whig paper denounced Strang. The Democratic paper was somewhat sympathetic. This fact added luster to the verdict of the jury because 10 Whigs and only two Democrats were serving on it.

The result of this trial again pointed out clearly that the persecuted Saints of Beaver Island and their Prophet James J. Strang were found consistently guilty in the nation's newspapers, although vindicated in courts of law.

It is difficult to understand the reason for continued punishment of the Beaver Island Mormons by the nation's press. Looking at it more than a century later clears the picture somewhat, but the realization now that national newspapers could arouse federal authorities sufficiently to arrest Strang unjustly for crimes against his own country is difficult to comprehend. This is not likely to happen in any United States court of law today.

These startling facts about the National political importance of Strang, along with a very brief outline of the incredible farce at Detroit, are important in an evaluation of him. The result of the trial has been disclosed prior to revealing what Strang, himself, thought of local and federal law procedure. That is, as it pertained to the Kingdom of God and himself in particular. This allows a personal judgment on the part of the reader before being influenced by the convincing pen of Strang.

Going back to April 3, 1851, a few months before the trial began in Federal Court, an issue of the *Northern Islander* published on that date carried a masterful summary of the legal protection the Beaver Island Mormons were unjustly deprived of. The new Michigan Constitution allowed all citizens this protection. It is obvious the Beaver Island Mormons never had it.

The *Northern Islander* rightfully stated:

> "Mr. Strang and various others, including all the principal men among the Mormons, live in the continual consciousness that there are men around them seeking their lives; and that should they be killed, the murderers would never be brought to justice by the authorities of the State."

This remarkable prediction came true in 1856. The shocking truth of this editorial statement was the cold blooded murder of

PHOTO BY PHYLLIS FITZPATRICK

Strang's Print Shop On Beaver Island

The only Mormon building left standing on Beaver, now a popular museum, managed by A. J. Roy.

Prophet Strang himself five years later. It happened on Beaver Island and the known guilty murderers were never brought to justice. Instead they were cheered and treated as heroes at Mackinac.

The *Northern Islander* continued:

> "We are not aware that they are in any particular fear of being murdered, but there is something very rotten in the institutions of this country, when men of respectability and of peaceful and industrious habits must live with the assurance that whoever pleases may murder them, and never be called to account for it."

Among the men marked for destruction were Strang, Miller, Graham, McCulloch, Johnson, Hopper, Chidester and Greig. McCulloch, four years later, dramatically supplied the necessary incentive to the actual murder of "King" Strang.

A quote from the same issue of the *Northern Islander* is indicative of the editor's grasp of the United States scene in commenting that the situation was not peculiar only to the Beaver Islands. He wrote:

> "This lawlessness is practiced on the weak and defenseless throughout the United States."

An interesting comparison was made between the then current administration with the foreign governments of centuries ago. Civil strife seemed to be swooping upon the North and the South. Strang felt that the nation would "perish in the anarchy of laws despised and trampled on by the whole people," even before Civil War disgraced our nation. In this, he was wrong, but it was said 10 years before the first shot was fired.

Strang had this to say about long established governments:

> "The old governments have a kind of heart; a body of people, generally among the most intelligent, who have a permanent interest in the integrity and respectability of the administration; men whose standing, property and even their personal safety depend on a respectable share of justice in the administration; and who at the same time, control its affairs. In the United States there is no such class."

Beaver Island — 1851

Does this sound like a man to be hated? Strang was a man of intelligence and quality, with an intense desire to help his fellow man. Yet, the memory of Strang has been allowed to remain unfairly judged for over a century.

Strang further stated that the new government in 1851 had weak administrators, whose:

> "Utmost interest is in the amount they can speculate out of the administration of public affairs. In the election the voice of the vicious counts equally with that of the virtuous."

Here, Strang does not sound like a man who would counterfeit money and commit treason. Yet, he was shamefully arrested for these crimes and, as already stated, though he was not found guilty, great character damage had been done. "Not guilty" meant only in the courts. The masses had convicted him long before the verdict was given. Most citizens today cling to this unjust evaluation of Strang.

The following report was published in the *Northern Islander* of May 1, 1851. It revealed that a new persecution of the Mormons had started on Beaver Island in the form of criminal warrants against 38 Saints. This ridiculous raid involved no resistance. It was perpetrated by the Sheriff of Mackinac County, using "a posse of 30 intoxicated Indians and eight or ten drunken Irishmen armed with guns."

ANOTHER OUTRAGE: HUNTING MORMONS LIKE WILD BEASTS, EMPLOYING INDIANS FOR A POSSE.

> "The O'Malley clique have commenced a new persecution of the saints at this place, with the aid of Mr. Granger, Sheriff of Mackinac county, but we believe without any aid or encouragement from any respectable part of the community. The process of persecution is a descent upon Beaver by the Sheriff with criminal warrants against thirty-eight persons, backed by a posse of thirty intoxicated Indians, and eight or ten drunken Irishmen armed with guns.

"Such an assault has a public officer made upon the peaceable inhabitants of this place, without one act of resistance, and before the slightest attempt was made to execute his process. Among the very grave charges upon which men are thus hunted like wild beasts by savages and drunken Irish, we are informed that Mr. Samuel Graham is charged with the very grave offense of standing by while somebody had some unpleasant words, and not interfering.

"Mr. Charles M. O'Malley is the Justice to issue warrants on such charges, and Mr. Sheriff Granger is the man to take every third man in the community on such pretences, and carry them fifty miles from home to be tried by an Irish bog trotter, who has declared beforehand that he will regard no testimony in their behalf.

"Some of the prisoners when taken into custody, were put in charge of the vilest drunken scoundrels that can be found on the wild borders, who were suffered to beat, abuse and threaten them at pleasure. They even went so far as to gather a rabble around Mr. Joshua L. Miller, who asserted with many assurances that the party who had been sent to arrest his father, Gen. Geo. Miller, when he was at work in the woods, had murdered him, and exhibited some portion of his clothing which they prepared for the purpose, as evidence of the truth of the assertion.

"From time to time the Indians were dispatched off in large parties, drunk, and well supplied with arms and ammunition, and led by such worthless wretches as Jim Lambert, to hunt over the adjacent Islands, on which it was supposed, that some of their victims might be found; and Mr. Sheriff Granger, hearing the savages boast how many white men's scalps they had taken, and that now they would have Mr. Strang's also, sent them on their errands of blood.

"Such a perversion of ministerial administration; such a prostitution of the powers of office to the purposes of crime, was never heard of in a civilized community. Let the citizens of the United States take this matter home to themselves. Let them imagine a tribe of wild savages, first made drunk, then provided with arms and ammunition, and then let loose on the peaceable inhabitants of a town, with authority to make prisoners of all the town officers and principal public men, having them whooping about your houses and swearing death against the men they are ostensibly sent to arrest, and you have but a faint picture of the scene that Mr. Sheriff Granger has created for his malignant pleasure upon Beaver Island.

"Whether this new outrage will meet with any rebuke from the publick press, or the constituted authorities, we have yet to see. Certainly we have seen nothing in the past to assure us that it will. Last fall the most vicious statements were made in many political papers, charging us with gross frauds in the election of the Hon. J. P. Irvine to the Legislature, and of the county officers. A Legislative investigation was had, in which we had no opportunity to offer one word of testimony, and yet the Legislature treated the complaint against us as merely ridiculous. Not one of all the papers that made and re-iterated the accusations has retracted them.

"We have a right to presume that in this case rumour, not on the wings of the wind but in the columns of the newspapers, will accuse us of a thousand crimes, and when a legal investigation vindicates us all, not one word of rebuke will be heard for the false accusations — none for hunting us like so many wild beasts.

"If the Mormons were really guilty of high crimes, this mode of proceeding against them is a violation of all law and of the principles of civilized government. It is the duty of the Sheriff, his officers and the posse comitatus, to protect as well as arrest the accused, and herein is the obligation of non-resistance. But in this case the Sheriff, instead of calling on the power of the county to arrest resisting culprits, calls on a tribe of Indians to murder those who do not resist an arrest, and have never shown the slightest disposition to do so.

"And what is the crime for which the lives of a whole community are thus put in jeopardy? Nothing but going with a Constable to assist in arresting a criminal with arms in his hands. Mr. Constable Field went with a few of his neighbours to arrest E. J. Moore on a criminal process. Moore with his friends, after firing several guns upon the Constable's party without effect, escaped to the woods, and fled to Mackinac, where he obtained warrants against them for that act, and that is the head and front of their offending. That is the crime for which the Mormons are hunted like wolves.

"We appeal to the sympathies of humanity — to the common feelings of the human heart against such wickedness. But we do not appeal as men begging for favours. We only ask some approximation to justice. And if we are not to have it, we only wish to be told so. We are able to take care of ourselves, by the help of God. If it is a settled principle that officers exist in this region not to protect but to murder us, we wish to be told so distinctly, and we will look to the rest."

Disclosing that the Saints of Beaver Island were "harassed" outside the courts is an understatement. These Mormons were living on this isolated island surrounded by enemies within and without, capable and eager to do bodily harm to man, woman or child, day or night.

A case in point: The trial at Detroit involved many Saints, most of them men. This meant a great part of the labor force of the colony was absent from the island during the farming season, of great concern to the Kingdom. In addition, scoundrels posing as authority plundered homes while the Saints were in Detroit. Believing conviction a certainty, even some of the farms were appropriated. This unique kind of robbery included livelihood as well as liberty.

How was it possible that the legal processes of Michigan and the U.S. Government were too blind to prosecute these admitted offenders? Both were eager to uncover "evidence" to prosecute a Saint. No wonder the Saints retaliated with violence. Eventually, the Saints had to be their own law for self-protection.

Early in the summer of 1851, a report was circulated that 60 Gentiles were on the island, ready and willing to shoot any Saint on sight. While this may have been an exaggeration, the news spread rapidly and had its effect. Many left the colony in

Beaver Island — 1851

fear of their lives, thinking the Kingdom was doomed, fully expecting collapse sometime during 1851.

Strang, however, was very much the symbol of courage. In the *Northern Islander* of August 14, 1851, three months after the Detroit verdict, this statement appeared for all to read and ponder:

"Prophet Strang sits quietly in his own house, without keeping one of his trusted friends by to assist him, and dispenses the law to these same men as a justice of the peace; and when business requires, goes along and unarmed in the midst of them, without molestation or danger."

It further stated, "a strong hand, never departing from the right, will secure respect anywhere, but vacillation makes us despised."

CHAPTER IX
Beaver Island 1852-1853

The size of the area Strang represented in the State Assembly to which he was elected dramatically on November 2, 1852, may surprise many who know he was a member. Strang represented approximately five percent of the lower peninsula in area. Citizens then were isolated, of course, making it difficult to communicate easily.

Personal isolation more than 100 years ago was a very serious problem. Strang solved this on Beaver by allowing each Saint a 160 acre farm, providing the family lived in one of the villages. This idea was not new. His own ancestors did the same in the early 1700's in New York state. Many of Strang's ideas were 50 years ahead of his time, however, evidenced by the thorough planning revealed in The Book of the Law of the Lord.

On Beaver Island in 1847, a rather complicated situation existed. The Township was called Peaine, after the Peaine Indians. It was part of Emmet County. All legal matters went to Mackinac, the election of state representatives to Newaygo and the election of state senators to Lapeer. It is difficult to comprehend the inconveniences pioneers had in early statehood.

Strang was a genuine pioneer and a very important one. Some of the best laws in Michigan were made while he was in the Legislature. How he was able to get himself initially elected is a charming salute to his unusual abilities and how he got to Lansing after being elected is an unbelievable tale. Compared with the freedom of an elected legislator today, his initiation was fantastic.

Conditions in the state were so isolated that the candidacy of Strang was kept a secret from non-Mormons until election day. Conditions were also such that he dared announce his election to the Saints ahead of time! The reason, of course, was assurance that the Saints would cast all 165 votes for him.

STRANG RECORD IN THE 1853 MICHIGAN LEGISLATURE

Bills introduced and passed by the 1853 Legislature

An act to organize the County of Emmet.
An act to organize the County of Cheboygan.
An act to organize the Township of Drummond.
An act to complete the organization of the County of Grand Traverse.
An act to complete the judicial organization of the State.

Bills introduced but not passed

A bill to extend and define the boundaries of certain counties (Placed on general order)

A bill authorizing the construction of a road from Croton, in the County of Newaygo, to the Straits of Mackinac (Mackinac Road) (Passed by the House, given immediate effect)

A bill to attach certain unorganized counties to counties which are organized (Placed on general order)

A bill to amend the Revised Statutes of 1846, concerning disturbing religious meetings (Reported back to the House and passage recommended)

A bill to change the names of certain townships in the County of Newaygo (Placed on general order)

Bills which Mr. Strang stated he would ask leave to introduce, but which were not introduced

A bill authorizing the construction of a road from the Straits of Mackinac to Sault Ste. Marie, in the County of Chippewa.

A bill to authorize the construction of a road from the mouth of Manistique River to Grand Island Harbor, in Lake Superior.

A bill to determine the qualifications of circuit court commissioners.

A bill to re-enact divers acts passed at the regular session of the Legislature, for the year 1851, but not completed and signed till after the adjournment.

When Strang was elected, there was great concern in the opposing camp. What they did to retaliate continued to prove that his life was one crisis after another. Gentiles were always after his hide, no matter what he attempted to do.

The crisis this time was a "stop Strang" movement, designed to intercept the supposed victim at Mackinac. Backers of this movement planned to do this by digging up an old indictment. It was really a "stalling for time" move on the part of his enemies in Lansing. They needed time to rally forces and plan an attack to keep Strang from occupying his seat in the assembly. No legislator today would enjoy going by boat to Green Bay, Wisconsin, from Beaver Island to reach Lansing, but Representative Strang did just that to avoid his rumored arrest at Mackinac.

Not to be outfoxed, his enemies made other arrangements in Lansing through the District Attorney for the Upper Peninsula to arrest Strang before the House of Representatives asked for a roll call. A unanimous vote to seat Strang followed. Still not to be outfoxed, immediately after the arrest was discharged, the opposition contested his seating directly to the bar of the House. Strang again won, this time by a vote of 49 to 11.

Strang was now treated with more respect. Even a few influential newspapers spoke of his abilities and backed his right to represent the district.

Strang had definite ideas about improving the area he represented. It was especially important to provide judiciary and municipal governments. This was accomplished in all districts of the counties he served. There had been only one organized township up to this time. Crimes punishable in Oceana and Newaygo Counties had been done so illegally. In Grand Traverse, there was no law at all. The loose administration existing was further strengthened by the organization of Grand Traverse County and the formation of two new ones, with a total of eight townships.

Quoting from favorable press notices, Strang was called "eloquent, honorable and the most talented ready debater in the House." His general fund of information became invaluable during two terms in the Legislature. When Strang initially fought for his rightful seat, he pleaded his own case. The Lansing *State Journal* said he spoke:

> "with a force of reasoning, energy and eloquence which, whatever may be the result, will leave a most favorable opinion of his personal qualifications for the position he claims."

The position Strang claimed successfully culminated in his ability to secure a separation of the Beavers from Mackinac County early in 1853. This was accomplished by organizing the new county of Emmet. In this county, the Pine River area was soon to become the scene of a ridiculous battle between nearly 90 participants over a few men serving on a jury at Saint James, then the county seat.

Later, from the newly organized county of Emmet, the following were separated and joined to organize the county of Manitou: the Beaver Islands, the Fox Islands and the Manitou. Restricting the Mormons to the islands by the Gentiles failed to materialize as planned, however. The Mormon ticket won without opposition.

Another result of these Gentile maneuvers was the acceleration of hostile feeling between two old enemies, Mackinac and Beaver Island. Strang was eager for vigorous liquor law enforcement from Old Mackinac west to Grand Traverse south, including Lake Michigan and its bays. Mackinac retaliated beyond the point of legality. Milo Quaife summarized the situation in this manner:

> "It would be charitable to suppose that the district attorney who presided over this gathering (called Committee of Safety), and the four magistrates who lent their influence to its proceedings, failed to realize the true character of their course. In all the turbulent history of the liquor business in America it would be difficult to find a more unblushing defiance of law and order, or a bolder condemnation of an announced intention to

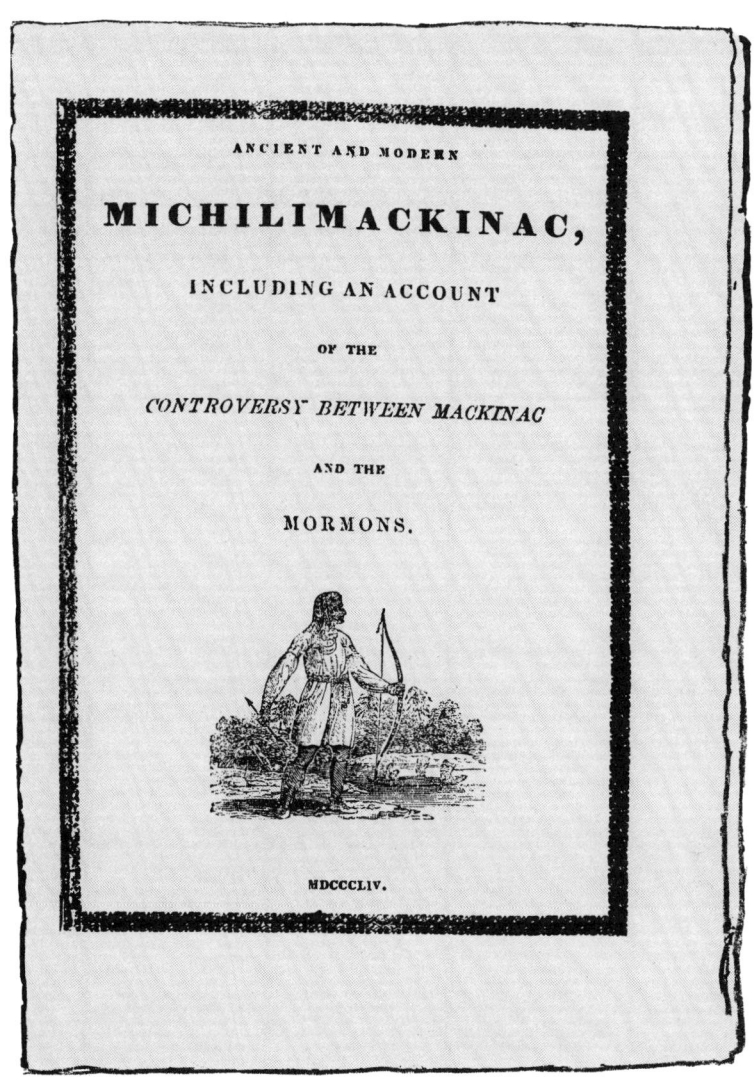

One page from Strang's "Ancient & Modern Michilimackinac, including an Account of the Controversy between Mackinac and the Mormons." One of the greatest books ever written by a Mormon leader.

defy it, than the one offered to the world by these magistrates and citizens of Mackinac."

The "Battle of Pine River" (now Charlevoix) several weeks later, July 13, 1853, may be said to have been caused by Gentile defiance of liquor law enforcement, the assessment of taxes and the approaching political influence of the Mormons at Mackinac. In addition, former Mormon church members who had been removed from the island bolstered up Gentile opposition by their eagerness for revenge and offer of assistance.

One year prior to the battle, warrants were issued at Saint James for the arrest of men at Pine River thought to be thieves. The *Northern Islander* of November 11, 1852, called the Pine River Settlement little more than a "band of vagabonds and thieves, and the sight of an officer of the law sets them all in a twitter," further adding, "almost the entire population fled when approached."

Milo Quaife observed:

> "It drew consolation from the fact that lack of provisions would compel the fishermen to scatter on the approach of winter, and the improbability that they would ever reassemble.
>
> "Contrary to this pious hope, the summer of 1853 found the fishermen assembled at Pine River in greater numbers than before, and animated by a common determination to resist the authorities of Emmet County. The issue came on July 12 (actually July 13), when the Sheriff of the county set out from Saint James for Pine River to summon certain of the residents there whose names had been drawn for jury duty in the circuit court at Saint James the following week. With the Sheriff was a boat's crew of five men. Stopping at Galilee (now non-existant but then a south end settlement), he learned that fresh threats had been made at Pine River to kill any man who attempted to serve any kind of process there. Accordingly he took along from here another boat and crew, all unarmed, thinking, if the Mormon narrative be credited, that the presence of so large a number of witnesses would prevent any act of violence until

he should have had time to explain the peaceful character of his business, when no further objection would be made."

No one will disagree with Quaife that 14 were too many if unarmed and too few if armed, since the settlement contained more than five times this number and the only possibility of retreat was across an open lake, a distance of about 25 miles.

Quaife continued:

"Gentile and Mormon narratives agree in at least one respect — that the denizens of Pine River were expecting trouble, and were prepared to meet it. The Sheriff's party reached the river mouth about two o'clock in the afternoon. As they approached the landing, armed men could be seen running about, and guns were heard, fired apparently by way of signals. The Mormons landed on a narrow beach, under a bluff which was covered with a growth of timber and bushes. The Sheriff quickly explained his mission, and in less than half an hour his party was preparing to embark for the return voyage to Saint James. Meanwhile armed men had been gathering on the bluff, and a party of thirty or more had filed down a narrow path to the beach and stationed themselves close to the boats. A considerable surf was breaking on the shore, and it was difficult to get the boats off. They had just been launched, and the last man was climbing in, when a murderous fire from both beach and bluff was poured upon them. In view of the closeness of the assailants to their victims, one must either suppose the fishermen to have been marvelously poor marksmen, or accept the Mormon theory that the escape alive of any of the Saints afforded an extra-ordinary instance of the care of God for his creatures. As it was, six of the fourteen Mormons were shot, all of them at the beginning of the attack, while the boats were pushing off."

The Mormons issued a statement that three Gentiles from the mob inspected their boats, reporting upon their return from the beach that no guns were on board. The "murderous fire" followed this disclosure, indicating the type of Gentile the

Mormons were dealing with. Quaife described the chase on Lake Michigan in these words:

> "Before these men lay twenty-five miles of open water. Behind them in hot pursuit, came three boatloads of fishermen, the largest manned by twenty-five men. For ten miles the Mormons, aided by a light wind, kept beyond the musket range of their pursuers. Then the wind dying down, the latter drew nearer and opened fire on the laboring boats. These were riddled with bullets and it seemed likely the occupants would all be slain, when the bark Morgan, bound from Buffalo to Chicago, came in sight, and in response to the frantic appeals of the Mormons, took them all on board. The pursuers thereupon gave over the chase and returned to Pine River."

The following day, the *Northern Islander* issued an extra with a full account of the battle, calmly reporting in part this remarkably restrained paragraph in light of the hideous action taken by the Gentiles against the powerless Saints:

> "A large number of the attacking party were recognized and measures are being taken to bring them to justice. There would be no difficulty in fitting out a party from here who would make Pine River settlement as bare as the palm of a man's hand; but the moral effect of sending a half dozen to State Prison is worth more than the death of them all. Legal remedies are better than violent ones."

The "murderous fire from both beach and bluff" may have been triggered by the young half-brother of Elizabeth Whitney Williams, Lewis Whitney. Though O. W. Riegel in "Crown of Glory" described the incident, he did not divulge the young man's name. Riegel gave this account as the Mormons took their places at the oarlocks:

> "At that moment a young fisherman (Lewis Whitney) who had lived a year or two on Beaver Island left the line on the beach and started toward the boats, perhaps to exchange a few words with his acquaintances or inquire about former friends on the island. When he was halfway to the boats, the boy for some inexplicable rea-

son hesitated, looked nervously around, and began to examine the hammer of his gun. A sharp report rang out. The boy on the beach gave a startled cry and clutched the calf of his right leg with both hands."

It is not difficult to imagine young Lewis, in his excitement, pulling the trigger of his own gun. Four Mormon guns were concealed by garments in one of the two boats to avoid disaster. Nothing less than suicidal tendencies could have induced a Mormon to have fired that shot, or picked up a gun for that matter.

In "A Child of the Sea; and Life Among the Mormons" Mrs. Williams claims to have been an eye witness to this battle. In fact, a participant, since she claimed to "run the bullets" for her father. Though a heavy surf was experienced when the Mormons launched their two boats in a successful attempt to avoid slaughter, Mrs. Williams claimed she heard "almost every word spoken by the leader "from her vantage point" a short distance from them."

"Fallacious" is a good word describing the Williams' version of "The Battle of Charlevoix," as she chooses to call it. Most of her Mormon stories are fallacious. A minor example revealing her lack of reputable reporting and one not included in the author's review of her book, is this careless statement:

"When the smoke cleared away I saw the men hurriedly push their boats off and jump into them, taking their oars and pulling with all their might."

Much of the Williams' narrative is composed in this manner. While an intense surf indicates an immediate clearing of smoke after shots were fired, the fallacy here lies in the fact that all Mormons except one were in the boats before a shot was fired. This example proves a point made in the first sentence reviewing her book: "Childhood memories, suffer an enormous lack of accurate separation."

Special attention given here to the "Battle of Pine River" is justified in view of its effect on Mormon morale. Though they lost the battle, the end result gave them self-reliance. Official arrests were attempted a week after the battle, but unsuccessfully, because the posse from Saint James actually did find the Pine River settlement "as bare as the palm of a man's hand."

A year after this July, 1853 battle, a situation developed between the new Pine River Gentile settlers and a small number of Mormon settlers, similar to the feud between Mackinac and Beaver. The Pine River settlement became firmly established at this time and marked the beginning of Mormon expansion in that area.

The year 1854 found the Strangite Mormons enjoying a wide majority in Charlevoix Township, the mainland section of Emmet County of which Saint James was still the county seat.

CHAPTER X
Beaver Island 1854-1856

The collapse of Strang's Kingdom of God came at the height of his career. What success he may have achieved in the minds of his Saints was in truth his downfall. In the period 1854-1856, the rule of Strang, while admittedly absolute, was not without affection for his Saints.

Two years after the coronation, the spread of Strangite Mormonism to the mainland alarmed the Gentile element sufficiently to promote a division of the Emmet County portion between two other counties, Cheboygan and Grand Traverse. Any semblance of fear that this would improve the Gentile position and deter Mormon settlement was published in the November 2, 1854, *Northern Islander*.

> "Before another election our settlements on that east shore will be large enough to control the politics of both Cheboygan and Grand Traverse. And having the power, under such circumstances we should not fail to use it."

As bold and autocratic as Strang now gave every evidence of becoming, the reason for his actions must be understood. The "Battle of Pine River" may be considered a prime example of the injustice heaped upon him in defiance of law and order. The Mormons were the law, whether the Gentiles liked it or not. They had earned the right to enforce obedience to legal authority. They did not misuse it, nor did they exercise every opportunity to prosecute it.

Within the Church, however, the Saints had every right to resent Strang's over-enforcement of authority. One whipping publicized in the *Northern Islander* of April 3, 1856, involved "lying, tale-bearing, and endeavoring to incite to mischief and crime." Prior to this, two identical punishments were administered for adultery, one of them to Thomas Bedford, making three known whippings.

The year 1855 witnessed two conferences of the Church, a general conference at Saint James early in July and one at Holy Island in Lake Mormon, July 15. It is interesting to note that 50 persons from Beaver attended the Holy Island Conference. Persecutions and dispossession attempts in the Lake Mormon area were the main topics of discussion, along with a good measure of asking God's help in solving their earthly problems.

The Saints' problems, specifically those of Strang, continued to multiply within the Church. Within the Church fringe, made up of a few disgruntled islanders who were never true Mormons, began a conspiracy to murder Strang. The conspirators were: Dr. H. D. McCulloch, Thomas Bedford, Alexander Wentworth, and "Doctor" Atkyn.

These names appear often in the Reviews. Nevertheless, at the risk of some duplication, it is proper to chronicle unsavory facts about them here toward a better understanding of their ability to murder.

There is little doubt that Dr. McCulloch's early pseudo-conversion at Baltimore to the doctrine of Strang was prompted only by material gain and personal exaltation. That he was a talented medical doctor, there is no doubt. In addition, he was not a poor man. On Beaver Island, his talents and means assured him a place of responsibility among the Saints.

In the Church, McCulloch was judge and confidential counselor. In civic affairs, he was coroner, clerk and register of deeds of Emmet County. Strang planned to send him to the Legisla-

Beaver Island 1854-1856   111

ture after completing his own first term. Unfortunately, a taste for liquor, even at the bars of vessels, contributed to his eventual dishonest behavior with public records.

The plan to send him to Lansing was dropped. Soon after Dr. McCulloch was removed from the Church roster for an accumulation of misdeeds, he and "Dr." Atkyn created the plan and provided the incentive to the weak and uncourageous Bedford and Wentworth in the assassination plot to kill James Strang.

Bedford had several grievances against the "King." His chief grievance was revenge for a whipping received for adultery, one of the most serious crimes against the Church. The adultery act is described in the review section, along with information about Wentworth, who was labeled a "dandy." Wentworth's close connection with Dr. McCulloch is due to his marriage to the daughter of Frank Johnson, a business partner of McCulloch.

"Dr." Atkyn was a professional "visitor" to Beaver Island between 1850 and 1856, though not a medical doctor. It is entirely possible Atkyn processed the daguerreotype of Strang illustrating the Frontispiece, a photograph taken sometime during the last two years of Strang's life. An uncomplimentary account of this "precious character," as Quaife called him, appeared in the last issue of the *Northern Islander*. He was presented as a:

> "cheap adventurer who sought, whether by fair means or foul, to sponge a living off the simple minded Saints. Having run his course at the islands, and being hopelessly in debt, he cooly proposed, unless they should pay his bills, to resort to a program of blackmail, and as evidence of his ability along this line, exhibited a specimen of lampooning handbill he had gotten out against certain reputable citizens of Council Bluffs. They did not comply and Atkyn proceeded to execute his threat by visiting Detroit, Lansing and other points, peregrinating the country, endeavoring to slander the Mormons and sponge his living."

Corrosive hatred of a few, bent on the destruction of Strang,

THE STEAMER *Michigan* COURTESY OF DOSSIN MUSEUM, BELLE ISLE

First iron ship of the United States Navy on the Great Lakes. From painting by Charles Robert Patterson.

Beaver Island 1854-1856 113

led to the complete annihilation of the entire Kingdom. The plot against Strang was public knowledge as evidenced by these courageous words in the *Northern Islander* a few weeks before the assassination:

> "We will neither purchase temporary peace and future calamities by dishonorable trafficking with political jugglers, nor will we yield our homes to enemies. If we live, here will we live. If we die, here we will die, and here shall our bones be buried, expecting in the ressurection of the just to possess the land forever, and dwell with the righteous during the lifetime of the eternal."

Courageous as these words were, it is apparent that no matter what preparations had been made to protect "King" Strang, the protection would not have been sufficient. Reason for such an observation is due to the appearance of the U.S. Steamer *Michigan* in the harbor at Saint James as part of the assassination plot. It is very obvious that Saints, viewing the United States vessel in the harbor, would not be aware it was on an evil mission. They would treat her appearance in a passive manner, regardless of the recent public defiance by Strang.

Historian Quaife gave a very clear personal opinion of government participation when he wrote these lines in "The Kingdom of Saint James" as a footnote to the furtherance of this plot:

> "What arrangement McCulloch made with this federal official or what justification the latter had for his course, is far from clear. One hesitates, in the absence of specific evidence, to charge a responsible official with prostituting an agency of the United States government to the furtherance of a private plot of assassination against one of its citizens; but the course of the commander of the Michigan before and after the assassination lends support to such a theory."

Details of the assassination appear in several reviews of this volume and need not be repeated or elaborated here. It is sufficient to say that when the news reached Mackinac there was great joy and public celebration. But on Beaver Island, the loyal and believing Saints were stunned and saturated with grief beyond description on that day, June 16, 1856.

In the eyes of his enemies, Strang's death was welcomed as something good. Though our laws did not permit any kind of evil deed that good might result, the known assassins of James Strang were set free without trial.

In the hearts of those who believed Strang to be a true prophet of God, his death signaled the end of a righteous cause. His death left the Saints stunned. Their mass expulsion from Beaver Island soon after created mental torture and physical hardships difficult to imagine.

"King" James Jesse Strang deserved a better fate, as did his devoted Saints. Instead, a lifetime of suffering and humiliation was dealt out to survivors, as though the northern Michigan breed of Gentiles in the 1850's had a personal right to exclusively occupy this entire island known as "Big Beaver."

They drove every Saint from it.

EPILOGUE

The Five Wives and Fourteen Children of James Strang

Disaster overwhelmed the Saints on the shores of Beaver Island's Paradise Bay in late June and early July, 1856, disillusioning the four polygamous wives of James Strang. It is impossible to comprehend their feelings, knowing then, that each carried a child of their shared husband and "King."

Strang's mortally wounded body, near death at the home of his parents at Voree, signaled chaos in the family and the end of the Beaver Island Kingdom of God.

MARY PERCE STRANG

The only legal wife of James J. Strang, Mary Perce, was not on the island during those fateful days. A requested separation took place during May of 1851 after Strang wrote to her on the island and asked her to leave. However, a semblance of their marriage still existed, perhaps as late as 1855. It is apparent that Mary remained passively loyal to her husband in spite of public unmasking of his polygamous revelation during July, 1850. Due to policy objections on her part, as a member of the Council, Strang requested her departure. She had been made a Council member early in 1851, nearly two years after her husband married Elvira Field in polygamy.

Strang's marriage to Mary on November 20, 1836, in New York State resulted eventually in his solemn disposition toward Mormonism. In 1843, the family moved west to Burlington, Wisconsin. A brother, Benjamin C. Perce, and a brother-in-law, Moses Smith, had moved there eight years earlier. Aaron, a brother of Moses, also resided at Burlington. All were devout Mormons, although Mary was a Baptist, her father having been a Baptist clergyman. With Strang and Mary went Myraette, their second child, born in 1841. Another child, Mary, died in infancy. Two additional children were born in Wisconsin, the first, William J. in 1844, and Hattie in 1847.

Aaron Smith and Strang made a journey to the headquarters of Mormonism at Nauvoo in February, 1844. Strang became a convert at this first meeting with Joseph Smith. Hyrum Smith and Sidney Rigdon were also present, and witnessed the baptismal.

Contrary to general belief, Mary was not present when Strang died by assassins' bullets at the home of his parents at Voree.

Mary moved temporarily to Elgin, Illinois, in 1851. She spent her last years living with her son, William J. Strang, a Terre Haute, Indiana, railroad conductor. Myraette lived with her brother and mother, never marrying. No record is available to this writer concerning the career of Hattie Strang. In "The Kingdom of Saint James," Quaife failed to record her name as the fourth child of Mary, though he mentioned a fourth.

ELVIRA ELIZA FIELD STRANG

Elvira Eliza Field was born in Streetsborough, Portage County, Ohio, July 8, 1830. At maturity she became the first of four polygamous wives of James Strang.

Elvira was a descendant of grandfather Thomas Field and father Reuben Field, born in 1801, both having lived in Massachusetts and Connecticut, as did her mother Eliza Granger, born in 1798. Two years after her mother and father were mar-

Home of Strang's parents at Voree, where Strang died.

PHOTO BY JOHN CUMMING

Marker on Strang's grave

COURTESY OF
STATE HISTORICAL SOCIETY OF WISCONSIN

Bronze map of Mormon settlement at Voree (now Spring Prairie). Marker sponsored by the Burlington Historical Society.

PHOTO BY EMMETT RAETTIG

ried in May, 1827, they moved to Streetsborough. A son, Albert, was born June 20, 1828, and a sister, Anna, December 26, 1832. Anna died six years after birth. Albert and Elvira moved to Eaton County, Michigan, with their parents in 1844, where Albert lived for nearly seventy years, except while on Beaver Island.

From 1844 to 1846, Elvira lived with an uncle, Israel Smith, in Washtenaw County, Michigan. Here she learned the tailor's trade while attending school. In nearby Milan, she became a Presbyterian.

At sixteen, Elvira signed a twelve week contract to teach school in Henrietta for $1.00 per week and her board. In 1847 she taught in Eaton Rapids, and in 1848, at a school in Eaton township, near Charlotte, where she received $1.25 per week and board for twenty-two weeks.

As a girl, Elvira enjoyed hunting with a rifle. She could kill a hawk on the wing. A love of outdoor life led to reporting weather data for the Smithsonian Institution at Washington, recording three times daily for five years.

The parents of Elvira were Mormon, even before Strang became a convert. After the murder of Joseph Smith in 1844, they became believers in Strang's prophetic succession. In the spring of 1848, Elvira, with her parents, attended a conference at Voree and met James Strang for the first time. Within a year, George Adams offered Elvira the honor of becoming the first plural wife of Strang. On July 13, after the 1849 conference held at the new City of James on Beaver Island, Strang and Elvira exchanged Mormon vows. This marriage represented the beginning of a new society, the reestablishment of the Kingdom of God, according to Strang, by commandment.

The establishment of plural marriage in the Kingdom meant gossip among its members was assured, especially after the conference when Strang and Elvira toured New York, Philadelphia, and Boston for converts. Confusion and scandal became paramount when secrecy of the marriage was attempted by grooming Elvira as a young "nephew" and dressing her in male attire.

Epilogue

In New York, one of the prime accusors was Lorenzo Dow Hickey. He had received a letter from his wife on Beaver warning him of "scandalous doings at the island." Mrs. Hickey renewed gossip which had been suppressed by Strang before he departed for the eastern mission.

In spite of her femininity, Elvira played this role of nephew and private secretary rather successfully, traveling with Strang as "Charlie J. Douglass."

The first of four children born to this union was Charles J. Strang, born April 6, 1851. Eva, who later married M. C. Baldwin, was born April 18, 1853; Clement J., December 20, 1854; and James J., January 22, 1857. James was the fourteenth and last child of "King" Strang.

Elvira was forced to leave Beaver Island with her three small children, aged five, three and two, during the violent turmoil following the assassination. She returned to Voree where she lived for several years in poverty and hardship. Elvira then moved to her former home in Eaton County, Michigan, where, in 1860, she was stricken with a supposedly fatal illness. As a result the children were given to the care of friends.

Four years later, fortunately having recovered, and again able to be independent because she was a skilled tailoress and a school teacher, Elvira was able to take care of three of her children. The youngest had been adopted into the family of Mr. David Grier, near Charlotte. His name was then changed to Charles J. Grier.

In 1865, Elvira met a widower with five children, a Mr. John Baker. They were married on November 26. On April 22, 1868, a daughter, Emma (Mrs. Jones), was born. She died at age thirty-one. A second daughter, May (Mrs. Buckley), was born October 1874 in Lake County, a location to which the Bakers had moved in 1873.

Later in life the Bakers moved to Kent County to be nearer the younger members of the family because of the infirmities of age. Elvira was confined only two days to her bed before she died on June 13, 1910 at the home of Mr. Warren Baker, in Courtland. She was buried in the Courtland cemetery.

Surviving Elvira was her husband, then past 91 years of age, five children, 21 grandchildren, and 12 great grandchildren.

The seven years that Elvira lived with James Strang on Beaver Island she considered very happy ones. Evidence that her life was influenced by Strang was her hatred of profanity and objection to tobacco and the use of liquor. She was a lover of nature, calling most of the common flowers and shrubs by their botanical names.

Elvira, as did Strang, led an honorable and industrious life, and she taught all her children to do the same.

BETSY McNUTT STRANG

Betsy McNutt, second polygamous wife of Strang, was born in Harrison, Pueblo County, Ohio, August 17, 1820. Betsy was further proof that polygamy on Beaver Island was far from being a harem of beautiful women trying to escape the clutches of a sexoholic.

Sunday supplements again reveled in the Beaver Island sex story after marriage to Betsy. In addition to plural marriages, untrue murders and uncounted whippings were double-spread stories in national newspapers, complete with illustrations depicting the Saints in all their violent pursuits. Sexual life on Beaver Island was actually serene by comparison. Physical violence was primarily caused by the incessant prodding by Gentiles. There was one murder on Beaver and that was the assassination of "King" Strang, himself.

Betsy hinted marriage to Strang, according to pious Wingfield Watson, when she bantered words with friendly Saints at one of their numerous social gatherings. After all, she was 31, plain looking and well on her way to becoming an old maid. Betsy considered it an honor to be marrried to Strang, as did the other three polygamous wives.

JOHN BAKER AND ELVIRA FIELD BAKER

Elvira married John Baker in 1865, living with him 45 years.

EVANGELINE

ABIGAIL

GABRIEL

Three of four children born to Betsy McNutt and Strang. A fourth, David, died in infancy on Beaver.

Epilogue 125

The McNutt-Strang vows were spoken two and a half years after Strang's marriage to Elvira Field. The ceremony took place on January 19, 1852. During the succeeding three years, three children were born; Evangeline, David and Gabriel. David died in infancy on Beaver Island. It is assumed that Betsy and her family left the Island on June 28, on the propeller *Louisville,* with her mortally wounded husband, who had been shot by assassins 12 days earlier. Betsy and her children were at the deathbed of Strang.

On January 1, 1857, her last child arrived, number 13 for Strang. Between that fateful July 9 and the birth of Abigail, Betsy had moved to Jackson County, Wisconsin, where she experienced difficulty in earning enough to hold her family together. When Evangeline married John Denio of Lamoni, Iowa, Betsy went to live with them. Abigail made her home in St. Joseph, Missouri and died there in May, 1921. Gabriel died in Texas in September, 1935, at the age of 82.

Though none of the Strang wives followed his teachings after death, Betsy did become a member of the Reorganized Church. She later joined another Mormon faction. Her four and a half years with James Strang were eventful and happy ones. Betsy never remarried, remaining faithful to his memory until her death on September 22, 1897.

SARAH ADELIA WRIGHT STRANG

Sarah Adelia Wright was the third polygamous wife of James Strang from their marriage, on July 15, 1855, to his death less than a year later. At the time of her marriage she was 19, having been born in Leeds County, Canada, November 25, 1835, according to her death certificate. Historian Quaife recorded her age at marriage as 17, though 19 appears correct.

This union, against the wishes of her father, Phineas Wright, she sincerely considered an honor. Though Sarah never followed the teachings of her Prophet-husband after his death, she did remarry a Mormon in Jackson County, Wisconsin, a Doctor

PHINEAS AND AMANDA WRIGHT

This couple arrived at Beaver Island from Potosi, Wisconsin. Phineas became the most influential of Strang's twelve apostles. Sarah Wright was one of their eight children. Phineas and two brothers, Benjamin and Samuel, married three Finch sisters, Amanda, Margaret and Rebecca.

In 1851, Phineas was charged with murder along with fourteen others. In less than thirteen months there were more than two-hundred criminal arrests charged to ninety Beaver Island saints. Not one was convicted.

Epilogue

Wing. Previously she had fled to Racine, Wisconsin, as a very disillusioned young lady.

Four months after her arrival at Racine, Sarah gave birth to child number 12 for Strang. The child was born on November 11, 1856. This son was christened James Phineas Strang. In "The Kingdom of Saint James," Quaife erroneously recorded his name as James J. Strang, Jr. It is not surprising, considering that the same name and initials appear so frequently in this plural family. James P. Strang was brought up as James P. Wing. Not until he was a grown young man did he have any knowledge of his real father.

Doctor Wing influenced the life of Sarah during their brief stay in Jackson County. After moving to Springville, Utah, his practice of medicine gave Sarah sufficient knowledge to become a medical practitioner, herself. It is fortunate she gained this knowledge, for Doctor Wing also had an interest in polygamy, causing a termination of the marriage.

In naming her son "James," Sarah followed the family tradition of honoring the father. Strang had seven sons, all of them named James as a first or second name. Six of them were from his plural marriages, their names undeniably complimentary to him. This should refute that animosity existed within the family. The Prophet was a sincere husband and a good father.

Hazel Strang McCardell, respectfully referred to several times in this volume, included the following paragraph in her letter of October 30, 1965:

> "My father was brought up as James P. Wing, for he was very small when my grandmother married Dr. Wing. It was not until he married my mother that he took his rightful name of Strang. He courted mother as "Jim Wing." He and my grandmother would have been persecuted had any of the Utah Mormons known of their Strang heritage. When my father and mother were married they were BOTH disenchanted with the Mormons and made no bones of the fact they were Strangs. In fact, I think they were both itching for a fight against Mor-

monism as it was practiced, for they had both suffered under polygamy."

The mother of Hazel McCardell, the former Lydia Houtz, was, herself, the daughter of a polygamous marriage. When Lydia wed James P. "Wing" Strang at Springville, Utah, she happily accepted the Strang name, although her husband had been "Wing" most of his life.

This speaks very well of "King" Strang. Respect felt for him within the family group is certainly worthy of special attention by any historian making a study of his life.

From the James P. Strang-Lydia Houtz union, seven children were born between 1880-1897. All arrived at Springville, Utah. The writer wishes to record their births in memory of the late Mark A. Strang, author of "The Diary of James J. Strang" and of his sister, Hazel Strang McCardell, without whose assistance many family observations would have been impossible:

James Jesse, October 8, 1880; Mark A., January 1, 1883; Jacob Claude, December 16, 1885; Vere, September 7, 1887; Anna Bebe, August 8, 1889, Sarah Hazel, April 24, 1891; Gail Eugenia, November 17, 1897.

Regarding the education of these children and further observations on her grandfather, Hazel McCardell wrote the following on October 30, 1965:

"We were never allowed to attend the public school. All seven of us were sent to private Mission (Presbyterian) school where tuition had to be paid. I don't know how my parents ever did it in those days of dire struggle, but we were all kept strictly away from any Mormon influence all of our lives. In those days of religious ferment no movement could hope to succeed unless tied to a religious motive... expediency if you like. These minor things, made so much of by writers, have never detracted in any way from his genius, in my view."

Hazel McCardell expressed her feelings about James Strang as a man, when she wrote:

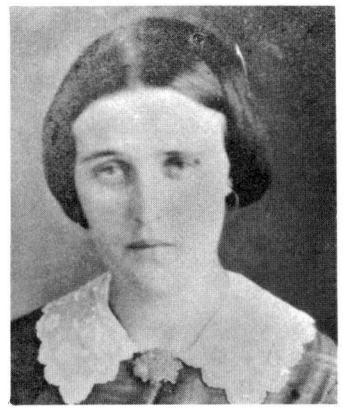 

Sarah Wright as Mrs. Strang and Mrs. Wing

As Mrs. Strang, this photo was taken about 1858. Her marriage to Dr. Wing was terminated because of his interest in polygamy.

FOUR GENERATIONS OF SARAH STRANG FAMILY
James Phineas   James Jesse   Sarah   James Lawrence

Sarah was the last surviving wife of James Strang. She bore him one son, shown on the left. All four polygamous wives gave birth to children after his death.

JAMES PHINEAS STRANG   EUGENIA JESSE (STRANG)

James Phineas Strang was the only child of James Strang and Sarah Adelia Wright, the third polygamous wife of Strang.

His introduction of strip farming and windbreaks in the great Western wheat country to preserve top soil, may be attributed to the influence of his father. Strang was one of the first to practice conservation of soil.

Eugenia Jesse was the only child of James Strang and Phoebe Wright, the fourth and last polygamous wife, and a cousin of Sarah. She never used the name Strang.

Epilogue

"All the sensational sordid things written and sold for gain cannot erase from my mind and soul the fine courageous and selfless image of the MAN who was my grandfather."

During her busy Canadian life, Hazel McCardell has lived this proud feeling. It is fortunate she inherited Strang qualities. To her credit, she developed these as a teacher, writer, musician and amateur astronomer. As Hazel Strang in Claresholm, before her marriage on November 9, 1917, she had won gold medals as a pianist at the Lethbridge music festivals. She also sang professionally as a lyric soprano. On July 1, 1921, Mrs. McCardell, with her husband and pilot Major Thompson, flew from Edmonton to Henry House, Jasper, thereby becoming the first woman ever to fly over the Canadian Rockies.

An examination of the Wright genealogy chart, especially prepared for this volume, reveals that Sarah's great-great uncle, Silas Wright, was Governor of New York state, 1844-1847. Wright was a considered candidate for the presidency of the United States at the time of his untimely death on August 27, 1847.

Sarah Adelia Strang Wing died at Boise, Idaho on August 18, 1923, at the age of 87. Through sheer determination, she won her fight for a good life. She had won in circumstances not imagined possible on that terrifying day 68 years before on the shores of Beaver Island.

PHOEBE WRIGHT STRANG

On October 27, 1855, James J. Strang, three months after his marriage to Sarah, took into his now crowded home on Beaver Island, a fourth and final polygamous wife, Phoebe Wright.

Phoebe, born in Leeds County, Canada, July 25, 1836, was a cousin of Sarah. She was a girl of 18 when she married Strang. The Wright genealogy clearly illustrates the branching off of these cousins who shared the same husband, along with Elvira and Betsy. Little is known of her private life. That she suffered a great personal loss due to her exile to Jackson County, Wisconsin, is understandable.

On October 28, 1856, Phoebe Strang gave birth to the 11th child of the Prophet, noting here that this was the final marriage of the "King." All polygamous wives gave birth to children conversely to their marriage dates, leaving a legitimate record of four single posthumous births.

The child of Phoebe was christened Eugenia, a family name. When Eugenia grew to womanhood, her mother lived with her as she was then beginning a teaching career at Black River Falls, Wisconsin. Previous to this, Phoebe had lived in the home of her parents at Black River Falls, helping to take care of her invalid mother. Because she also had a brother at home and because of the teaching position, Eugenia was able to move into a rented house.

In a letter to Hazel Strang McCardell, dated June 6, 1936, Eugenia wrote of the lifelong devotion of her mother to the memory of her father. Phoebe never remarried. Her life with the Prophet of eight months' duration was one of devotion, though she admittedly felt some dissatisfaction with polygamy during this short marriage. For 48 years, Phoebe lived with a mixed memory of Beaver Island love and hate and the memory of being among the mourners at the deathbed of her husband at Voree.

Phoebe died on November 9, 1914, at age 66, another disillusioned wife and Saint who had abandoned the Church and teachings of her earthly Prophet in the flesh.

Eugenia Jesse never used the name Strang, nor did her mother after the death of her husband. She called herself Mrs. Phoebe Jesse during her remaining life.

When Rev. A. N. Somers wrote his narrative "An American King" for the May, 1901, issue of National Magazine, his "Princess Eugenia" was this same daughter of "King" James Strang. Rev. Somers, later of Westboro, Massachusetts, had been a preacher at Black River Falls, Wisconsin, about 1890. Here he became familiar with this segment of the Strang family history, accounting for this brief narrative.

HAZEL STRANG MCCARDELL AND HUSBAND, WILLIAM H. MCCARDELL

On July 1, 1921, Hazel Strang became the first woman to fly over the Canadian Rockies. Her father was Strang's only child by third polygamous wife, Sarah Wright. William McCardell, born in Anthracite, Alberta in 1892, was a member of the Royal Canadian Artillery, Royal Flying Corps, Royal Air Force and the Canadian Air Force from 1917 to 1919. In 1923 he obtained a commercial pilots license. From 1931 to his retirement in 1957, he was a member of the Alberta Forrest Service.

The father of McCardell was one of three credited with the discovery of the Cave and Basin, and Upper Hot Springs, resulting in the creation of the world famous Banff National Park in Canada in 1883.

Wright Genealogy Chart

NATHANIEL — Nathaniel was a London merchant. Founded the Winthrop Colony in America.

DEACON SAMUEL WRIGHT — Samuel Wright was sent over to America by his brother Nathaniel in the interest of the Winthrop Colony about 1634 (founded). Record of his being juryman in 1639 at Southhampton, Mass. Moved to Springfield, Mass. In later years and was a deacon. Died in 1670's.

SAMUEL *

NEW YORK STATE — State Senator, Congressman, Comptroller, U.S. Senator, Governor. Offered Supreme Court seat by Pres. Tyler and Sec. of Treas. by Polk. Mentioned for Pres. at death.

- **SILAS, JR.** B-1795 * D-1847 — Officer in the Revolution. He married Elinor Waybridge in 1782.
- **SILAS** B-1759 D-1843

PHINEAS

- **BENONI** — Married to * Zilpha Downer. Captain in the Revolution under General Sullivan.
- Composer and teacher of music. Oldest of nine children. Born 1765 or 1761.
- Captain in the Continental Army. Killed in battle with Indians.

*Educated midwife, daughter of physician. · Or Barrona.

Children of Silas (Jr.)

- **WILLIAM**
- **PHINEAS**
- **JOSEPH**
- **GEORGE** B-5-25-1789 D-2-23-1859 — M- Phoebe Whitley
- **LUCY** — M- James Blakeslee
- **EUNICE** — M- Henry Elliott

Children of George (M- Margaret Finch)

- **BENJAMIN G.** B-3-6-1839 D- M- Margaret Finch
- **PHINEAS** — M- Amanda Finch
- **SAMUEL** — M- Rebecca Finch
- These 3 children died in infancy or youth.
- Through second marriage **HENRY C.** — Married Mary Carpenter. Henry died at 35 leaving his wife and daughter.

Children of Benjamin G.

- SAMUEL
- GEORGE
- AMANDA
- MOSES
- ZILPHA
- LOUISA * Died in infancy
- **PHOEBE** — Fourth of thirteen children above.
- MARGARET
- * EUGENIA
- BENJAMIN
- * WILLIAM
- * DOOLESKA
- THEODORE

DOOLESKA — Born 3-26-1853 at St. James on Beaver Island. Died 11-7-54, B.I.

THEODORE — Born 12-24-1855 at St. James on Beaver Island. Died 1-17-1954 Tacoma, Wash.

Phoebe married James Jesse Strang
PHOEBE WRIGHT

Sarah Adelia married James Jesse Strang
SARAH ADELIA — Married Dr. Wing

Children: ELIZABETH, ZENAS, PHINEAS, AMANDA, SILAS, MARY, EDGAR

Amanda died. Mary Carpenter. These four were young.

Eugenia Strang
Born 10-28-1856 Black River Falls, Wisconsin, died in Tacoma, Wash. — After 40
Married 9-10-1879 to Thomas H. Philips

- **THOMAS R., JR.** B-1-10-1877 D-10-20-1930 — Moved to Duluth, Minn. in July, 1892 and moved to Salt Lake City, May, 1896 and then to Tacoma, Washington 1-1-1898.
- **ZILPHA EUGENIA** B-8-9-1878
- **BENJAMIN W.** B-1-27-1894
- **THEODORE**
- **JOHN W.** B-1-31-1897
- **JAMES G.** B-6-29-1900 — Twins. B-1-31-1897 John died a baby, James at birth.

James Phineas
Born 11-11-1858 Black River Falls, Wisconsin. Died in Claresholm, Alberta, Canada 11-1-1937.
Married 12-3-1878 to Lydia Houtz in Springville, Utah. Lydia was born on 1-28-1862, died in Claresholm on 9-1-1923.

All children born in Springville, Utah.

- **JAMES JESSE** B-9-8-1880 D-7-30-1952
- **MARK** B-1-1884 D-JULY 22,1965
- **JACOB CLAUDE** B-12-16-1885 D-MARCH 27,1965
- **VERE** B-9-1-1887 D-9-3-1970
- **ANNA BEBE** B-5-5-1889 D-
- **SARAH HAZEL** B-4-24-1891 D-
- **EUGENIA GAIL** B-8-17-1897 D-

MISCELLANY

A Sampling of Strangite Impostures: George J. Adams and John C. Bennett

During his lifetime, George Washington Joshua Adams represented many things to many people. Romantically speaking, it may be said this lecherous charlatan was the John Alden of Strang's Kingdom of God on Beaver Island. To him fell the honor of asking Elvira Field to be the first polygamous wife of James Strang, soon to be James the First to his Mormon Saints.

In no respect is it an exaggeration to tag this imposture "lecherous." If readers wish a confirming opinion of this pious fraud, the descriptive words of another author lend credence and additional censure of Adams. In his attempt to interpret the incredible career of this complicated and unsavory "minister" of the gospel, author Peter Amann exposed him as a crook, a psychopath and a fanatic, adding: "these labels do scant justice to the complexities of the man who lies buried in a long forgotten grave in Philadelphia's Cedar Hill Cemetery."

Author Amann deserves much credit for researched information disclosed in this brief chronicle about Adams, beginning at age 55. His thoroughly documented article appeared first in "The New England Quarterly," under the title "Prophet in Zion: The Saga of George J. Adams." Those who wish to pursue this scholarly work may find it in Vol. XXXVII, No. 4, December, 1964.

George Adams launched numerous celestial careers. His most ambitious plan, inaugurated at age 55, further exposed his life of religious hypocrisy. This exposé begins at age 55 revealing his later career, followed by a review of his earlier careers with claimed Prophets of God, Joseph Smith and James Strang.

The most ambitious celestial career for Adams began when he planned to transport most of his church members to the Holy Land from Jonesport, Maine during August, 1866. On board would be Adams, his wife and about 156 colonists bound for Jaffa to launch a new American religious settlement in Palestine. Specifically, this was to be the nucleus of a spiritual-minded agricultural society. This possibility began to shape in the mind of Adams four and a half years earlier, at the time of his arrival in New England to preach the second coming of Christ. Having founded and ministered in the "Church of the Messiah," his appetite now whetted for bigger and better things. There is no question that Adams considered his talents and abilities boundless. Establishment of a colony in Palestine was a scheme worthy of his unique talents, though it was highly unsuccessful as this story unfolds.

Between the removal of George Adams from Beaver Island in 1850, when Strang turned him over to the "buffetings of Satan," and the year 1861, Adams had been a Campbellite preacher in Vermont. Then, as throughout his ministry, his career was often burdened by addiction to alcohol. At Rutland he was once publicly drunk on the street while his wife was delivering a lecture on temperance in a local hall.

The year 1862 was spent at Springfield, Massachusetts, where Adams was unmercifully rebuked by a newspaper editor who recalled his earlier Mormon career with Joseph Smith. Editorial persecution drove the entire "Church of the Messiah" to the State of Maine. Here, the Prophet began exhibiting his energetic preparation of misadventure to the Holy Land. He began a monthly news magazine, a rather successful publication promoting all manner of schemes toward the glorification of his Church. The purpose of the magazine was to insure the recruiting success of his plan.

During 1864, a move 200 miles east to Indian River, on the coast of Maine, emerged as another turning point in Adams' life. At Indian River, Adams met a new angel, prosperous A. K. McKenzie, whose multiple business interests included ship building. Important, spiritually, was their mutual interest in the second coming of Christ, a point Adams now pressed to advantage by suggesting a return of the Jews to Palestine. This idea met with favor on the receptive ears of McKenzie, by now an influential member of the Church. He agreed to assist in the preparation for the establishment of an American colony at Jaffa.

An intensive drive for funds publicized the proposed colony as an agricultural society specializing in fruit. There was no mention of a temple in their plans, although the purpose of building Mormon temples at Kirtland, Nauvoo, Salt Lake City and elsewhere was to receive Christ bodily. Adams had been a Mormon for many years and his avowed purpose in colonizing was to prepare for the second coming.

Adams and McKenzie left for Malta from Boston Harbor early in 1864 to investigate properties deemed appropriate for the "glorified production of fruit." Outside the walls of Jaffa, a six-acre plot prompted a down payment of 40 pounds. The two partners were gratified to find such a promising acreage, though it is doubtful their research needed the six or seven months they were gone. Not until October did they return home bearing the good news.

As soon as Adams arrived back at Indian River, his agile mind concocted the "Palestine Emigration Association" and he, of course, accepted the Presidency. He was thoroughly competent in matters of this kind. His concern for legal status involving the "Church of the Messiah" in Jerusalem included the assistance of Secretary of State Seward. Not only did Seward promise assistance, his office expedited all legal preparations.

Shortly before, a letter from Adams' Senator in Maine gained him entrance to the White House and a brief reception by President Andrew Johnson!

The clipper *Nellie Chapin,* still being constructed at Addison, Maine was chartered to transport the 156 strangely enthusiastic colonists to their promised land. When completed, the sailing date was set as August 11, 1866.

While the ship served well to store enough lumber for 20 small homes, it was not designed for passenger service. A great deal of discomfort and dissatisfaction gave the colonists plenty to grumble about. In addition to lumber, an important commodity aboard was a good stock of brandy, not merely for the consumption of the addicted false Prophet but for economic reasons as shall be revealed later.

Once at sea, it was graphically evident that this ill-fated voyage was to be far less comfortable than anticipated. Not only crowded conditions prevailed, but food was poor, a most unhappy situation. Adams' cloak of respectability and charm vanished. The quarrelsome, brandy-loving dictator, constantly at odds with Mrs. Adams, revealed his true self for all to behold. There was nothing for them to do but ignore his drunkenness and hope for the best. Control of their savings in the form of goods gave him the power he so dearly loved. Another 19th century display of religious gullibility was about to be unveiled.

A jolt of major proportions greeted the unwary colonists upon their arrival at Jaffa. Faith in sanctimonious Adams suffered another setback when the naive congregation found out something he had known before sailing from Jonesport. The government of Turkey refused to authorize transfer of the six-acre tract! Arrival on September 22, heralded many bitter things for many bitter tomorrows.

Relief from this predicament was temporary. In addition, it entangled individual property ownership beyond belief. In spite of Turkish Government authority, red tape was cut when local circumvention of ownership involved engagement of a native as holder of a nominal title. Local officials also allowed goods on board to be put ashore duty free. Though this combination of unlawful maneuvering and looking the other way, so to speak, meant freedom to land, it allowed them to begin establishment of a colony many wished later had never been permitted.

Many resultant legal entanglements were almost beyond solving. To make matters worse, if indeed they could be, Mrs. Adams became a third party on many deeds. Not only were the properties entangled illegally, oftentimes they were even smaller than the size agreed upon by the Prophet. As a result, more than one member held deeds to the same piece of property.

The first day on the beach a baby was born. In contrast to this added member of the colony, 18 died the first year. Conditions were unsanitary and almost unbearable. Land was parched and exceedingly poor. Glorified production of fruit, promised by Adams and McKenzie less than a year earlier, could not have been further from reality. Adams lied and the colonists knew it. Nothing would grow to satisfactory maturity. The quality was poor and the quantity extremely low or nonexistent.

During the first six weeks, improvised tents offered meagre protection from severe elements, especially downpours, which were common. Luckier colonists lived in shacks. Their position on the beach was not unlike an open sewer. Garbage, human excrement and rotten seaweed brought dysentery. Fever was a very common ailment. All necessary food and water left the colonists at the mercy of Adams or the Arabs, with very little hope for livelihood outside the colony itself. Destitute members were at the mercy of their claimed God-appointed Prophet.

The first home constructed on the beach belonged to Adams himself. Not only the first, but the second. From this, he dispensed, at a profit, among other things, his imported store of brandy. Colonists were at his mercy in many ways. Adams was adept at subjugation, a lesson most learned too late.

Only eight months after arrival at Jaffa, 52 members swollowed their pride and started for home. During October, 1867, the U. S. State Department assisted repatriation of all remaining members who wished to leave. The $3,000 offered by the State Department sparked individual contributions, allowing an additional 42 members to embark on the liner Quaker City.

Surprisingly, the following year, 20 members of the American colony at Jaffa still braved its rugged climate, unproductive land and local authorities, Mr. and Mrs. Adams among them, protecting their investment no doubt. In a short time, however, this quarrelsome couple sailed for England. There, Adams again failed to establish a following in proportion to his self-projected talents as Prophet and spellbinder, and the couple left for home.

George Adams dedicated still another "Church of the Messiah" in Philadelphia in 1873. His return from England three years previous allowed him to prepare his son, an ordained Baptist, for the role of minister.

On May 11, 1880, at the age of nearly 70, Adams died of typhoid fever in Philadelphia. He was buried in Cedar Hill Cemetery.

The writer now wishes to digress 40 years to 1840 to examine the career of George Adams, Mormon.

The cloak of early Methodism was worn lightly by Adams. From birth about 1811 to the year 1840, his entire being craved attention, and in later life, power. Therefore, he shed his career as a Methodist spellbinder of the gospel at age 29. Adams then left New Jersey with great aspiration to perform on the stage. If these great aspirations had been matched by an equally great talent, perhaps the chance meeting in New York State with Mormon Heber Kimball might have been less impressive. Adams' introduction to missionary Kimball ended for all time his cherished hope of a professional acting career.

Within a month, Adams became an elder of the Mormon church. His meeting with Kimball during February, 1840, was the beginning of a pseudo-prophetic entry into the realm of heavenly hypocrisy. In 10 short years, Adams had progressed from Campbellism, to Methodism, to Mormonism, to Strangism, to his own "Church of the Messiah." Drunkenness and immorality were the primary reasons for being "turned over to the buffetings of Satan" by Brigham Young and James Strang, though Strang, in addition, charged embezzlement.

Readers may ponder the question, "Why did Joseph Smith and James Strang indulge Adams, obviously a man of disreputable character?" Actually, both indulged a good number with poor reputations, Strang primarily inheriting his by choice from Smith.

Many pre-Salt Lake City Mormons were of questionable character. Strang, in his eagerness to organize a following to bolster his own claim of God-given prophetic succession, jeopardized his church by welcoming some of these early Mormon cast-offs. George J. Adams was one of them. John C. Bennett, who supposedly influenced Adams to seek a high position in Strang's church, was another. A brother of Joseph Smith, William, whom Bennett urged as patriarchal see at Voree, was cleverly recommended by sentimentally suggesting he bring his mother, the mummies and papyrus, and the bodies of Joseph and Hyrum!

The mummies and papyrus referred to are capably narrated by Milo Quaife in "The Kingdom of Saint James."

> "The allusion to the papyrus and the mummies recalls one of Joseph Smith's most amusing impostures. While he was still at Kirtland, a traveling showman came along, exhibiting, among other objects, two or three Egyptian mummies. Smith had them purchased for the Church, and when it was discovered that some papyri had been acquired along with the mummies, the Prophet proceeded to "translate them." In due time he announced that one of the writings was by Abraham of Old Testament fame, and thereafter until Smith's death the mummies were treasured and exhibited (for a price) to curious visitors. Unfortunately for the credit of Smith's translation, however, he published along with it a picture of the document he had translated; thereby he enabled certain future scholars who really possessed some knowledge of Egyptology to expose the measure of Smith's pretended knowledge of the subject."

At Voree, Strang's "Garden of Peace," John Bennett became the Prime Minister for the Imperial Primate of the Order of the Illuminati and chief advisor to Strang. At Nauvoo, Bennett had been Mayor, the Nauvoo Legion's Major General, President of Nauvoo University and member of the First Presidency, all appointments showered upon him quickly after becoming a Mormon. Prior to baptism, he had shown political skill in lobbying the unique Nauvoo charter through the Illinois Legislature.

The assumption that Bennett and Adams discussed the possibility of personal power by joining Strang suffices a brief chronicle on Bennett. His capabilities seemed endless, a quality Smith looked for in choosing aides regardless of adeptness in the art of conniving.

In this connection, the successful inheritor of Joseph Smith's regime, Brigham Young, chose aides in the same manner and was, himself, a ruthless organizer. Testimony by actual Mormon participants in affairs of the Church accused Young of accepting as policy the false interpretation of scripture, quoting him as saying, "I don't know and I don't care whether it is correct or not, so good grows out of it." One witness claimed Young said he "would not give a straw" for the Book of Covenants. Another witness testified an accepted policy included any act, even killing a man if necessary, to save a Mormon brother in danger. As Major General of the Legion, Bennett, of necessity, became involved in policies of expediency.

It has often occurred to the writer that Mormon policies of expediency in many matters may very well have included the purported "Letter of Appointment" to Strang from Joseph Smith as his prophetic successor. As pointed out, Bennett was a known coniver. He was made a member of the First Presidency within weeks of his baptism as a Mormon. Does it not seem a possibility that Joseph Smith did not trust any member of the Council of Twelve and, in fear of his mortal life, appointed the capable James J. Strang as his successor, even though he had personally baptized him only four months previous?

Conjecture about the genuineness of the letter persists to this day. If the entire contents are genuine, the only conclusion possible is this: Brigham Young was a fraudulent usurper of the Joseph Smith regime. Only one month before his assassination, Smith received a requested report from Strang on the desirability of a Mormon center at Voree. That Smith needed immediate action of some kind is well known. Although Gentile persecution persisted, the greatest threat toward disintegration of his Mormon regime was internal dissension, lending further support to such a theory. The letter has never been proved fraudulent.

Dr. John C. Bennett began life at Fair Haven, Massachusetts, August 3, 1804. Like Strang, he accumulated a wealth of knowledge beyond his medical profession. Among varied capabilities, other than being a physician, may be enumerated these activities: President of the Medical Faculty and Professor of the Principles and Practice of Midwifery and the Diseases of Women and Children at Willoughby University on Lake Erie; a similar position at the Literary and Botanico-Medical College of Ohio in Cincinnati; and a politician of proved ability as already noted. Bennett suggested the establishment of a "University of Wisconsin", to Strang, as early as 1849.

Bennett remained with Joseph Smith for only 18 months. His meteoric rise to influence in the Mormon hierarchy ended abruptly without public explanation, possibly because Smith wished to avoid another quarrel within the Church. If true, his wish was short-lived. Though Bennett wrote Strang in March, 1846, that he had "withdrawn" in the Spring of 1842 with "best of feelings subsisting between all parties," this must be considered false, for within the year, he published his book on "The History of the Saints; or an Exposé of Joe Smith and Mormonism." This was the first important book encompassing charges of immorality against the leaders of the Mormon Church. The first edition leads one to believe much of it was compiled and authored by Bennett while yet a Saint. It is doubtful he joined the Mormon Church for this purpose, although he freely claimed to be a spy. He loved pomp, as did Smith, and this he found at Nauvoo. Like Adams, he craved power and public attention.

On May 19, 1842, the City Council of Nauvoo tendered a complimentary vote of thanks to Bennett upon his resignation as mayor. The following notice appeared in the "Wasp" and was reprinted in the Voree "Zion's Reveille" issue of February 11, 1847, six months before the arrival of Bennett at Voree:

> "New Election of Mayor and Vice-Mayor of the city of Nauvoo, on the resignation of General Bennett. On the 17th instant, Gen. John C. Bennett resigned the office of mayor of the city of Nauvoo, and on the 19th, Gen. Joseph Smith, the former vice-mayor, was duly elected to fill the vacancy; and on the same day Gen. Hyrum Smith was elected vice-mayor."

> "The following vote of thanks was then unanimously voted to the ex-mayor, General Bennett, by the city council to wit: Resolved by the city council of the city of Nauvoo, that this council tender a vote of thanks to General John C. Bennett, for his great zeal in having good and wholesome laws adopted for the government of this city, and for the faithful discharge of his duty while mayor of the same."

Joseph Smith, Mayor

In the same issue of "Zion's Reveille" appeared these curious lines about "Exposé" authored by Bennett:

> "When General Bennett had his unfortunate difficulty with the Church, he published an Exposé. As the pseudoes lack brains to edict original articles, we suggest to them the propriety of furnishing some extracts from that racy work, or Tom Paine's "Age of Reason," for the benefit of the infidel patrons, of the Anti-Mormon New Era, in lieu of the quack advertisement reprints from the Elkhorn Western Star. Pseudoes, will you take the bait?"

"Exposé" revealed Bennett for what many knew him to be, a demagogue and knave. Yet, on March 9, 1846, knowing Bennett to be an unprincipled knave, Strang wrote a letter offering him a position in the Church at Voree. With little hesita-

George J. Adams and John C. Bennett

tion, this malcontent began dictating terms of enlistment, including a desire to serve the Imperial Primate, as he called Strang, as his General-in-Chief. A close tie with Joseph Smith had made him aware that he wished appointment by revelation and commandment! In July, 1847, Bennett arrived at Voree, a newly baptised and supposedly penitent man.

Bennett and Adams had been living in Cincinnati prior to the Voree period of their lives. It was natural for them to meet and to discuss the situation of the Strangite Saints. Knowledge that Bennett had been approached by Strang prompted Adams to suggest appointment to a similar position he held with Smith. A recommendation by Bennett assisted Strang in his decision, undoubtedly, but Strang was careful to point out, "I have only to say *now* that if you are guilty (drunkenness, loose women, etc.), you must do so no more."

Perhaps caution should be used in stating that Strang thought himself able to forgive Bennett and Adams, and also be able to rescue both for some service to his Saintly flock. Admittedly, such belief on the part of Strang toward either man would tax his utmost patience. Bennett was not a religious man. Adams, as already pointed out, was addicted to drink and women and his religious fervor was not genuine. Both continued their evil ways at Voree. Adams went with the Saints to Beaver Island, spending most of his time in the East, however, seeking new recuits and promoting acceptance of Strang as Smith's successor.

While Adams was a member of the Smith Mormon regime, he accompanied Orson Hyde on a trip to Jerusalem. At the time of the Prophet's assassination at Carthage jail, another trip, this time to Russia, was apparently planned but cancelled because of Smith's murder. Perhaps the projected trip to Jerusalem gave Adams the idea for his attempted colony at Jaffa, previously narrated.

From the day Joseph Smith was assassinated, Brigham Young did everything possible to ward off acceptance of Strang as prophetic successor. His fear of Strang was clearly paramount. Any Saint from Voree, or from Nauvoo for that matter, who spoke up for Strang was removed from the Church roster. Members were offered no opportunity to even defend their removal. Orson Hyde, with whom Adams had gone to Jerusalem, heard a resounding "Amen" even before he made a motion that "if any man investigate Strangism or talk with them on the subject he should be cut off." Adams was cut off, of course, and within a few years joined the only one who claimed divine appointment to succeed Smith.

Until the death of Smith, the Mormon Church had never been without a Prophet. Its very existence converged upon one thought: their Prophet in the flesh in truth was God's own representative on earth. James Strang was the only claimant professing to be called of God. If his claim was fraudulent, God failed to reveal a successor-Prophet through Smith or by direct revelation. If God failed by revelation at the time of assassination, as Brigham Young vigorously maintained, the Church had no Prophet, nor could they have, according to their beliefs, except by direct appointment from the Omnipotent to the individual or by angelic messenger directed of God.

Strang claimed such a miraculous vision on June 18, 1844. This date precedes the purported "Letter of Appointment" by nine days, a letter Strang claimed was processed on Smith's authority to designate him as successor. The "Letter" was hand printed, not written, supposedly by a secretary. Certainly, this must be considered unusual, but the claimed appointment, itself, is no less so. On June 27, 1844, Smith was murdered. On July 9, the letter was received at the Burlington, Wisconsin, post office. It is now in the Coe collection at Yale University Library.

John Bennett and George Adams benefited by Strang's claim of prophetic succession. That is, if joining him may be considered a benefit. It is doubtful either believed Strang divinely appointed. However, there were many who sincerely believed God chose Strang to be His Prophet at Nauvoo, including most of the Smith family.

Smith's Mormon Church harbored many malcontents and many demagogues. Among the worst were John Bennett and

George J. Adams and John C. Bennett

George Adams. It was no compliment to Strang, unless he was sincere in thinking he could save their souls and rehabilitate them for the work of God, that their presence become a reality at Voree. Joseph Smith, however, as the claimed mouthpiece of God, had accepted Bennett into his Church knowing he was not a religious man.

Soon after the Kirtland, Ohio, Stake was reorganized as a Strangite Mormon possession, including the Temple, James Strang and George Adams, among others, held meetings in eastern churches to win support and to disclaim Brigham Young.

The Mormon Church, up to this time, had not only survived, but seemed surprisingly to enjoy verbal conquests with skeptics. Strang, though not in the role of skeptic, was eager to debate his claims, and at Philadelphia defied Orson Hyde and John Taylor to air their differences publicly. Their refusal to debate was a compliment to Strang. It is easy to understand refusal. While their purpose in the East was to repudiate Strang publicly, it did not please them to clash with so brilliant a debater and student of the Bible.

Orson Hyde and John Taylor followed their eastern tour by proposing discussion with less able debaters in England, among them Lester Brooks and Martin Harris, who were no match at all. Harris was one of the three original witnesses of the Book of Mormon, but later a Strangite Mormon. The English Strangite delegation crumbled. Hyde and Taylor were successful in their effort to back the existing Council of Twelve at Nauvoo, accomplished by withering editorials in the Liverpool Millenial Star, their Church organ. A sample of strong public denunciation of Strang included this description of him:

> "successor of Sidney Rigdon, Judas Iscariot, Cain (the brother and murderer of Able) and Co. Envoy Extraordinary and Minister Plenipotentiary of His Most Gracious Majesty Lucifer the I, assisted by his allied contemporary advisors, John C. Bennett, William Smith (a brother of Joseph), G.

J. Adams, and John E. Page (former member of the Council of Twelve)."

Name-calling between early Mormon members never has been equalled by any other American religious sect, nor have many of its impostures. Earlier, a quote from Milo Quaife's "Kingdom of Saint James" related the mummies and papyrus story incriminating Prophet Smith. Since the writer felt the "amusing imposture" might add a bit of human frailty to the "Story," it now behooves him to include a "somewhat curious reflection" relating to Prophet Strang taken from the same source:

> "In the Strangite Bible, the Book of the Law of the Lord, which purports to have been translated by Strang with divine aid from the 'Plates of Laban' which the ancient Jews kept in the Ark of the Covenant, verse 6 of chapter XX on the "Calling of a King" reads:
>
> "He hath chosen his servant James to be King; he hath established him a Prophet above the kings of the earth; and appointed him King of Zion; by his own voice did he call him, and he sent his angels unto him to ordain him."

Quaife continues:

> "Two alternative deductions from this statement are possible: either the divine author of the Law of the Lord did not know that the future king of the earth would be named Jesse by his parents; or the finite author of the reputed sacred record had forgotten, when composing it, that in earlier life he had gone by the name of Jesse rather than James Strang."

Name-calling appeared to be a trait any male Mormon worth his salt should be capable of exercising at any time. While Bennett and Adams were champions at such vitriolic expressions, hardly an early influential Mormon lacked this audible weapon. In England, during the period when Brigham Young had his Strangite opponents crushing Strang's prophetic claim, words of the most degrading description possible were heaped upon apostles of God, recent faithful servants to Joseph Smith. Church leaders, including Strang, were purged by Young to bolster his own claim of succession. Young's quest for leadership spared no vile English word known to crush an opponent, even within his own Church.

A trial at Voree, involving John Bennett as the accuser, included charges of "schism, heresy, mischief-making, diabolism, libel, and supererogating the spiritual wife doctrine." Moral delinquency accusations, such as the last charge involving incest with a daughter, may have been rare, but early Mormon adult delinquency was astoundingly constant, even at Voree.

Two important Saints not allowed to remove themselves to Beaver Island in 1847 were John Bennett and William Smith. William, a brother of Joseph, was an apostle and successor-patriarch at Nauvoo after the death of brother Hyrum by assassins. The office had been created by Joseph for his father soon after founding the Church in 1830. Late in 1847, Bennett and Smith were cut off from the Strangite Church, both somewhat mysteriously, the latter for questionable adultery at Voree and the former for conspiracy to establish a Mormon Stake, deception and immoralities.

Zion's Reveille of July 8, 1847 published a removal notice of Prime Minister Bennett in this manner, as it appears in the copy in the Clements Library, University of Michigan:

> "John C. Bennett has been removed from all official standing in the Church, for the following reasons: 1st. Suppressing letters addressed to Pres. Strang. 2nd. Giving instructions to the Saints, purporting to be by the authority of the First Presidency, which were entirely unauthorized, and directly contrary to their known instructions and settled policy. 3rd. Teaching unsound doctrine."
>
> James J. Strang

George Adams, however, cleverly remained in Strang's good graces in spite of his poor reputation in the East. His faults were kept in check while on Beaver, but from Baltimore, where he was a leader, scandal filtered back to the island, revealing escapades unworthy of any Saint.

Prior to joining James Strang as counselor, this frustrated personator of Richard III had been counselor and spokesman to Joseph Smith. At least Adams stated this in a letter to the Saints "scattered abroad in all the World" for publication in the Voree Herald. The full letter, written from Lewisburgh, Ohio, July 6, 1846, exposes Adams as a pseudo. His ill-omened mission to Jerusalem lends credence to such a conclusion when comparing his misdeeds to these written words:

> "I feel it a duty that I owe to God, the Church, and the age in which I live, to make known to you, some facts in relation to the present situation of the Church of Jesus Christ of Latter day Saints; first then be it known unto all men that James J. Strang is the President, Prophet, Seer, and Revelator, to this Church appointed by Joseph Smith, according to the Book of Doctrine and Covenants, before his martyrdom and confirmed by the ministry of Angels, according to the order of such callings and priesthood. The question may be asked, how do you know that such is the fact; I answer that I know by the same testimony from God by revelation. I know he is the only man that has claimed that calling according to the order of the Church and Book of Doctrine and Covenants. I know he is the only man that is now giving proof to the Nations of the Earth, of such Calling's, Priesthood, and Authority.
>
> "My beloved brethren: You all know that previous to the death of brother Joseph, I was acting as his counselor and spokesman; you also know that as soon as the Twelve usurped authority, I withdrew from their unholy, and pernicious councils — after which they attempted, in their illegal and usurped authority, to cast me off and blacken my character, and injure my usefulness. But you among whom they and myself have traveled, can judge of their conduct and mine, and you know the "errors" that I committed were by their teachings and direct commands, which "errors" I have forever renounced and forsaken, God being my helper. If they had done the same, God would not have forsaken them; "but they love darkness rather than light, because their deeds are evil." After I withdrew from them and their wicked ways, I determined never to take a stand until I could take one in righteousness and truth, according to the order of the House of God. The time has come and the man also. After calling on God in the name of Son Jesus, he con-

descended in a glorious manner to manifest his will and purpose to me, concerning brother James J. Strang; and I now bear testimony to all the world that he is a Prophet, Seer, and Revelator, appointed and chosen of God, to stand in the place of brother Joseph; to give the word of God and hold the keys and power that is to bear off this last dispensation."

George J. Adams

This letter to the Saints was obviously edited before publication. Not only was Adams emotionally unstable and a man of excessive zeal, but he was also an uncultured man, creating such phrases as "base phalshoods" and "whereaver and wheneaver I lift up my voice."

The July, 1846, Voree Herald also contains the certificate advocating James Strang as the true prophetic successor to Joseph Smith. This was written by William Smith and signed by the whole Smith family, except the widow, seven in all, and includes Joseph's mother. Fifty-three years later, one of the signers repudiated the certificate as noted in the Saint's Herald of Lamoni, Iowa, March, 1899.

This same July issue also revealed that John P. Green, City Marshal of Nauvoo, died mysteriously soon after Joseph and Hyrum were assassinated. He was heard by numerous individuals to say that Joseph had appointed Strang.

Others turning away from Brigham Young included John E. Page from the Council of Twelve. Even more importantly, the president of the Nauvoo Stake, itself, William E. Marks. Both advocated James Strang the true appointed leader. Marks, along with Strang and Adams, signed the "Memorial" of April 6, 1850, "To the President and Congress of the United States, and to all the People of the Nation," requesting forever "all the uninhabited lands of the islands in Lake Michigan."

During November, 1846, George J. Adams launched a short-lived but ambitious publication in Baltimore called "The Star in the East."

In the prospectus, Adams' 24-page magazine promised to spread the pure doctrine of Christ; to teach men to fear God,

THE

STAR IN THE EAST.

EDITED BY ELDER G. J. ADAMS.

VOL. I.   NOVEMBER, 1846.   NO. 1.

PROSPECTUS.

THE present is one of the most important eras that have yet taken place in the history of the Church of Jesus Christ of Latter Day Saints. After having struggled for years against persecution, opposition and oppression, and been compelled to witness the martyrdom of her prophet and patriarch, and more recently to behold the usurpation, tyranny and misrule of some of her apostles and professed leaders, who, by their wicked acts, unholy and false teachings, have spread misery, disorganization and ruin in many of her branches throughout the United States, and even in England, she is now just emerging from a night of darkness and desolation; a brighter day is dawning than she has yet known. She is being renovated and purified by the Word of God, and the pure teachings of the prophet James J. Strang, the regularly appointed successor of Joseph Smith, whose claims are now becoming generally acknowledged by the Saints of God throughout the nation. Faithful elders are

PAGE ONE OF 'THE STAR IN THE EAST'

From the only copy known in a private library, now in possession of the writer. Three other copies are known: New York Public and State Libraries and Yale University Library.

respect and obey laws, contend strenuously for the principle of "non-resistance," beware of drunkenness, the emancipation of slavery and pray for an eternal law of "brotherhood." And in conclusion, "we shall ever pray that God will give us wisdom and understanding, that we may be able to do some little towards establishing peace and righteousness on the face of the earth."

Knowledgeable Ernest J. Wessen, recently retired rare book dealer, in a letter dated September 20, 1965, commented on the brief existence of "The Star in the East" by stating the inserts on page 23 "were quite enough to put the STAR out of business." The following paragraph speaks for itself, keeping in mind the publication office was in the same building:

> "The NEW BOSTON MUSEUM; we are extremely glad that this establishment will soon be open, as it will give the hypocritical and long-faced professor of religion an opportunity to witness a good play without having any one accuse them of going to the theatre, as the name of MUSEUM will wipe off all of the stain; we mean those characters who have not moral courage enough to know what is right and then do it."

Dale L. Morgan, who compiled "A Bibliography of the Church of Jesus Christ of Latter-day Saints (Strangite)," indicated a possible second issue of the magazine. He pointed out that anti-theatre members did drive Adams out of business. Morgan recorded a broadside prospectus for a new Adams' publication dated the same month and year, adding credence to the Wessen conclusion that only one STAR was published. The broadside, now in the Coe Western Americana collection at Yale University Library, announced the forthcoming "Independent Inquirer and Journal of the Times."

From 1846 to the coronation, July 8, 1850, George Adams continued as a Strang-pampered member of the Beaver Island colony. During four years as Prime Minister, second only in authority to Strang himself, Adams continued to handicap Strang by his impropriety. And yet, the Prophet continued defending him, as he had many others, though his moral interruptions were embarrassing. Strang claimed Adams was called of God and used this to exonerate himself from personal responsibility. He also defended Adams by quoting comparisons from the Bible, such as "King David dancing naked before the maids of Israel."

Earlier it was pointed out that the Strangite Mormon penalty for adultery was death. Though such a penalty could never be carried out, it nevertheless defines to what extent adultery was condemned. Thus, when Adams failed to use discretion in his introduction of a woman of ill fame he had met in Boston, to associates in Baltimore, the flouting of decency could not be ignored by Strang because it was learned Adams had lied about his wife having died. This fact was unknown until after the concubine was brought to Beaver Island as Mrs. Adams.

In this instance, discipline to Adams was unavoidable and came in the form of divesting his divine right in the First Presidency, a shocking degradation to a revelation-appointed man of God. Degrading Adams in this manner only a few months after the coronation caused a sensational breach in the Church.

In typical early Mormon fashion, Adams became a turnabout and joined the Gentile enemy at Mackinac. Only a few months before, he had suggested "a generous letting of Gentile blood" in retaliation for their determined, but completely frustrated, attempt to annihilate the colony.

The Gentile plan, in the words of Quaife, was to:

"attend the Mormon meeting, armed with concealed weapons, and at the proper moment start a disturbance, and overpower or kill the Mormon men; after which the women and property of the Saints would be at their mercy."

On July 8, 1850, James Strang was crowned in a dramatic ceremony in the tabernacle, which only four days earlier had been garrisoned to repulse the Gentile fishermen. George Adams placed a crown on the head of the new "King." The bright red robe Adams used on the stage, which characterized King Richard III, draped the shoulders of "King" James the First.

George J. Adams and John C. Bennett

Turnabout Adams reappeared at Beaver Island on October 20, a sworn enemy of Strang. With him was the Mackinac County Sheriff, fully prepared to arrest the "King" on a trumped-up charge of threatening the life of his pretended wife. Arrest by the Sheriff took place at Mackinac a few days later. Here, the burlesque legal procedure, played by a satirical cast of legal minds, ignorant of proper law, finally ended in a trial, after first witnessing several commitments and an equal number of releases of the victim.

The prime accuser, of course, was Adams. From the lips of a man who repeatedly claimed James Strang a divinely appointed Prophet of God, his testimony appeared especially shocking. Because of these repeated claims and his own violations in the Beaver Island colony, the accusations seemed a mockery. Strang knew that Adams' sensational charges permanently condemned the colony in the eyes of the public. Although this colony did not deserve such a fate, justice, as far as Strang was concerned, was dead.

During the 1851 federal trial of Strang and his Mormon colony at Detroit, Adams continued his private war on the Saints by appearing in court as a prosecution witness. In addition, he lectured in Detroit on the subject of Beaver Island wickedness. These charges were published in the Detroit Free Press of May 26, June 10 and June 28 of that year.

There is no record revealing the expressed feelings of either Adams or Bennett upon hearing of the assassination of Strang. Dr. Bennett had remained silent when expelled from the Church. Adams continued bellowing about the evils of Mormonism, though having held several important positions in two distinct branches for 10 years. On extensive lecture tours, his evil tongue wagged eternal about the Voree plates being made from an old brass kettle.

It is extremely improbable that James Strang ever asserted that biblical miracles were fakes, though Adams said as much publicly. Nearly all prominent Mormons were brutally tongue-lashed by apostates after separation from the Church, a rather crude method of character assassination since their charges included self-accusation, whether conscious of it or not.

George Adams was 39 years of age when he was cut from the rolls of the Strangite Church in 1850. Sixteen years later, his most ambitious celestial career, already narrated, began. These years were chronicled first to impress readers as to the general type of visionaries many Mormon branches subscribed to during this period in their turbulent history.

While Adams and Bennett were typical of the worst visionaries, they represent but two of hundreds in the spiritual regimes which Joseph Smith and James Strang founded. Both firmly expounded the Mormon Church as the only one on earth founded on commandment and revelation from the Omnipotent. Both also confused society by constantly accepting known demagogues into Church authority as divinely appointed.

An average span of life may said to have been experienced by fanatic Adams and Dr. John Bennett. In contrast, their Prophet, Joseph Smith, was assassinated at age 38, ironically at a time when most of his church leaders were away from Nauvoo campaigning to gain him the presidential nomination. Prophet James Strang was later assassinated at age 43.

Although the most frightful curse in life may be no death, mortals never cease to ponder grim assistance by assassins, of claimed Prophets of God especially.

A Sampling of Strangite Defenders: Bishop George Miller

Rivalry and greed caused enormous dissension within the Mormon Church after the assassination of Prophet Joseph Smith. Caught in the midst of this dissension was an able and trusted friend of Smith, George Miller, who had been "revelation-appointed" of God in 1841 as Presiding Bishop of the Church. After Joseph Smith was assassinated in 1844, Miller and Newell Whitney were unanimously voted trustees-in-trust for all properties owned by the Church. Miller held this office until his final break with the "arrogant usurper," Brigham Young.

While a great many events transpired in the life of Bishop Miller immediately prior to 1844, interest in him is due to his eventual arrival at Beaver Island in 1850. He was a faithful believer in "Brother Strang being called of God to lead his people."

How Miller arrived at Beaver Island, starting from near Austin, Texas, with his family, his son Joshua and family, and the Clark Whitney family, is a story of hardship, courage and determination. This group included 23 persons traveling with four wagons, horses, oxen, baggage and household goods. They crossed Texas, Arkansas, Missouri, Illinois and into Wisconsin, toward their temporary goal, Voree.

The trip started on October 12, 1849. Bishop Miller was then 55 years of age. The small group wintered in Arkansas. They were forced to remain until July 22, 1850, before continuing to Voree, arriving there the following September. Voree was known as "Garden of Peace," the Mormon Stake established by James Strang in 1844.

Prior to sympathetically reviewing the life of Bishop Miller, it is important to relate, in Miller's own words, one vision and two dreams experienced by him and pertinent to those who put faith in them. All have reference to Joseph Smith. One dream-like mental image embraced Smith and Strang.

The vision took place after sunrise the morning following the assassination of Prophet Smith. Bishop Miller, then in Mercer County, Kentucky, on preaching and political engagements, had not yet heard of the assassination. Reports of civil strife in Nauvoo, thought to be highly exaggerated, had appeared in the newspapers and read by Miller and his companion.

Miller described the vision in these words:

> "I was lying on my bed, and suddenly Joseph Smith appeared to me, saying 'God bless you, Brother Miller.' The mob broke in on us in Carthage jail and killed Brother Hyrum and myself. I was delivered up by the bretheren as a lamb for the slaughter. 'You ought not to have left me; if you had stayed with me, I should not have been given up.' I answered, 'But you sent me.' 'I know I did, but you ought not to have gone'; and then approaching me he said, 'God bless you forever and ever,' making as though he was about to embrace me, and, as I was in the act of extending my arms to return the embrace, the vision fled, and I found myself standing on the floor in the midst of the room."

Bishop Miller and his traveling companion, Brother Thomas Edwards, were together in their room of the Saunders residence when this vision was projected in the mind of Miller. One week later, still in Kentucky, they read the assassination account in a Nauvoo paper handed them by a tavern keeper from whom they had asked a drink of water.

Bishop George Miller 161

The first of the two dreams was experienced by Miller in Texas. He had gone there to be with Lyman Wight after the murder of Smith. Wight earlier formed his own Mormon colony near Austin. Miller's son, John, had married one of the Wight daughters. Although the "Association" of 150 Mormons appeared to be thriving, it was heavily in debt. This indebtedness, combined with Wight's false teachings, and drinking, caused discontentment between the two. In urgency, Miller spoke to Wight about these conditions, regretting he did so as noted here:

> "But I soon found my mistake, and it was made doubly manifest to me that, by a multitude of transgressions of the laws that God has given for the purifying and guidance of his people, the transgressors will lose the spirit that directs the mind to all truth, and become wholly darkened, and will invariably persecute those who point out to them the errors with the most bitter feelings."

For more than a year following this break, life was nothing but constant trouble for Miller: illness in the family, trying to earn a living outside the Association where he had placed his monies and equipment in good faith, and continued suffering and privation.

> "But when I could look about me and realize the distracted condition of the church in their scattered situation, without a shepherd that I knew of, I felt in my heart that I was a mourner, and became almost weary of life. While in this state of mind I had a dream, in which I saw Joseph Smith in the heavens in a glorified state, together with countless numbers of glorified beings shouting hallelujah, praising God and the Lamb, and bidding me welcome to the celestial abode. A thin veil separated us, and their brilliancy was whiter and brighter than the sun. Joseph spoke to me and told me that if I would come I might, but I had better not come, as my work was not yet finished on earth. At this time the spirit of praising God came upon me, and I shouted, whereupon part of my family not having retired to bed, hearing me supposed I had a nightmare, and pulled me from my bed. When I awoke my eyes were so affected from the light I had seen that I could not for a time distinguish the surrounding objects."

The second dream is justifiably argumentative, but nevertheless remarkable. Each reader places individual value on these mental images and thoughts while sleeping. This dream, therefore, is included for personal pondering and evaluation.

> "On another occasion I had a dream that I saw Joseph Smith sitting in a room talking to a person whom I have since seen. (James Jesse Strang) Upon my entering the room Joseph looked at me, saying 'God bless you, Brother Miller; I am instructing my successor in the prophetic office — how to manage and conduct the affairs of the church.' The appearance of the person shown me by Joseph Smith in the dream was so stamped on my mind that I could not keep it from my view for a moment, and it was secretly whispered to me that I should soon hear news that would cheer my drooping spirits."

Immediately following the narration of this second dream, Miller penned a few lines, giving a clear picture of his state of mind. More importantly than this, perhaps, is Miller's first word picture projecting James Strang as the true and rightful successor to Joseph Smith.

> "Whilst pondering in my mind the scattered state of the Saints, and the fact that I could hear of no shepherd that I believed was authorized of God to lead the church, I was really in a state of gloom and despondency.
>
> "One afternoon after the toil of a warm day I came to my house to rest, and found some papers setting forth the appointment of J. J. Strang to the prophetic office, instead of Joseph Smith, deceased. It is true that I had heard his name spoken of as leader and prophet, but in my mind I numbered him with other pretenders; as I had not wholly abandoned the belief that Joseph Smith had appointed his successor in one of his own posterity.
>
> "I therefore wrote to Brother Strang a letter questioning his assumption of authority, and requested him to publish my letter. But the next day after mailing my letter I received another package from Brother Strang containing a small tract setting forth Brother Strang's appointment and calling to the prophetic office. On a close and critical reading and investigation of this tract I changed my opinions, and wrote to Brother Strang countermanding the publication of my former letter. From this time, I had frequent manifestations of Brother Strang's being called

Bishop George Miller

of God to lead his people, even as Moses was to lead the Israelites out of Egyptian bondage, and I began to set myself earnestly to make preparations to gather* with the Saints. I was prospered in all my undertakings, and managed so as to be well provided with teams and four or five hundred dollars to bear my expenses to Beaver Island."

*Note: In the 1917 Annual of the Southern California Historical Society, Page 152, the line reads "to make preparations 'together' with the Saints." The manuscript reads 'to gather with the Saints,' as indeed it is in the earlier Watson booklet of 1916. (See "Letters of George Miller" below)

Arrangements were completed to acquire suitable equipment and provisions to continue their journey to Beaver Island, by then the seat of the First Presidency. In the "Bishop Miller Letters," written at Saint James during 1855, is found this soul-stirring paragraph:

"No one can possibly realize my gratitude to God of heaven for my safe deliverance from the perplexity of mind and burning anxiety for respite from the misrule of the haughty and arrogant usurpers of authority in the Church and Kingdom of God, and my eager expectations of being in a week or two placed again under the guidance of the true shepherd (Strang) of the flock of God's people on earth, but those alone who have passed through such ordeals as I have in the last six years, subsequent to the death of Joseph Smith, and up to the time of my arrival at Voree."

While "arrival at Voree" concludes the "Letters of George Miller," as published in the 1917 Annual, this particular one continued for seven additional paragraphs, telling of their arrival at Beaver Island. They were published at least one year earlier by Wingfield Watson, titled "The Correspondence of George Miller." The two publications vary considerably in text for some reason. Prior to these two publications, they appeared in the *Northern Islander,* Strang's island newspaper.

Note: Those wishing to evaluate Bishop Miller more fully may do so by reviewing the 1917 Annual, pages 112 through 156. Copies may be borrowed from your state library. A few are available at the writer's home at Saint James, Beaver Island, if those interested care to write. The full title of the chronicle is "De Tal Palo Tal Astilla," meaning "A Chip of the Old

Block," and was edited by Dr. H. W. Mills after discovering the existence of the Miller diary.

Dr. Mills presented George Miller, Jr. to the Southern California Historical Society, honoring him for his character, accomplishments and historical contributions as a worthy "chip" of his esteemed father.

There are a few errors in the Dr. Mills two-page introduction to the Miller story, pages 86 and 87. Although respectful of Dr. Mills, these should be pointed out. But how fortunate it is to have the opportunity to read the Miller diary. This is primarily due to the friendship between Dr. Mills and George Miller, Jr., and their appreciation of the manuscript's historic value.

At the outset, Dr. Mills said, "Fragmentary notes on the life histories of the two George Millers, father and son, the former of whom started for California in 1846." On page 87, Dr. Mills uses the date 1841. The former is correct. In 1841, three years before the assassination of Smith, Miller had been made the Bishop, replacing Edward Partridge who had died on January 15. Also during that year, on October 15, Bishop Miller was issued a dispensation to form a Masonic Lodge at Nauvoo. This was established finally on March 15, 1842, and the temple dedicated April 5, 1844, about six months prior to the assassination.

Although the meaning is clear in paragraphs four and five on page 87, there is a disarrangement of lines, making it difficult to follow. This will be explained a few pages later.

BISHOP MILLER AND BRIGHAM YOUNG

Bishop Miller was one of the most able men in the Mormon Council of Fifty during the immediate years prior to Smith's murder. It may be proper to call him the "talented work horse" of the Saints, although this term rightfully could be applied to others. A more industrious group of righteous and not-so-righteous people would be difficult to find. However, without

MOTHER OF GEORGE MILLER, JR.

BISHOP GEORGE MILLER

Bishop George Miller was an able and trusted friend of Joseph Smith, and a faithful believer in "Brother Strang being called of God to lead his people."

James Strang was the only Mormon who claimed 'being called of God' to hold the prophetic office after the assassination of Joseph Smith.

question, Miller was one of the most obedient, able and trusted of all the Prophet's friends.

No period in American history had more worshipers who thought they personally walked with God, talked with God and received God's revelations than that following the birth of Mormonism. Nor has any period produced a group with more tenacity for religious independence than the Mormons.

It is not difficult to understand the need for each other during America's post-colonial years. Conditions created a need for religious leaders. This great religious hunger opened up avenues of fraud, deception and false prophesy. The great problem seemed to be to separate good from evil. History has shown that this separation, as far as the early Mormons were concerned, never took place.

Early Mormon history continually proved that good did not always conquer evil. Many good Mormon men were buried and almost forgotten, whose good deeds far outweighed their Mormon enemies who, though corrupt, arrogant and capable of murder, still live memorably in the hearts of present-day worshipers. The memorable survival of Brigham Young and the all-but-forgotten Bishop of the entire church body, George Miller, and the remarkable claimant to prophetic succession, James J. Strang, are striking examples.

There was no rivalry between Young and Miller for Church power. Bishop Miller was a key man, however, not only in the Church, but in the civil government as well, and was a great believer in the importance of prophetic succession. The sudden and violent death of Smith left the Church without a named successor, unless the "Letter of Appointment" to Strang be considered genuine. A final analysis must place Strang as the leading contender, although his name appears in few histories in that role. He was the Mormon Brigham Young feared most.

Miller first believed Smith may have left something in writing in appointing his son as head of the Church. One indication of this was expressed by Miller when he wrote:

"I had no one in whom I could implicitly confide in all things, as he to whom I sought in all times of trouble for counsel and advice was now no more. Oh, who can appreciate my feelings? Let me be excused from saying more on this painful subject.

"Subsequent to these times of intense excitement I had frequent attempts at conversation with Brigham Young and H. C. Kimball in regard to Joseph leaving one to succeed him in the prophetic office, and in all my attempts to ascertain the desired truth as to that personage I was invariably met with the innuendo, "Stop, or hush, Brother Miller; let there be nothing more said in regard to this matter, or we shall have little Joseph killed as his father was;" implying that Joseph Smith had appointed his son Joseph to succeed him in the prophetic office. And I believe that this impression was not alone left on my mind, but on the bretheren's in general, and remains with many until this day."

George Miller had been with Joseph Smith only two years before he became the Bishop. He met Smith in 1839 and became converted to Mormonism at their first meeting. Miller was somewhat older than most influential Saints, having been born on November 25, 1794.

THE LIFE OF GEORGE MILLER

George Miller was born in Orange County, Virginia. The family moved several times to other areas, first when he was about four, followed by moves in Kentucky at ages 11, 12 and 14. The latter move was to Boone County, an area where his father owned 3,417 acres. He experienced earthquakes there in 1811 and 1812. At age 19, Miller learned "the housejoiners trade and carpenters trade" in Richmond, Kentucky. He took his knowledge to Lexington in April, 1814, where he became even more adept while working another year.

At this time, Miller's father lived a short way from Cincinnati. Illness of his father made it necessary that he go there to help with the crops and follow his trade in nearby Cincinnati. His father died in August. Miller, now 21, waited until the following year to make a trip by boat to New Orleans, sailing eventually around Florida in the ship "Balize" to Baltimore. In all of these places, Miller was able to earn the highest wages in the building trade.

The latter part of 1816, Miller was back home in Virginia visiting relatives and working as a carpenter in Charlottesville. The following spring, he returned to Baltimore for a short time, after which he assisted a contractor in building a home for a Mr. Mitchell in Lancaster County, Virginia. A severe illness forced him to leave in October before the job was completed. His decision to recuperate at his sister's home, back in the county of his birth, resulted in a planned attempt on his life, or so he surmised after reviewing the events that took place on the schooner voyage to Fredericksburg, Virginia.

The reason for this attempt on his life was the belief that Miller carried a large sum of money. The would-be culprits, surprisingly enough, were members of the crew: the captain and the mate, his brother. Miller writes, "By my decisive and prompt action, their design was baffled."

It is interesting to note this planned attempt on his life at age 23 was only the first of four or five during his lifetime. Another attempt, according to Miller, involved Brigham Young, whose desperation for complete subjugation to his will tested the patience of many. In this instance, orders were given through one of the Council members, Hosea Stout. This incident took place just before one of their nightly councils while on their westward trek from Nauvoo. This was narrated in Stout's diary as though intended as a joke. Miller knew better, however, as did many others.

In November, 1817, Miller recorded that he was again working in Charlottesville. There is some question about the year being correct. He tells us that:

> "I went to Charlottesville, Albemarle County, Virginia, the proposed sight, at that time, of the Central College. But before the erection of the college buildings had begun, the Legislature of Virginia changed it into the University of Virginia, and applied the literary fund to its endowment and the erection of its build-

ings, which were on a very large scale. I was employed until 1820 in the erection of these buildings. The first year of my labor at the university was very arduous, for I did not get clear of the ague until the latter part of the August following."
(The same illness suffered at Baltimore).

Although the University of Virginia may be considered to have been legally established in 1819, Miller is correct in saying he was employed there from 1817 to 1820. An informative letter from William B. O'Neal, Chairman of the Division of Architectural History at the University, dated October 27, 1965, clears the discrepancy of dates:

> "Although the University of Virginia was founded in 1819, it was preceded by two other institutions. First, the Albemarle Academy which transformed itself into Central College which in turn became the University of Virginia in 1819.
>
> "The original buildings were started in 1817 and eventually became the permanent buildings for the University of Virginia.
>
> "It will be most interesting if you can determine the actual presence here of George Miller, a name which, as yet, has not been recorded as one of the University workmen. There was a large group of carpenters that came down from Pennsylvania, but only the name of their foreman, Richard Ware, is listed in the accounts. Perhaps, George Miller was a member of this group."

Although Mr. O'Neal stated that the University of Virginia was founded in 1819, as indeed literature from the University attests, evidence substantiates 1818 as a thoroughly qualified founding date.

The five-volume "History of the University of Virginia" by Bruce confirms 1819 as the beginning of its statutory existence. However, the Act of the Virginia Assembly in establishing a Board of Commissioners was passed in 1818, according to the February, 1819, issue of the "Analectic Magazine."

The Act of the Virginia Legislature, entitled "An Act appropriating a part of the revenue of the Literary Fund, and for other purposes," required the formation of the Board of Commissioners for the "University of Virginia." The first meeting took place, by law, at the tavern in Rockfish Gap, on the Blue

Ridge, on Saturday, August 1, 1818. All duties charged the Commission were completed the following Tuesday, August 4. Its report was presented December 8, 1818, and the Board immediately dissolved. Two of the 21 members were ex-presidents James Madison and Thomas Jefferson.

The first duty of the Commission necessitated choosing a proper site "in some convenient and proper part of the state for an University, to be called the 'University of Virginia' "

A second requested duty was to propose plans for its buildings. It was on these buildings that young George Miller labored as a carpenter for three years. According to Miller, they were "on a very large scale."

The third entailed what "branches of learning which should be taught," and the fourth "the number and description of the professorships they will require by first considering at what point university education should commence."

The fifth duty included proposals for such general provisions as may be properly "enacted by the Legislature for the better organizing and governing of the University."

Thomas Jefferson was the guiding light of the University, as well as its founder. There is little doubt that George Miller saw him many times during these years, and may have had opportunities to converse with him. Jefferson was vitally interested in every detail, whether construction from his plans or the selection of the faculty. Close observation at the site was as often as health permitted. Jefferson gave his very life to the University as, indeed, he did his modest wealth in entertaining at Monticello. There, he died a poor man on the 50th anniversary of our country's independence. Another ex-president, John Adams, died the same day, July 4, 1826.

During the Fall and Winter of 1819, Miller again visited relatives in Kentucky and again returned to the University to work. Since the Miller narration was written 35 years after leaving Charlottesville, and the name "University of Virginia" was given to it a year before he left, it is not unusual for Miller to record this as "University of Virginia" instead of "Central College."

FIVE GENERATIONS OF THE MILLER FAMILY

George Miller, Jr., on the left was honored by the Southern California Historical Society as a worthy chip of his esteemed father.

The review of "The Life of George Miller, Written by Himself," has now reached a gap. Historically, it is fortunate to be able to examine this diary — the sections surviving destruction, that is. Dr. Mills rescued this bit of history for future generations.

It is now time to relate the rescue story of the diary, as told in the words of Dr. Mills, and to reveal the reason for the gap. The copy in brackets the writer has supplied, due to the omission spoken of previously. The deleted line is also properly placed in the paragraph below. The "George Jr." referred to was a son of Bishop Miller's second polygamous wife.

> "George Jr., was a baby — an uncommonly husky, self-reliant and sturdy boy, incidentally, — but too young to be interested in family documents. (It was decided, therefore, to entrust this manuscript) into the keeping of a female relative. The keeper of the archives forgot in the course of many years its very existence until, in the year 1916, the log was brought to her memory by the fact that the mice ate through the seventy-six year old trunk and disturbed her sleep by rummaging in the documents contained therein during the starry night.
>
> "Did she instantly take measures to protect and preserve these documents? By no means. Being of a prosaic and practical turn of mind, she instantly consigned the trunk and its contents to the rubbish heap, and applied a match — casually, some days later, informing George Jr. of what she had done.
>
> "George, who had never heard of the log, but who entertained profound respect for his father's memory, was greatly shocked and at once essayed to rescue the partially destroyed and tattered remnants of what was left of his father's bequest.
>
> "From this fragmentary salvage I have transcribed what follows: — many gaps occur; — the pages are yellow with age, and whole segments have gone by the board; frequently a portion of a page is torn off, and other parts are so charred as to be utterly undecipherable. Nevertheless, what remains is of such historic interest that I have thought it worthy to be brought to light before this Historical Society."

The "Letters of George Miller" in the Annual concluded with the communication of August 10, 1855. While the date is correct, there is no explanation for the omission of the last seven paragraphs from that particular letter. They are included here. Properly placed, they follow the paragraph ending . . . "and up to the time of my arrival at Voree" quoted shortly after the second dream.

"The remembrance of my feelings on the occasion herein alluded to, awakens anew in my bosom the liveliest sensations of gratitude for the past, and also praise and thanksgiving for the glorious prospects of the present and future blessings, that the God of heaven is so graciously bestowing on the little flock. And were the Saints, under surrounding circumstances to withhold their gratitude and praise, it does really seem to me that the very stones, seas, mountains, brooks, rills and forest trees would cry aloud in praise to the God of our fathers Abraham, Isaac and Jacob, for his matchless blessings in his deliverance from Gentile oppression, and the sustaining us in the dominion and inheritance he has given us, as also the blessings and bounteous yield of our crops and present prosperity.

"Although at the present time I am heavily borne down with disease and bodily infirmity of long standing, nevertheless in my heart I feel to magnify and praise the God of Heaven for the blessings I have received at his bounteous hand, as also for the blessings and good things he is daily bestowing on his people who have congregated on the God-given possession, that they may keep his law.

"After a necessary time had elapsed to procure an outfit to go to Beaver Island, near the last days of September, by the assistance of brother Wright and the brethren at Voree, we set out for the seat of the first Presidency with light hearts and buoyant spirits, of so soon realizing our expectations in seeing a prophet called of God and ordained by angels to lead the church of Christ.

"We lay at waiting at Racine for a boat to convey us to the Island a day or two, but none calling as we expected we engaged a passage on the brig Boston and went aboard. She was bound for Grand Traverse Bay, and not having a full freight, the master agreed to take us at about propeller rates. There were other brethren aboard beside my family, which made it rather an object to take us to Beaver. There was nothing occurred on our voyage. It was rather of a pleasant kind to me, but those of my family who had never been on large waters on a sail vessel, had a good deal of sea sickness.

"On our arrival at Beaver Harbor, our vessel came to anchor, and in a short time Brother Strang came on board giving us a hearty welcome. I knew him from description or otherwise, before he got on board. ("Otherwise" here means the second dream previously narrated.) He and brother Phineas Wright rendered us all the assistance in their power in getting us and our effects landed, and getting a cabin to shelter us from the weather, which was somewhat boistrous at this time.

"I did not, it is true, act as the pilgrim fathers that landed some centuries ago at Plymouth Rock, but I have no doubt in my mind that I felt quite as much or more gratitude and heartfelt joy for my safe arrival and landing at this place as they possibly could have felt on that memorable occasion.

"I may at some future time resume my narrative, as subsequent events are fraught with some of the most thrilling incidents of my life."

Most truly and sincerely,

George Miller

With regret, it must be recorded that there was no resumption of the writings of "General" George Miller, as he was called on Beaver Island. His arrival late in 1850 was a great event in the island Kingdom, as indeed it was to his own personal "gratitude and heartfelt joy."

If the five and a half years he spent with James Strang before the expulsion were not the happiest of his life, they were at least as fruitful as the equal number spent with Joseph Smith at Nauvoo.

On June 28, 1856, the 12th day after the assassination, the "King" was removed from Beaver Island on the propeller *Louisville*. With him were several of his loyal followers. It may be assumed that George Miller and Betsy McNutt Strang were also on board. Miller was at the bedside of Strang when he died July 9 at Voree.

Milo Quaife, listing those at the bedside of Strang in "The Kingdom of Saint James," meant to say "General" George Miller instead of Sheriff. This is stated correctly in his Index, however. "Sheriff" would be his son, Joshua.

Personal respect for George Miller by the present writer equals his respect for Wingfield Watson, the young man who guarded Strang on the dock at Beaver Island to prevent further violence after the shooting. Watson was a sincere believer in Strang for over 70 of his 94 years. While Watson's life was just beginning in the Strangite Church, the life of "General" Miller was soon to end at age 62.

A letter dated October 11, 1965, from Barbara Drew, granddaughter of Wingfield Watson, comments interestingly on her own feelings toward Miller.

> "Bishop George Miller was a wonderful man. My grandfather said that if there had been more men in the church on Beaver Island like him, the members never would have been driven off."

Miller died during 1857, never completing his planned journey to the great west. His young son, George Jr., grew to manhood there and became a successful owner of one of the finest orange groves in California.

To the end of his life, George Miller respected his earlier belief that James Strang was indeed the rightful successor to the prophetic office of Joseph Smith.

A Sampling of Strangite Defenders: Wingfield Watson

The memory of Wingfield Watson is one of profound respect in the diminutive Strangite Church today. There would possibly be no Church of Jesus Christ of Latter-day Saints (Strangite), but for the staunch faith of Watson in the teachings of James J. Strang. His ability and willingness to devote his long life as disciple and presiding elder created unity, dignity and purpose among the scattered Saints.

Watson was 24 years old when he went to Beaver Island, the year Strang was elected to the Michigan Legislature. To this young man and his wife, Beaver Island in 1852 was a paradise of self-help, economically as well as spiritually. At 28, Watson experienced the shooting of his "King" by Wentworth and Bedford, and he "stood guard over him lest the enemy, thinking he was still living, might rush in upon him to finish him."

Watson was a man whose talents were sufficient to have earned him a measure of success in earthly affairs had he chosen to do so. One of his brothers became politically important in Wisconsin, resulting in his election to the State Senate.

The photograph chosen to illustrate the Watson "Autobiography" exemplifies restrained dignity typical of this very humble man whose life was not only devoted to God, but also to James

Strang as God's representative on earth. Credit for availability of the photo belongs to Mrs. Stanley L. Johnston of Lansing. Originally, Mr. Watson gave the print to her father, S. T. Maloch, then a citizen of Louisiana. The lower border includes the autograph of Wingfield Watson. This picture was taken in 1917 and sent that year as a present to Mr. Maloch, a member of the Strangite church.

The original manuscript of the "Autobiography of Wingfield Watson" is owned by a granddaughter, Mrs. Guy Throe. Permission to publish part of this personal narrative for the first time, nearly 90 years after it was written, is gratefully acknowledged to Mrs. Throe and to her sister, Mrs. Barbara Drew.

AUTOBIOGRAPHY OF WINGFIELD WATSON

Beginning with his departure from Nauvoo for Beaver Island and representing the closing fifth of his autobiography, narrated in 1881.

> "We stopped at Mr. Timmins' house in Nauvoo three days or thereabouts. He had some kindness and humanity about him, notwithstanding his spiritualism. He charged us the moderate sum of a shilling a meal each for my son, my wife, and myself.
>
> "We put out on a boat for St. Louis and then took another boat for La Salle, Illinois, where we took the Canal boat for Chicago. There we took passage on the Sciota for Beaver Island. We paid $3.50 each for deck passage on the Sciota.
>
> "The captain, an Irishman, a Mr. Hyans, made it his business to ridicule the Mormons to me; but it was like rain on a duck's back. It was labor lost on his part, for I knew that Mormonism was true and he could not shake it out of me. We soon landed at M. M. Aldrich's dock on the west side of Beaver Harbor, where I remember receiving a cordial handshaking from Brother J. J. Strang, George Bronson, and James Smith. We landed at 3 o'clock in the afternoon of the 23d of June, 1852, according to my wife's memory, which is very good on dates.
>
> "I regret now very much that we did not keep a journal of all of our proceedings; but it never seemed at that time nor for years afterward that there was anything in my life that was

LORENZO DOW HICKEY

WINGFIELD WATSON

Wingfield Watson, staunch supporter of James Strang as the only true prophetic successor to Joseph Smith, for over seventy years. Watson was ordained presiding high priest in 1900 by Lorenzo Dow Hickey, and served gracefully in that capacity until his own death in 1923.

really worth recording. This I have since realized is not a small error.

"I was still sad in my feelings and gloomy in my thots; and I used to express my feelings to one and another; and many kind words and encouraging advice did I receive while I was stopping at Brother Aldrich's. We moved our things, which consisted of a box of clothing and some bedding, into Brother Aldrich's at the end of the dock a little to the north and stopped there about 24 hours. He shewed me the Book of the Law, translated by James J. Strang over two years before, and "The Baptism for the Dead." I thot that it was a great and good thing; but I was too sad in my feelings to rejoice.

"From Brother Aldrich's we moved to another house where Brother Shaw's things were and which an old man and his wife, by the name of Case, had also moved into. It was a large hewed log house and was about 24 by 16 with a short story overhead. It was large enough for the three families of the saints.

"I began after a time to grow in grace. I paid tithes out of the money which I then had, which was about $75 and did everything required of me so far as I could. Brethern and sisters were kind and just, generally speaking, but there were some evil speakers. Some took pains to tell me of the prospects of peace and the chances of making a living, thinking perhaps that I might not like the look of the land along the beach which was nearly pure sand.

"I did not come there for the chances of making a living; and this did amount to much with me. Still, I can't say that the looks of things pleased me at first. However we gradually came to like the place, not for the nature of the soil around the beach with its scrubby pines here and there, but for the many advantages and blessings which it really possessed.

"The Saints there were free from the contamination of Gentile vices such as drunkenness, swearing, fashions, and foul language. There was health, refreshing breezes, pure water, splendid grass, potatoes, grain, and root land, tho grain had not yet been grown there to any extent so that much could be known how it would do there. There were splendid cedar swamps for fencing, shingles, etc. The poor had thus plenty of material for building and for firewood.

"The inland lakes abounded with fish of many kinds, there were pleasant streams for cattle to quench their thirst, and to run sawmills and grist mills. There was grateful shade and forest land and lake riches to support a large and teeming population.

"To many, who were used to the prairies of the West, it seemed a very trying and forbidding place. At first they did not like it. But time and perseverance brought even them to like it. The Eastern people got along with it very well from the first.

"I see now advantages that I did not then. All of these blessings associated with the having a prophet raised up by the Almighty in fulfillment of prophecy to translate and reveal unto us and to the nations his law and the order of God's house, the pleasant greetings of the saints, the happy conversations with the children of God, the happy gathering together of the people, and with all these, the glorious teachings of prophets and apostles and priests, gave the whole a glorious charm.

"Ah yes: pleasant indeed were all these associations, reminding one of the inspired sayings of a prophet of old at the contemplation of Israel under Moses and in the Latter Days. "How goodly are thy tents, O Jacob, and thy tabernacles, O Israel. As the valleys are they spread forth, as gardens by the riverside, as the trees of lign-aloes which the Lord hath planted, and cedar trees by the waters. He shall pour the water out of his buckets and his seed shall be in many waters, and his king shall be higher than Agag, and his kingdom shall be exalted." (Numbers 24: 5, 6, 7)

"And again, "Happy art thou, O Israel; who is like unto thee, O people saved by the Lord, who is the shield of thine help, and the sword of thine excellency. Thine enemies shall be found liars unto thee and thou shalt tread upon their high places." (Deut. 33: 29)

"Alas! that such a people should have ceased to deserve such a blessing. For truly were they blessed and truly did they possess a peace, a rest, a freedom, and an enjoyment unknown among men: unknown to those who serve not God.

"The 8th of July was coming on, the day that James was crowned and sat upon the throne of David, something that I knew then as little of as a three years' old child; but which long years since I have learned the necessity of in order to fulfill prophecy. For says Hosea 3: 4, 5: "The children of Israel shall abide many days without a king, and without a prince, and without a sacrifice, and without an image, and without an ephod, and without teraphim. Afterward shall the children of Israel return, and seek the Lord their God, and David their king, and shall fear the Lord and his goodness in the latter days.

"Again: "Simeon hath declared how God at the first did visit the Gentiles to take out of them a people for his name. And to this agree the words of the prophets; as it is written. After this I will return and will build again the tabernacle of David, which is fallen down; and I will build again the ruins thereof, and I will set it up; that the residue of men seek after the Lord, and all the Gentiles, upon whom my name is called, saith the Lord, who doeth all these things. (Acts 15: 14-17)

"And again in Amos 9: 9-12: "For, lo, I will command, and I will sift the House of Israel among all nations, like as corn is sifted in a sieve, yet shall not the least grain fall upon the earth. All the sinners of my people shall die by the sword, which say, The evil shall not overtake nor prevent us. In that day will I raise up the tabernacle of David that is fallen, and close up the breaches thereof; and I will raise up the ruins, and I will build it as in the days of old; That they may possess the remnant of Edom, and of the heathen, which are called by my name, saith the Lord that doeth this.

"Jeremiah alludes also to the subject of the Gathering and here again a king of the house of David is promised: "In those days shall Judah be saved, and Jerusalem shall dwell safely; and this is the name wherewith she shall be called, The Lord our righteousness. For thus saith the Lord; David shall never want a man to sit upon the throne of the house of Israel." The city seemingly is to take the name of this great king of the lineage of David; and the whole earth is to be brought into subjection to him.

"In many respects I cannot utter my feelings with relation to the good work on those Islands. I can only touch upon many things. As in all ages when God's people began to increase in riches, they treated lightly the many great and glorious things revealed. Many violated the Word of Wisdom, or in other words they never left off their old heathen practices of the use of hot drinks, tea and coffee, and the use of pork and other kinds of flesh in hot weather, intoxicating drinks in some cases, and the use of tobacco. And for these many shortcomings the enemy received power over them; and they were scattered to the four winds.

"It is now some 25 years past since all were driven from there; and there seems to be no sign or indication of a living prophet anywhere altho much by dreams given show that there is a living prophet somewhere and that one has been at the head all the time, altho to all intents and purpose we have been left without one.

"I saw James J. Strang a few minutes after he was martyred and stood guard over him lest the enemy, thinking he was still living, might rush in upon him to finish him. After laying a week or so in his wounds on Beaver Island, he was removed to Voree, Wisconsin, where he was buried about three weeks after being shot.

"It seems that the assassins shot him in three different places. One bullet struck him in the right side of the top part of his head and glanced out at the other side near the top of his head. A second shot entered at the right side of his nose and lodged somewhere beyond and could not be taken out. This so swelled up and blackened that side of his face that he could scarcely be recognized. A third bullet entered the right of the spine, leaving him palsied from there to his toes.

"Many were unwilling to believe that Mr. Strang had been fatally wounded and strongly expected that he would recover from his wounds. I was myself; and when I heard that he was laid in the grave it was a great shock to my feelings; for we had looked for much to be accomplished by him and were not at all prepared to believe in his being taken from us.

"But so it has happened, plainly showing that our thots are not God's thots and that in many ways, when we feel that all is well, we are sadly and strongly disappointed, as were the Jews in the days of Jesus, expecting great things of him. So it was with us.

"Indeed we thot that we had much more reason to expect much of Mr. Strang than former day Saints had for expecting so much from Jesus. It seems that in both cases each had to suffer martyrdom before the great work promised to be done by them could be accomplished.

"In our case it was galling to the last degree to see mobocracy and lawlessness triumph seemingly over the Saints who had so faithfully clung to the hope that the poor would be redeemed from deceit and violence, and the oppressor broken in pieces in all the earth thru Mr. Strang's ministry and faithfulness. "Where is your God and your Kingdom and Prophet now, that you trusted in so much?" was as it were on every enemy's lips.

"I suppose that there have been similar triumphs in all ages by those who slew the prophets and robbed and scattered the Saints. However "the triumphing of the wicked is short. (Job 20:5)

"Many buildings were under construction and much in the way of improvement and settlement had been accomplished and was going on when all at once the murderous echoes of the assassin's fire-arms are heard and consternation seizes upon all. Little by little the general progress stops until finally the sound of the axe and the hammer and the busy clatter of the teamsters' wheels and the general stir of business of all kinds is hushed and still; and a heartless mob is seen busily tramping here and there, commanding, driving, threatening, and pillaging all before them.

"All the Saints are warned and threatened with whiskey-inspired curses and oaths to "get your things down to the harbor by tomorrow at 2 o'clock or by --- your house will be burnt down over your head." Remonstrance was useless. It was in vain to say that your wife was confined yesterday, that you had no team and you were sick and couldn't walk. "Get your things down, G-- d--n you, get your things down." There was no plea except the denial of our faith that would prevail with the mob to let us stay on our improvements.

"The grand scheme of the mob was to have the Mormons get all their chattels and movable property down to the harbor under the belief that we were all to be sent off with our cattle and movables on the first boat, but in reality it was simply that they might rush us all aboard in as great hurry and bustle as possible and then retain our cattle and goods as a booty while the boat shoved off.

"Thus were we left in destitution and landed in a couple of days and left on the dock at Chicago to go where we pleased and find a home how and where we could. Here we were left without shelter, the sun beaming down at fever heat. Here we were made a gazing stock for all kinds of people to stare at.

"One man began to swear at the mob for sending the people there and robbing them; and with some manly feelings he shoved the large warehouse doors apart and said, "Here, ladies and gentlemen, come in here out of the sun and stay till you can find places." This was the first kind word that we heard from any one during the whole proceedings and indeed we could appreciate it."

The narrative ends during 1856, at which time Watson was 28 years of age. Composition of it, however, was not completed until 1881 upon reaching age 53.

Between 1856 and 1866, Watson lived comfortably in Grant County, Wisconsin; Black River Falls, Wisconsin; and Coldwater, Michigan, prior to moving to northern Michigan. There, he eventually settled in the Boyne City area, where he lived in simple comfort for about 25 years.

During his many years in the Boyne City area, Watson published a series of pamphlets expounding the Strangite Mormon faith and the right of James Jesse Strang to prophetic succession in the main Mormon body after the murder of Joseph Smith. Some of his pamphlets were reprints of articles appearing first in the Strang newspaper at Saint James, the *Northern Islander*.

Perhaps the most noted of the reprints is the Prophetic Controversy, known as Number 1, a letter from James J. Strang to Mrs. Corey. In this, Strang defended his claim to head the Mormon Church against the Twelve led by Brigham Young. This was first reprinted in 1856 at Saint James by the publishers, Cooper & Chidester. According to Dale L. Morgan in his Bibliography of the Church of Jesus Christ of Latter-day Saints (Strangite), this was further reprinted in 1878, 1886 and 1893. A total of 13 different pamphlets were published in this series by Watson. Several were issued later by others.

Watson returned to the Strangite settlement site at Spring Prairie (Voree), in 1891, continuing to farm for another 16 years as he had at Boyne City. At 79 years of age, he decided to devote full energy to his office as presiding high priest of the Church. The former high priest, L. D. Hickey, one week before

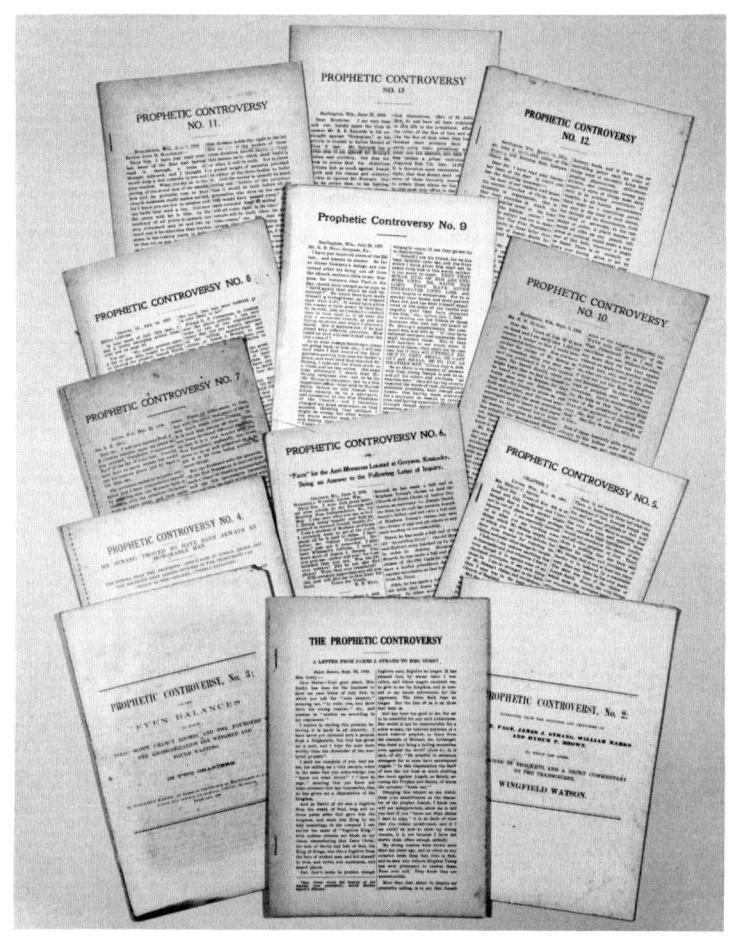

FROM THE COLLECTION OF THE WRITER

THE WINGFIELD WATSON PAMPHLETS

Wingfield Watson published this series of pamphlets attempting to prove that James J. Strang had indeed been appointed to succeed Joseph Smith as head of the Mormon Church.

his death in 1900 at Coldwater, Michigan, ordained Watson to this office.

In 1918, at 90 years of age, Watson issued his last pamphlet, "The True Gospel." The following year, the young man who had stood beside the riddled body of James J. Strang in 1856, returned to Beaver Island for the first time in 63 years as a guest of Milo Quaife, author of "The Kingdom of Saint James."

Wingfield Watson died on October 29, 1922. His 70-year devotion to an almost lost cause, through adversity few men endure, had come to an end. Now, nearly half a century after his death, adversity yet stalks through the diminutive Strangite Church. Dissension has arisen regarding the legal heirs to the Watson farm property left in trust for the expected new Prophet of God on earth.

Rescue of a Strang Portrait

Early in June, 1966, a granddaughter of James Strang, Anna Bee Bevan of Portland, Oregon, sent this vignette as her personal contribution to "The King Strang Story:"

"I am a trained nurse, and was depended upon, all my life, by all my families, far and near, to attend and lend a hand during any and all illnesses, just as my grandmother, Sarah Wright, was called upon and expected to do, during her generation. No one thought anything of calling upon Grandmother at any time or any place, and so it was with me. Especially was I invited, as a house guest, when new arrivals were expected. Even after my own son was born and my own home established in the States I was still expected to travel to Alberta and beyond when the need arose, which I did cheerfully, for it was a Strang tradition.

"It was on one of these occasions, while visiting my brother Claude and his family in Alberta, that I quite accidently ran on to this portrait, which I remembered from childhood had always hung in our living room.

"This brother Claude and his family had returned from Montana where under my brother Mark they had tried to become established.

"My parents had vacated their home leaving it lock, stock and barrel to Claude and family, to help him get established again on the farm. He had a young family to raise.

"I guess none of us ever dreamed of the day when that picture of Grandfather Strang would NOT be hanging there in the living room of the home on the original homestead.

"Meantime a daughter-in-law and very young children could not possibly feel the same sentiment about original Strang things as we did, so it was not really surprising when the older boy having developed a deep love of horses decided that the oval frame which held the very old picture, would be just the thing to frame his favorite picture of a horse's head, and so it was. Out came grandfather's portrait and in went the horse's head, and no one appeared to notice or inquire after the portrait until that fateful day when I had a bit of leisure and happened into the old shed which was originally the blacksmith shop in the old homestead days.

"I was so shocked I was positively ill. Saying nothing which might disturb the household I lovingly packed the portrait, minus the frame, into my suitcase and brought it home with me where it has been ever since. I have not even cleaned it up, but did loan it to the others, and I believe Mark, Vere* and Hazel all have copies of it. The original is still here with me filled with memories of those far off days, when it was lovingly carried across the plains of Utah and survived those hectic days, then just as lovingly taken to Alberta, then rescued by me and just as reverently and lovingly brought with me to Portland.

"When the portrait was missed by the Claude Strangs they immediately decided that Hazel had it. (She was the collector of the family) but she was just as shocked to find it missing as I was to find it in the trash box. In her grief at the loss she checked with me and learned that after all, all was well."

Anna Bee Bevan

---

*Vere died on his 83rd birthday, September 7, 1970.

Strang's Beaver Islanders

Listed here are more than 350 saints, most of them adults, who were members of the Kingdom of God on Beaver Island. Nearly 300 of these attended the coronation of Strang. The original coronation record, in the Coe Collection of Western Americana at the Yale University Library, has many signatures difficult to read accurately. Only those on the island are included in this list ... the most complete ever compiled and published.

ACKERMAN, F.
ADAMS, GEORGE J.
ADAMS, MRS. G.
ADAMS, JAMES M.
ADAMS, OLIVE
ALDRICH, ALANSON G.
ALDRICH, LUTE
ALDRICH, MARVIN M. JR.
ALDRICH, MARVIN M. SR.
ALDRICH, RACHAEL ANN
ALDRICH, SALLY M.
ALDRICH, TEMPERANCE
ALLCOTT, R.
ALVORD, DAVID B.
AUSTIN, BENJAMIN
AUSTIN, LOIS L.
AVERY, DANIEL

BACON, ELIZABETH
BACON, SAMUEL P.
BAXTER, BARTON
BAXTER, CORNELIUS
BAXTER, DELANAH
BAXTER, HARRIET
BAXTER, HENRIETTA
BAXTER, HYRAM
BAXTER, SAMUEL

BAXTER, WILLIAM
BEDFORD, THOMAS
BEDFORD, MRS. THOMAS
BENNETT, ELIZABETH I.
BENNETT, SAMUEL
BENNETT, SELINA
BEVIAR, FRANKLIN
BICKLE, SARAH J.
BICKLE, WILLIAM
BLAKESLEE, JAMES
BOTSFORD, DANIEL F.
BOWER, PRAISEWORTHY
BRIGGS, LEWIS
BRIGGS, ORLANDO P.
BRONSON, GEORGE
BROTHERTON, HULDA E.
BROTHERTON, MALVIN
BROWN, ALBERT
BROWN, DAVID
BROWN, MRS. DAVID
BROWN, ELISHA C.
BROWN, GURDON
BROWN, HARRIET
BROWN, HIRAM P.
BROWN, JOHN H.
BROWN, JOHN S.
BROWN, JOSEPH M.

Brown, Lucretia
Brown, Orria
Brown, Ruth M.
Brown, Sarah
Brownson, George
Burgess, James

Campbell, Emily
Campbell, Morrill E.
Campbell, Orrin
Campbell, Orson
Campbell, Sally
Campbell, Silas
Campbell, Susannah
Carpenter, Egbert
Case, Mr. and Mrs.
Chambers, William
Chase, Moses
Chidester, Dennis
Chidester, Edward
Chidester, Eliza
Chidester, Sarah E.
Clark, Abegail
Clark, Anngenett
Clark, Charles
Clark, Eliza D.
Clark, William I.
Clark, William M.
Cleveland
Cole, Galen B.
Cole, George
Cole, John
Cole, Lucinda
Cole, Sarah
Comstock, John S.
Cook, Luther
Cooper, Catherine A.
Cooper, Francis
Cooper, Frank

Cooper, J. W.

Davis, John A.
Deery, Charles
Delap, Jonathan
Demares, Mary or Demarie
Dinnel, Chester
Dixon, Christopher
Doan, Jacob
Dobson, Thomas
Doty
Duncan, Thomas
Dunham, O. P.

Eaton, George W.
Ellsworth, Benjamin C.
Ellsworth, Josiah

Farage, Catherine
Field, A. B.
Field, Albert
Field, Ann E.
Field, Eliza
Field, James H.
Field, Joel S.
Field, Loretta Octavia
Field, Maria Howe
Field, Reuben
Field, Rhoda Stern
Field, Samuel C.
Fillmore, Daniel
Finch, David
Forscutt, M. H.
Foster, Nathan
Fox, Cynthia
Fox, Francis
Fox, Henry
Fox, Ralph O.
Fox, Sally Ann

Strang's Beaver Islanders

Fox, Stephen R.
Franklin, Mrs.

Gamer, Henry
Garnet, David M.
Garner, John
Gaylord, Elijah B.
Gaylord, J. C.
Gaylord, John
Gibbs, Henry
Gifford, Ichabod B.
Goodale, Jackson
Graham, Brigham Y.
Graham, Jeb.
Graham, Samuel
Green, Harvey
Greenwood, Charles
Greig, Ellen E.
Greig, Ellen O.
Greig, James M. Jr.
Greig, Judge James M.
Grierson, John W.
Grierson, Martha T. A.
Griffiths
Gunningham, John
Guthrie, D.
Guthrie, John

Hale, Alden
Hale, Andrew J.
Hall, Augusta
Hall, Catherine
Hall, Hyrum G.
Hall, Serena H.
Hazzard
Heath, David
Heath, Margarett
Henderson, B. T.
Hendrickson

Hickey, Lorenzo Dow
Hickey, Mrs. L. D.
Hickox, Betsy
Hickox, Daniel
Hickox
Hickox, Julius A.
Hickox, Mary Jane
Hill, Cecelia
Hill, George
Hill, Harriet
Hill, John C.
Hill, Ludlow P.
Hill, Mary L.
Hill, Oren R.
Hill, Susanna
Hopper, A. G.
Hopper, Heziah H.
Hosmer, Albert Newell
Hosmer, Joseph
Howe, A.
Hull, Agnes F.
Hull, Oscar W.
Hull, Samuel E.
Humphrey, Ermina E.
Hutchins, James

Jennings, Chauncey
Johnson, Franklin
Johnson, G. F.
Johnson, P.
Johnson, P. F.

Kendall, Charles
Ketcham, Albert
Ketcham, Ezra
Ketcham, Joseph
Ketcham, Joseph S.
Ketcham, Mary
Ketcham, Mary P.

KIMMINGS, WILLIAM S.
KINNEY

LAKE, ANSEL
LAWRENCE, ALPHEUS
LAWRENCE, MARY JANE
LEE, A.
LINNELL, JUDSON
LOOMIS, CHAUNCEY
LOOMIS, MARTHA
LONGFIELD, F. W.
LYONS, G.

MARKS, WILLIAM
MCCULLOCH, HEZEKIAH D.
MCCULLOCH, MRS. H. D.
MCLEAN, WILLIAM R.
MCLELLIN, WILLIAM E.
MCNABB, HORTON
MCNUTT, MARY
MCNUTT, HULDAH
MCNUTT, JOHN
MCNUTT, SARAH JANE
MCNUTT, TOBIAS
MILLER, GEORGE
MILLER, MRS.
MILLER, JOSHUA L.
MILLER, P.
MILLS, R. F.
MOON, DAVE
MOORE, ERI JAMES
MOORE, SOPHIA AMELIA

NICHOLS, ELIZA ANN
NICHOLS, NEPHI
NICHOLS, REUBEN T.
NICKERSON, V. C. H.

OSTRANDER, HYINA
OSTRANDER, WALTER

PAGE, ANGELINE
PAGE, EBENEZER
PAGE, FINLEY
PAGE, MARY
PAGE, NANCY
PAGE, RACHEL
PAGE, SERVILIA
PAGE, SEYMOUR
PACKARD, NOAH
PARRISH, A.
PARRISH, ELMIRA
PARRISH, UARIAH
PEIRCE, JOHN
PIERCE, ELIZABETH
PIERCE, ESTELLA
PIERCE, ISAAC
PIERCE, JONATHAN T.
PIERCE, MARTHA ANN
PORTER, ANDREW J.
PORTER, ELIJAH
PORTER, ELIZABETH A.
POST, LEONARD
POST, STEPHEN
POST, WARREN
POWERS, MELINDA
POWERS, SIMON
PRESTON, BENJAMIN
PRESTON, CAROLINE M.
PRESTON, CORDELIA A.
PRESTON, GEORGE T.
PRESTON, O. H.
PRINCE, JOHN
PRINCE, RACHEL
PRINDLE, ANSON W.
PRINDLE, LUTE
PURNELL, MARTHA

RENFEL, JAMES
REYNOLDS, HENRY

Rice, Elias
Rice, Eliza
Rogers, Catherine
Rogers, John L.
Rogers, Sarah E.
Rogers, Stratton
Rogers, Violetta
Richmond

Savage, Jehiel
Sea, Adam
Sea, Sam
Scott, Christopher
Scott, Horace
Seaman, Murray
Shaw, Mary
Shaw, Samuel
Shippy, John
Small
Smith, James
Smith, John
Steele, Eli
Steinolm, A.
Strang, Betsy
Strang, Charles J.
Strang, Clement J.
Strang, David J.
Strang, Elvira Eliza
Strang, Evaline
Strang, Evangeline
Strang, Gabriel J.
Strang, Hattie
Strang, James Jesse
Strang, Mary Perce
Strang, Myraette
Strang, Phoebe Jesse
Strang, Sarah Adelia
Strang, William J.

Thomas, Lewis
Thorton, Henry
Townsend, Mrs.
Tripp, Deborah
Tripp, Hannah M.
Tripp, Johnathan
Tripp, Margureth E.
Tripp, Martha Ann
Tripp, Rebecca
Tripp, Solomon
Tripp, William H.
Tubbs, Lorenzo, D.
Tucker, Catherine M.
Tucker, Royal
Tucker, Sarah M.

Wagener, Liddy
Wagener, Nathan
Wait, James M.
Wait, Nephi
Wait, Semour
Wait, Zadiaett
Watson, Cynthia
Watson, Gilbert
Watson, Wingfield
Wentworth, Alexander
Weston, Milo
Wheelock, Daniel G.
Wheelock, George C.
Wheelock, Lorenzo D.
Wheelock, Ruth C.
Whipple, C. T.
Whipple, David R.
Whipple, Martha A.
Whitlock, John
Whitney, Fancis
Wright, Amanda
Wright, Benjamin G.
Wright, Elizabeth

WRIGHT, GEORGE
WRIGHT, MOSES
WRIGHT, PHINEAS
WRIGHT, REBECCA

WRIGHT, ZENAS

YOUNG, BASS
YOUNG, JAMES

It is of genealogical importance to update this list of *Strang's Beaver Islanders* and to correct errors in this list. Should readers care to contribute any information toward improving this list, please do so by writing to the author. Anything about James Strang or his career will add greatly to a better understanding of his unique personality.

REVIEWS

"The King of Beaver Island"

By: Charles K. Backus

This short narrative about James J. Strang and his island kingdom originally was published in Harper's Monthly magazine, appearing in the March, 1882, issue. The title was "An American King."

In 1955, this was reprinted as "The King of Beaver Island" in a copyrighted, limited edition as a 25-page story, attractively printed and bound by Westernlore Press of Los Angeles.

"An American King" was a briefly written study, and a remarkably accurate one, apparently researched very carefully by Backus. There are a few unfavorable personal observations. However, it could have been just another article of careless reporting. Certainly, most accounts written about Strang in the past 100 years have been unreliable.

Why the title of this narrative was changed from "An American King" to "The King of Beaver Island" is not known. The original may be considered correct, while the latter is not. Strang was never the "King" of Beaver Island, he was only "King" of his Saints, and there were others who lived on Beaver. Strang made no demands on friendly Gentiles. This includes religion, as well as tithing, in spite of reports to the contrary that he attempted to force all non-Mormons to become Mormons and, whether they did or did not, pay into the treasury for the privilege of living there.

A footnote on page 17 indicates the name "James" was added to Jesse Strang in early manhood. His full name at birth was Jesse James Strang. He was named for his grandfather, Jesse James. In early years, he often used the names reversed and did so permanently when he reached maturity.

In speaking of the murder of Strang, Backus, on page 37, states:

"His death was not immediate, and in a few days he was removed to Voree (his parents home) where he received the devoted care of the lawful wife of his purer days, an estimable woman, who had rejected his gross "revelations" but clung to her personal belief that death alone could release her from the obligations of the marriage vow."

Strang was not cared for by his "lawful wife," nor was she at Voree when he died. Two of his four polygamous wives were there: Betsy, with two of her children, and Phoebe. Others at the bedside included George Miller, the former Bishop of the original Joseph Smith Mormon Church; Edward Chidester, to whom Strang spoke his last mortal word, "Yes," and Lorenzo Dow Hickey, who was once considered somewhat unbalanced, but who eventually headed the Strangite Church with unfailing devotion until his own death at Coldwater, Michigan, in 1900.

In 1882, it was factual for Backus to relate that Strang was still buried in an "unmarked grave." However, even this was not his first resting place. The original burial place was neglected for twenty years, resulting in publicity that the "King" was "resting in a cow pasture." On September 18, 1876 the body was moved to lot 6, block 4 of the Burlington cemetery through the efforts of Hattie, daughter of Strang and Mary Perce. About 1925, another daughter, Eugenia, whose mother was Phoebe Wright, successfully requested assistance from the Burlington Historical Society in erecting a suitable marker. Thus, after nearly 70 years, a headstone was finally placed on his grave.

The Foreword by Westernlore labeled Strang a "character." This is a personal opinion of the publisher. Strang was far from being what this writer considers a "character." "Genius" would be nearer the truth.

It might be said that Strang was a "regulator of fashions," but not "to the point that men wore his particular cut of pantaloons." The source of this information is unknown. It is very doubtful such a garment was worn by any Mormon. A pantaloon is a tight-fitting combination of trousers and stockings. In

The King of Beaver Island

respect to the women, they did wear "Strang" bloomers, as stated in the Foreword.

It should be understood that James Strang was a man 50 years ahead of his time. Many of his ideas dating back to the Beaver Island period of 1847-1856 are commonplace today. It is not surprising that Strang would suggest, yes, even decree, that Mormon women wear "bloomers."

Mrs. Amelia Bloomer advocated this combination of short skirt and loose trouser nearly fifty years after Strang suggested this femine undergarment. These were gathered at the ankles to make them a little more refined.

A letter from Hazel Strang McCardell, granddaughter of Strang, had this to say about bloomers:

> "As regards the 'Bloomers,' even the most skeptical will acknowledge that a revision of women's clothing was long overdue, what with unsanitary skirts sweeping up the filthy streets, the shorter skirts, with the modest bloomers was the logical first step in the right direction."

Before concluding this brief review, here is a quote from page 38, of great importance to present Strangite Mormons:

> "The kingdom did not survive the assassination of the king."

Actually, the kingdom did survive and, to this day, while very few in number, does still exist. From it also emerged the present Reorganized Church of Jesus Christ of Latter-Day Saints, founded by several former Strangites who, before the death of Strang, were anti-polygamous and withdrew because of their objection to plural marriage.

"A History of the Grand Traverse Region"
By: Dr. M. E. Leach

This partial review covers only the seven Mormon chapters of the Dr. Leach, "A History of the Grand Traverse Region," Chapters 18 through 24. Knowledgeable historians will understand it cannot be a favorable "Review," though few, if any, have forcefully brought its inaccuracies to the attention of readers for more than 80 years.

Leach, himself, called it a "thorough and accurate history of the Grand Traverse Region." This may well apply to the 25 remaining chapters, but certainly does not apply to those on Strang and his controversial Kingdom of God.

Historians interested in factual information about the hated Mormons of Beaver Island cannot get true, unbiased facts from newspapers, the original recipient of the Leach history. By repeating biased stories from old settlers, Leach compounded hateful injustice to the memory of Strang.

Only 27 years after Strang's murder, this "History" began serially in the Grand Traverse Herald. The year was 1883. Dr. Leach missed a great opportunity when he failed to record more than a one-sided narrative. Any attempt to record both sides would have required an open mind and a very sympathetic understanding of a depressed and angry religious people. Had such an attempt been made, Leach may possibly have found himself an enemy of the old Grand Traverse settlers. They enjoyed these horror stories and believed the worst. That most of the stories were false meant very little to these Gentiles. Because Leach failed to investigate fairly, he merely added another research source of falsehoods to the libraries of circulation-hungry tabloids of the 19th century.

There was a second printing of "A History of the Grand Traverse Region" prior to publication in the "Michigan Pioneer and Historical Collections." Following this in Volume 32 of the Collections is a brief history of the Beaver Islands. The Henry E. Legler article, "A Moses of the Mormons" then appears, followed by the 1877 Detroit Tribune story by the Hon. Geo. C. Bates, entitled, "The Beaver Island Prophet." Bates was the United States District Attorney prosecuting Strang and his associates at Detroit in 1851, when all Saints, including Strang, were acquitted. The political party opponents on this jury out-numbered the other jurors, eight to two. This fact, alone, added genuine luster to the acquittal.

The fourth printing of the Leach "History" is a facsimile reprint by Central Michigan University Press, Mount Pleasant.

On the Preface Page, Al Barnes of the *Record-Eagle,* Traverse City, has erroneously stated that the University Press reprint allows the Leach History to become available "for the first time to libraries." Since 1903, Volume 32 has been on the shelves of many Michigan libraries.

Continuing, Mr. Barnes writes, "His (Leach) History of the Grand Traverse Region is undoubtedly the best researched paper of its kind ever published."

It is unfortunate that those responsible for the reprint failed to enlighten the reader by footnoting the seven Mormon chapters. The Clarke Library is well known for its Strang collection. They are aware that the Mormon Chapters are far from being "the best researched paper of its kind ever published."

Dr. Leach said he "carefully and impartially weighed the evidence, and gave what appeared to be the truth without fear or favor." He obviously attempted to get the truth from Gentile participants, and he wrote a most commendable work excepting the Strang section. However, the key words in his own evaluation explains this precisely, "what appeared to be the truth." There was another side to the Strang story, however, and he failed to appreciate its significance. Dr. Leach may never have really understood the Beaver Island Gentile mind. These Gentiles were capable of burning down their own homes! Factual information exists, revealing that comparable acts were committed, all carefully planned to make it appear the Mormons were the culprits.

In Chapter 18, Dr. Leach estimated the maximum number of persons on Beaver Island at no more than 1300, having a legal vote of 370. The census taken in 1854 showed a population of 2,068 on Beaver. That same year, 695 votes out of 696 in Emmet and Cheboygan counties were cast for Strang in his bid for a second term in the Michigan Legislature. Most of these votes were cast on the island. Numbers may appear unimportant here, but if an honest visual picture is attempted in portraying the exile of those helpless Saints from the island in 1856, no minimizing should be done to lessen the monstrous crime the legal processes of the State of Michigan not only failed to hinder, but failed to prosecute, including the murder of Legislator Strang.

In his "History," Dr. Leach divided the Saints into three classes:

1. Sincere believers of the early Church.
2. Influential ones who joined for personal gain.
3. "Once faithful," unable to leave because of financial loss.

It is true there were a few influential Mormons on Beaver Island for personal power. Some of them were real scoundrels. They were a source of constant trouble for Strang and a major cause of the Kingdom's downfall. Some were from the Church at Nauvoo. They had been accepted early at Voree as repented sinners, in good faith and expedient to the cause.

There were many unsavory characters in the early Mormon Church. The projector of Mormonism himself had identical problems. Joseph Smith had high personal aspirations toward power. Did he not claim authorship in the first edition of the Book of Mormon though it was purported to have been the word of God translated from Golden Plates? While searching for rare Americana, Charles P. Everitt found sections of the Book of Mormon in *"The Reflector"* published in Palmyra before the first edition of 1830.

Joseph Smith claimed to have received a message from the Lord Jesus Christ in his very first vision in answer "to his earnest prayer to know which of all the religions was true and which should he join." The Lord Jesus, according to Smith, answered:

> "He must join none of them; they were all wrong; their creeds were an abomination in His sight; the professors thereof were corrupt; they drew near the Lord with their lips, but their hearts were far from Him; they taught for doctrines the commandments of men, having a form of godliness but denying the power thereof."

The third class designated by Dr. Leach, "unable to leave because of financial loss," were isolated cases. Extenuating circumstances may have made this appear true. There were a few disgruntled Mormons on Beaver Island, of course, but many Gentile stories were spread to discredit the Church. Many Saints left for personal reasons. These cases are unworthy of this classification, considering that none had any evidence of accumulated wealth when they arrived at Beaver. Most of them, including Strang, were very poor and none was financially secure when exiled.

Near the close of Chapter 18, Dr. Leach writes this of polygamy: "Marriage by the civil law was not held to be binding, but only the marriage ordained by the Church." Strang, himself, is the best refuter of this, when he informs us he knew it was legally possible to have but one wife.

Dr. Leach was merely playing with words when he said:

> "Of the number of concubines falling to his share by the voluntary choice of dutiful widows, we have no authentic record, but it is reasonable to conclude that, from the regard in which he was held by all good Mormons, male and female, he enjoyed a monopoly of that luxury."

This is nonsense. Island Mormon law regarded adultery so serious that Church punishment could not legally be carried out. That is why the notorious Thomas Bedford was whipped. The penalty was death. The partner of Bedford, by the name of

Brown, appeared unexpectedly one day and found Bedford in the act of adultery with Mrs. Brown.

Dr. Leach discredited his own narrative when he stated that Strang enjoyed this monopoly. "Desperate, unsuccessful efforts of young, unmarried women trying to escape Beaver" was a Gentile fabrication and a direct contradiction to the Dr. Leach statement, "the supply of available women was limited."

Robbery on Beaver Island was an established practice for nine years, according to Dr. Leach. There is not one single shred of evidence that the Saints had even a hint of a plundering operation. It must be remembered there was a fight for the good life on Beaver Island, especially after federal laws opened it for homesteading. The Gentiles did everything in their power to discredit the Saints. The Mormons tried to fight back, and were rather successful for a few years, but the Gentiles finally won. Plundering on Beaver was Gentile-inspired, carefully planned for Mormon blame and persecution.

One malignant thread weaving through the century old Strang story is that called "destroying angels." Dr. Leach became one of the expert weavers by recording the Gentile tales almost exclusively. He stated that Mormon plunderers were "under the control of a class of officers called in the Church 'destroying angels', but known to the outside world by the harmless name of deacons." And he further writes that these angels "were under the immediate direction of Strang himself."

Visualize, if you will, a man laboring day and night for his earthly flock of Saints as minister of the gospel, editor, lawyer, author, teacher and state legislator, and able to travel many months of the year in the eastern states, devoting time on Beaver Island directing plundering operations for the benefit of his own Church! In addition to this, he was a faithful husband to several polygamous wives who cared for six small children at home.

It would take only one plundering operation by Gentiles wearing the garb of deacons, leaving tell-tale "Mormon evidence," to create many shocking stories for the nation's Sunday supplements that the Mormons constantly terrorized the island.

Many lurid stories have been written about Mormon piracy. Dr. Leach records his thoughts when he writes:

> "To what extent piracy was carried on is not known. During a considerable period previous to Strang's death several vessels were lost, none of the crews ever returning to tell their fate. It was generally believed that they had been plundered by the Mormons, the crews murdered, and the vessels sunk."

The treacherous waters of Lake Michigan have engulfed countless crews and boats of every description during its recorded history. In nine years of this history, Dr. Leach conveniently blamed the Beaver Island Mormons for most of the robbing, scuttling and murdering, one such episode merely to acquire a load of whitefish!

That the Mormons were never found guilty of any criminal act by the courts did not seem to deter Dr. Leach from believing all he heard. Here is a typical Gentile story told to him and later published in the Grand Traverse Herald:

> "Some men by the name of Martin were compelled by stress of weather to land on the island. A watch was always kept to report the approach of strangers. The arrival of the Martins being reported, Strang, with a party of men, went to interview them. Chris Scott, who was a secret friend of mine, was one of the party and gave me an account of what was done. On arriving at the place where the Martins were, some of the party proposed putting them to death, but the measures were strongly opposed by Strang. It was finally decided by vote that they should be robbed of everything and sent adrift. Accordingly, everything valuable was taken out of the boat, the men were forced into it, and it was shoved off. As it was shoved off Chris threw into it a pair of oars."

Little is known of Christopher Scott. He may have become one of the disgruntled Mormons. If so, this story may have been told by him to discredit Strang. Numerous members were turned over to the "buffetings of Satan" when they committed acts contrary to Church law. To get even, they helped the Gentiles in their battle with the Saints. Christopher Scott was one of the Mormons in the Pine River battle of July 12, 1853, in which six Mormons were injured and nine, including Scott, escaped unharmed.

In Chapter 22 Dr. Leach mentions the *Northern Islander* newspaper of Strang. This was the first newspaper in Northern Michigan. It also was a well-edited newspaper, edited with more than ordinary talent and truth. The initial number was published at Saint James, December 12, 1850. Dr. Leach states in Chapter 30: "The Herald was the first newspaper published in northwestern Michigan." The Herald, however, did not issue its first number until November 3, 1858, nearly eight years later. In fact, the *Daily Northern Islander,* published last on June 20, 1856, was the second newspaper in Northern Michigan. The issue of January 24 publicized that both the weekly and the coming daily would be published as a joint effort. Therefore, the Herald was the third newspaper published in Northern Michigan. In December of 1867, a brother of Dr. Leach purchased the Herald, but sold it seven years before the Dr. Leach history began serially at the request of Thomas T. Bates, the editor. Dr. Leach, himself, owned it for nine years.

The whipping of Thomas Bedford, an insincere member of the Church on Beaver, is reported in Chapter 22, along with highly inaccurate details of the Strang assassination by Thomas Bedford and Alexander Wentworth. Dr. Leach gives us this reason for the whipping:

> "The Mormons had stolen a boat, for the recovery of which the owner had offered a reward of $50. On one occasion Bedford remarked to a young man, whom he met in McCulloch's store, that if he wanted to make $50, he would go to Mackinac and give information of the whereabouts of the stolen boat. Bedford's friends were frightened at his temerity. Several persons were present, and the remark was no doubt reported to Strang. It is supposed that this was the immediate cause of the whipping that followed."

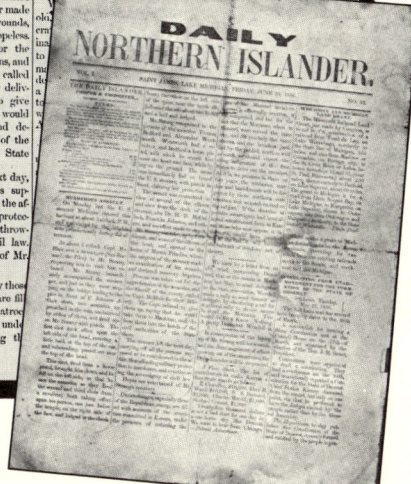

COURTESY OF
YALE UNIVERSITY LIBRARY

LAST ISSUE OF THE DAILY NORTHERN ISLANDER

Strang published ninety issues of the Northern Islander from December, 1850, to June, 1856. The Daily above began on April 1, 1856. Thirty-three issues of the Daily and seven of the Weekly came off the island press after January 24, 1856.

A supplementary footnote on this page by Dr. Leach is interesting:

> "The statement has been widely circulated that Bedford was whipped as a punishment for unlawful intimacy with another man's wife. A careful investigation of the facts has convinced me that there is not a shadow of truth in it."

Careful investigation by Dr. Leach did not apparently include anyone sympathetic to the case. Had he done so, he would have realized the footnote was the factual story. Sarah Strang gave the true facts to historian Milo Quaife, telling him that Bedford was a partner of David Brown in a fishing business and, coming home unexpectedly one day, Brown found Bedford and Mrs. Brown "in the act of adultery." One of those whipping Bedford publicly was David Brown, himself. According to Quaife, Wingfield Watson informed him that Strang remarked to those demanding punishment, "Whatever you do, let it be done quickly." Watson certainly did not oppose Strang for this comment. However, it is certain that Strang would have been willing to accept all responsibility for such a whipping, in view of the death penalty for adultery as part of Church law.

Events of this kind were greatly exaggerated in the newspapers all across the land. This particular incident had much to do with the downfall of the Kingdom in the sense that, because of it, Bedford, Wentworth and Atkyn, became tools in the hands of Dr. McCulloch in the eventual assassination of Strang.

It is inconceivable that Dr. Leach reported as factual, what actually were fictional tales about the assassination of Strang. He did not weigh the evidence fairly, especially as it involved federal authorities. Investigating federal officers sent to Beaver Island on the steamer *U.S.S. Michigan* were weak. While they did not assist in the assassination plan of Dr. McCulloch, it is known that the ship's officers, on two earlier occasions, had been in the harbor to lend moral support to assassin Bedford in a lawsuit. This steamer was part of the United States Navy, the first iron ship built for duty on the Great Lakes.

The vessel came to the harbor at Saint James about 1 p.m. on the afternoon of June 16, 1856. Strang was sent for about six hours after arrival. When Strang appeared at the dock, he was shot by Bedford and Wentworth with no interference from officers and crew of the *Michigan*. The commander even refused Sheriff Miller jurisdiction of the murderers, though the crime took place at Saint James, the county seat. At 10 o'clock the following morning, the steamer, a fully armed vessel of war, complete with several cannon, sailed for Mackinac with the entire group of conspirators who, upon arrival, were treated as heroic men of the hour. Whether planned or not, James Strang was assassinated with moral federal assistance.

Strang was shot after seven o'clock in the evening, not in the afternoon as Dr. Leach has written. Though the wound was pronounced mortal on that fateful day, death did not occur until 23 days later. Strang died at Voree, at the home of his parents on July 9.

Had Central Michigan University Press, in their reprint, annotated at least the Mormon sections of the Dr. Leach history, they would have corrected numerous century-old errors, among them:

"During his (Strang) last days, he was tenderly nursed by his first and lawful wife."

This type of reporting was highly effective, of course. The statement has been repeated in countless newspapers, magazines and books for more than 100 years, though it is completely false.

Dr. Leach has written a very interesting narrative in Chapter 23, describing the last days of the Kingdom. It is regrettable that he dulled some of its effectiveness by including a few fanciful tales. Gentiles allowed him to believe that they were only reimbursing themselves "for losses sustained by Mormon robberies."

Much of this chapter is written by Wingfield Watson, staunch supporter of Strang's teachings for nearly 70 years. Watson was an eye witness to Strang's prostrate condition, lying with assassins' bullets in his body at the Beaver docks. Dr. Leach included the Watson narrative verbatim, except that initials are given instead of full names.

Even the initial "W" was used, though obviously Watson. Should researchers care to include the reading of these four and a half pages of the "History," the following four names may add interest. These four are particularly important: M.M.A. — Justice Marvin M. Aldrich, T.B. — Thomas Bennett, O'D — Richard O'Donnell, and H — James Hoy. O'Donnell and Hoy were the Gentiles who assaulted Mormon Samuel Graham, breaking his arm and fracturing his skull. This incident led to the death of a Beaver Island Gentile, one attracting unfavorable national attention on the Saints. It also revealed the extent to which the Michigan legal system went in harassing Beaver Island Mormons. As far as public condemnation was concerned, the shooting of this man was murder.

The victim of this incident was Thomas Bennett, a man of unsavory reputation. A Mormon, Samuel Graham, had business one day with unsympathetic Sheriff Granger at Whiskey Point. This Beaver Island area was noted for Gentile brutality, and Granger, a non-Mormon, was a great hindrance to justice, in spite of his official duties. When Graham went to see Granger on business one day, he was beaten severely on the skull by O'Donnell and Hoy. Two warrants were issued for their arrest, one by Judge Greig and one by Justice of the Peace, Aldrich. Granger refused to serve the warrants because the victim was a Mormon. This prompted an appeal to Michilimackinac Prosecuting Attorney William McLeod, who then gave both warrants to the Constable of Michilimackinac, William Chambers.

Constable Chambers stopped at the home of Thomas and Samuel Bennett on his way to the fishing grounds to serve the warrants on O'Donnell and Hoy. There he met with unexpected armed resistance. Chambers then secured warrants for their arrest. He was able to form a posse of 30 or 40 to assist him, although meeting with some opposition by the Gentiles. Obstructing justice in the performance of duty did not please Con-

A History of the Grand Traverse Region 213

stable Chambers. Returning with the posse, his intent was to arrest both Bennetts. Instead of surrendering, however, they fired on the Constable. The posse quickly responded, wounding Samuel and killing Thomas.

During this defiance of law by the Bennetts, the intended prisoners, O'Donnell and Hoy, attempted to escape. While Hoy was successful, O'Donnell failed to avoid the officers when his boat was approached and he was placed under arrest.

The cry of "cold-blooded murder" echoed throughout Michilimackinac. The entire country condemned the Saints unmercifully. Facts were merely confusing. This is what they wanted to believe and they believed the worst.

Milo Quaife felt the untenable Mormon situation on Beaver Island at this time was one to be pitied, not persecuted. In commenting on the Bennett killing, Quaife narrated:

> "It is a sad commentary on the popular voice, which has been frequently supposed to be the voice of God, that it uniformly condemned whatever the Mormons might do, misrepresenting their acts, however innocent, to their disadvantage. A large number of Mormons were arrested for complicity in the killing of Bennett, and held in durance at Mackinac for many weeks. At length they were discharged, no bills having been found against them. Since the administration of justice was at this time wholly in Gentile hands this outcome of the affair tends strongly to establish their innocence of wrongdoing."

Dr. Leach could not have written the Bennett affair with any degree of sympathy without researching the Mormon version of the incident. This he failed to do. He failed to comprehend that Beaver Island Mormons could be innocent of any wrongdoing. Strang's own writings, or those sanctioned by him, may have been somewhat biased, but they were much more accurate and believable.

In "A History of the Grand Traverse Region" are found many short punches aimed as though the author, himself, believed the Mormons were a long way from being anything better than most Gentiles thought. Dr. Leach revealed exactly how he felt when he included such phrases as: "Young girls who tried to escape; robbing an established practice; right to own the earth; elections by fraudulent votes; wives believed their husbands were murderers; dead men tell no tales." In addition, Dr. Leach believed Gentile testimony "conclusive."

There is little doubt that Dr. Leach received many denials of wrongdoing from Wingfield Watson, to whom he owed a debt of gratitude for his vivid description of the violent July, 1856, exodus. If such denials had been publicized, their access today would go far in contradicting the numerous derogatory Gentile fantasies, with wisdom and truth.

As thorough as Milo Quaife was as an historian, it must be assumed that he knew of the Dr. Leach history, as would O. W. Riegel, author of "Crown of Glory." Both authors failed to quote a single important item from the "History."

Whether or not ignoring it meant a lack of factual respect is not known, but it is very significant in view of the fact it was published 14 years earlier than Legler's "A Moses of the Mormons." That is reason enough for stating earlier that Dr. Leach missed a great opportunity for research. Most of the Saints were still living. In fact, Strang's four polygamous wives were still living: Elvira, 53; Betsy, 62; Sarah, 48; and Phoebe, 46.

In closing the Beaver Mormon history, Dr. Leach summarized his research in this manner:

> "The history of the rise and fall of the Mormon kingdom of Beaver Island affords a striking example of systematic, organized and wide-spread lawlessness lawlessly punished."

If "The King Strang Story" enlightens historians by planting seeds of truth, thereby encouraging a reevaluation of James Strang as a man and public servant, this work will have accomplished its purpose.

"Beaver Island and its Mormon Kingdom"

By: Charles J. Strang, son of James J. Strang

The title of this very brief Strangite sketch might well have been used on a volume much larger than "The King Strang Story." The writer's purpose in reprinting it in full is to eulogize the author, Charles J. Strang, son of the famous or infamous "King," depending on the individual point of view.

Mr. Strang was christened "Charles," apparently after his mother, "Charlie Douglass," the notorious first polygamous wife of "King" Strang.

"Beaver Island and its Mormon Kingdom" appeared in "The Ottawan," a paper-back written by J. C. Wright. It was published in 1895 by Robert Smith & Co., Lansing, Michigan. No doubt this booklet was well received as a "Little Traverse Bay Souvenir." If it wasn't, it deserved to be. It is a delightful short history of villages and resorts surrounding Little Traverse Bay and the Indian legends connected therewith.

A few inaccuracies appear in the narrative. Much of it is necessarily repetitious. However, its value lies in the fact that Charles Strang, a former Lansing printer and oldest polygamous son of "King" Strang, narrated it. Here is the brief article complete:

> "Beaver Island, the largest in Lake Michigan, lies about thirty miles northwest of Little Traverse Bay. From 1850 to 1856 this island was the headquarters of a band of people who assumed for themselves rights and prerogatives contrary to the spirit of our constitution and laws, and whose acts made a considerable portion of the history of the Traverse region for that decade. The rise and fall of the "kingdom" which then flourished there will always be a prolific subject for writers who visit this northern country.
>
> "These people called themselves "Latter Day Saints," but they were better known as Mormons. Their leader was James J. Strang, who called himself a "king," and assumed many of the prerogatives of a monarch.

"Mr. Strang was born in Scipio, New York, March 21, 1813, but grew to manhood in Chautauqua County. His education was obtained in the public schools of the county, closing with a course in the Fredonia Academy. He studied law, and was admitted to the bar. In 1843 he settled in Burlington, Wisconsin, and some time before the death of Joseph Smith, in 1844, he visited Nauvoo and became a Mormon. After Smith's death, Strang disputed with Brigham Young the right to lead the church, and succeeded in gathering quite a large following at his "stake of Zion" in Wisconsin. In 1847 he visited Beaver Island, and decided to establish his people there, founding the village of St. James, which was named in honor of himself. On July 8, 1850, he reorganized his church and established the "kingdom" and from that day he was known as "King Strang." His authority was respected and obeyed by the "Saints," and as cheerfully hated and opposed by the "Gentiles." He controlled the Mormon vote, and was elected to the Legislature of 1853, and again in 1855.

"The practice of 'consecration' led to many conflicts between the Mormons and Gentile fishermen in that vicinity. Such expressions as "The earth is the Lord's, and the fullness thereof," and "We are the Lord's chosen people," stilled the consciences and justified the use of property lawfully owned by others, yet it is undoubtedly true that many depredations were committed by irresponsible persons and deliberately charged to the Mormons.

"Mr. Strang had frequent collisions with the authorities at Mackinac, but with his knowledge of the law, and his readiness in debate, he cleared himself of every charge. At one time the Sheriff of Mackinac County hunted him three days in the wilds of the island with a posse of ten whites and thirty Indians, and offered a reward of $300 for his body dead or alive, but Mr. Strang eluded them and avoided arrest.

"In the spring of 1856 matters reached a crisis. A resident of the island, Mr. Thomas Bedford, had been publicly flogged by Mr. Strang's authority, and he determined to have revenge. He enlisted the support of a few others, among them Mr. Alex Wentworth and they decided to kill Mr. Strang. The opportunity came on June 20, when the U. S. Steamer Michigan was in the harbor at St. James. Strang was fatally shot, after which Bedford, Wentworth, and some others were taken to

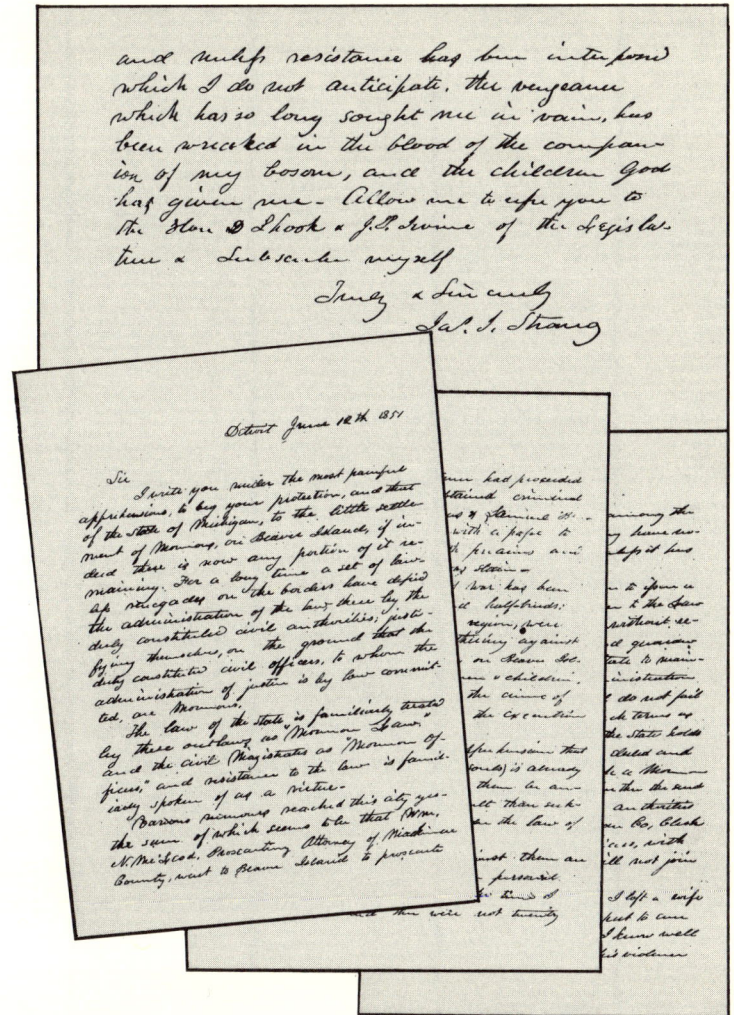

STRANG FEARED ANNIHILATION OF 700 SAINTS IN 1851

James Strang was elected to the Michigan Legislature less than seventeen months after sending this plea to the Governor for protection from the lawless gentile renegades on Beaver. "You will forgive my anxiety, I left a wife and children there. I do not expect to ever see either this side the grave."

Mackinac, 'tried' and acquitted. After the acquittal, Bedford and his friends organized a company at Mackinac and other points near the islands, and returned to St. James and drove from their homes every Mormon except a very few who were willing to renounce their religion. Strang's house and printing office were ransacked and robbed of everything of value; the tabernacle was destroyed and the property of the Mormons, confiscated and divided among the raiders. Warning was served on the Mormons to leave the island within a specified time. The warning was heeded, a few going to the mainland near Charlevoix, but the main body proceeded to Milwaukee and Chicago. Mr. Strang was removed to Wisconsin, where he died July 9, 1856.

"Strang's house, which has been raised by recent writers to the dignity of a "royal palace," was substantially built of hewn logs, and after the dispersion of the Mormons, it became the mecca of relic hunters, and so continued until 1892, when it was destroyed by fire.

"Of the present residents of the village of St. James, the majority are Irish Catholics, many of them having gone there directly from Ireland. The principal occupation of the people is fishing, and they live happy and contented in their island home."

"King" Strang and his Saints, in this writer's opinion, were not people who assumed for themselves rights and prerogatives "contrary to the spirit of our constitution and laws," with but few exceptions.

One possible exception may be trespassing on Government lands for lumber and firewood. Gentiles objecting to this as flagrant breaking of the law were merely concerned that the Saints were beating them to it. Furthermore, in early pioneer days, this kind of appropriation was generally accepted. But hatred of the Mormons made a difference in viewpoint.

Perhaps Charles Strang included polygamy as "contrary to the spirit," but polygamy was a choice of the women on Beaver Island and not one of force. Strang's wives considered it an honor to marry their "King," and this marriage in the Church broke no law. Men could not have more than one legal wife

Beaver Island and its Mormon Kingdom

at a time, to be sure. "King" Strang would have married them legally if he could have. Polygamy was not illegal at this time.

Plural marriage on Beaver Island was far different than polygamy practiced secretly at Nauvoo by Joseph Smith and Brigham Young. The "arrogant usurper" Young not only had his own wives, but inherited those of the Prophet after Smith's assassination.

During his lifetime, Brigham Young had 27 wives and 54 children, a veritable beehive of activity. The beehive was his Utah trade mark, in fact, although it had nothing whatever to do with bees. Actually, there was not a single bee in the entire territory of Utah.

This writer is not aware of any "personal property encroached upon by the Saints." The Saints did farm some of the Government land, a very common practice. It is incorrect to say, "justified the use of property lawfully owned by others," without some explanation or incident to prove the statement.

Charles Strang paid his father a great compliment when he wrote, "with his knowledge of the law, and his readiness in debate, he cleared himself of every charge." This is true, not only at Mackinac, but also Detroit where legal competition was a real challenge. "King" Strang was in the enemy camp at Mackinac.

Commenting on the "posse of 10 whites and 30 Indians," it should be pointed out this was a drunken posse, hunting Strang down like a dog. Whether or not the public liked this brand of Mormonism on Beaver Island, or their polygamous beliefs, did not justify that Strang be treated in such a manner. There were few to sympathize with his treatment during nine precarious years on Beaver.

The correct date of Strang's assassination is June 16, 1856, not June 20, as Charles Strang recorded, and as did Quaife when he wrote that Strang lived 19 days. Both were apparently misled by the *Daily Northern Islander* account of Friday, June 20. Strang was shot the previous Monday.

The impression given by Charles Strang that his father was

driven off the island should be corrected. Twelve days after being shot and beaten, "King" Strang was removed to the home of his parents at Voree, a few miles from Burlington, Wisconsin. The Gentiles drove the helpless Saints off Beaver Island a few days later. See "A Sampling of Strangite Defenders — Wingfield Watson" for his story of this episode of sorrow and horror for which no legal action was ever taken on behalf of those helpless men, women and children.

Feature writers for Sunday supplements and lurid magazines wrote every word-picture depicting life on Beaver Island as they imagined it to be, nearly all of it highly colored, sensational, and false.

Charles Strang said that the home of his father was dubbed "royal palace" after July 8, 1850. It was also called a "royal castle." The four polygamous wives who lived together in this home with their chosen and mutual husband, considered it much less than a palace or a castle. Though a frame home of simple construction and small, they were quite content to live together as one family.

While paying tribute to Charles Strang by reprinting this brief article, the writer also wishes to add a short eulogy to the memory of Clement Strang, his brother. Like his father, he, too, lived a life of service to his fellow man . . . a life of genteel poverty.

Clement Strang lived in Benzonia, Michigan, for many years. He taught physics, chemistry, botany and zoology part time in its High School and was an instructor for two years in North Carolina and a year in Texas before going to Benzonia. Three years were spent in the Science Department at Buchanan, Michigan, High School. A commendable position was accepted by him as School Commissioner of Benzie County.

In all the years devoted to teaching, Clement Strang found time to preach as a Congregational minister. He also wrote a scholarly work, entitled "The Living God." Ten precious years of his life were devoted part time to this contemplated book.

"The Living God" was never published for reasons unknown

CHARLES JAMES STRANG

CLEMENT JAMES STRANG

CHARLES J. GRIER
(JAMES JESSE
STRANG, JR.,
ADOPTED
AT AGE TWO)

James Jesse Strang, Jr. was the last child born to Strang. Charles, Clement and James were sons of Elvira Field, Strang's first polygamous wife.

to this writer. Perhaps the mental strain in later life did not allow sufficient effort or knowledge to complete its presentation to the public. Perhaps the subject was too risky for a publisher to chance a profit.

A full typescript copy, comprising 215 pages, deserves and has a cherished niche in this writer's library. Under its title reads:

 Research Study for the Basis of Biology
 Exposition of Psychophysical Philosophy
 Exploitation of Psychotropic Evolution
 New Twentieth Century Christian Science

"The Living God" typescript reveals a triple Dedicatory to the Memory of August F. Bruske, past President of Alma College; William James Beal, famed past Biologist at then Michigan Agricultural College; and Charles Carroll Everett, once Dean of the Harvard University School of Christian Theology.

"Prove all things; hold fast that which is good." — Clement Strang.

"A Moses of the Mormons"

By: Henry E. Legler

This brief, 32-page study of the Strangite movement is historically important because it was the first serious study, excluding the biased chronicle "A History of the Grand Traverse Region" by Dr. Leach. Milo Quaife used the word "hitherto" evaluating Legler and has every justification, since his "Kingdom of Saint James" is monumental in its own right. Quaife narrated:

 "But one writer, hitherto, has made a serious effort to produce a comprehensive and unbiased account of the

JAMES JESSE STRANG

This was the only portrait known to Legler in 1897.

Strangite movement. Henry E. Legler, in his later years librarian of the Chicago Public Library, was greatly interested in the study of local history. He was long a resident of Milwaukee, and a member of a small group of Milwaukeeans of like tastes who associated themselves under the name of The Parkman Club. The members prosecuted a number of local historical studies which were subsequently published as the Parkman Club Publications. Mr. Legler's contribution to the series was a study of the Strangite movement published in 1897 as Nos. 15 and 16 of the series under the title, "A Moses of the Mormons." Mr. Legler enjoyed a rare opportunity to make an exhaustive investigation of his subject, since many of the actors in the story were still alive and accessible for interviews. However, he contented himself with a comparatively slight study of 80 pages, only half of which is the author's own contribution. Slight as it is, Mr. Legler's investigation still remains without a competitor, the only one ever made of Strang's prophetic career. It has been several times reprinted, and is frequently utilized by the newspaper feature writers, as the quarry from which their tales are derived."

Although "A Moses of the Mormons" was published in Milwaukee, May 11, 1897, 41 years after the death of James Strang, it must be considered an early study of the Strangite movement. Being early, certain statements do not now agree with facts known today. Its greatest fault lies in its brevity.

The Coe Collection of Western Americana at the Yale University Library is the best source for Strang research. In it, one will find information not available or even known to Legler. During his time, the material was in a scattered state.

On the Frontispiece of "A Moses of the Mormons" is a reproduction of a line drawing made, as Legler states, "from the only photograph known to be in existence." There are now several known photographs.

It is interesting to insert here Quaife's comments on one of the four ringleaders promoting the downfall of Strang in 1856 by the name of "Doctor" Atkyn, a Beaver Island photographer.

A Moses of the Mormons

"What he was 'doctor' of is not now in evidence, but he had paid various visits to Saint James from 1850 on, coming finally, in the autumn of 1855, to open a daguerreotype gallery. In the last weekly issue of the Islander ever published, occurs a two-column account of Atkyn's career, which presents him as a cheap adventurer who sought, whether by fair means or foul, to sponge a living off the simple-minded Saints. Having run his course at the islands, and being hopelessly in debt, he coolly proposed, unless they should pay his bills, to resort to a program of blackmail, and evidence of his ability along this line, exhibited a specimen of lampooning handbill he had gotten out against certain reputable citizens of Council Bluffs. They did not comply, and Atkyn proceeded to execute his threat by visiting Detroit, Lansing and other points, "peregrinating the country, endeavoring to slander the Mormons and sponge his living."

It is fair to assume that Atkyn, at some time, must have taken a daguerreotype of Strang. The small portrait chosen as the Frontispiece of this volume may have been one of them. It is on glass encased in a metal frame, indicating a patent date of July 4, 1854. The line drawing used by Legler is from a similar one.

Legler makes this interesting observation:

"Of his temple and his so-called castle, the only vestiges now are a few splinters in the collections of relic hunters."

At least one item exists larger than a splinter. Because the home was not burned when torches set fire to many of the Mormon buildings, one door, taken from the home in 1857, is still on the island. Reports that the "castle" burned in 1893 were due to the fact that the home replacing it burned shortly after it was built. It was torn down. Very few buildings escaped the torches in 1856, mainly simple homes. These the Gentiles could use. Only the museum remains standing today, formerly the print shop.

Earlier it was stated that Brigham Young, to gain full power for himself, eliminated the Council of Twelve, and that Strang made the most vigorous bid. Legler recorded it better by saying:

"He (Brigham Young) was one of the all-powerful Council of Twelve, and at first fed the enmity of his colleagues towards outside aspirants by ingenously suggesting to each individually hopes of personal aggrandizement. It was a shrewd scheme at first to crush outside aspirants, and then narrow down rivalry at home by cajolery or intimidation till his own elevation became possible."

Legler mentioned the political manipulation of Strang to secure a seat in the legislature as the election of 1853. The correct date is 1852. This was a very interesting maneuver, indeed. It added stature to Strang as a man to reckon with in anything he set his brilliant mind to do.

An additional 32 pages beyond the Legler narrative consists of an Appendix. This includes several worthwhile historical writings, including Strang's fragmentary autobiography, except the cipher.

The remaining sections include:

Ludlow P. Hill: a member of "a disaffected family by the name of Hill" in Strang's "Ancient and Modern Michilimackinac"

Mrs. Cecelia Hill's Recollections: wife of Ludlow P. Hill

The Battle on the Lake: E. S. Stone's dictated narrative of the rescue of the Mormons from the battle of Pine River (Charlevoix)

Interview of Judge Lyon: an acquaintance of Strang at Burlington, Wisconsin

Voree Plates: description of one side

The Buried Plates of Laban: a Strang revelation

Strang's Books and Pamphlets and the Bibliography

"Assassination of the King"

By: Ivan Swift

In 1904, Ivan Swift composed an uncomplimentary poem about James Strang, called "Assassination of the King." It is strictly character assassination and it is quite apparent Mr. Swift did little research beyond Chapter XVIII of "A History of the Grand Traverse Region."

The Dr. Leach "History" ran serially in the Grand Traverse Herald in 1883, as noted previously. No doubt a copy of this important area history was in the Swift library. The more reliable Strang narrative, "A Moses of the Mormons," was either unknown to Swift or he chose to ignore it. Dr. Leach and Mr. Swift were residents of the same area. The former lived at Traverse City, Michigan; the latter, at Harbor Springs.

In 1909, Mr. Swift, artist and poet, published some of his compositions in a book called "Fagots of Cedar." These poems had been accepted for publication previously by at least 10 national magazine and newspaper editors.

"Assassination of the King" was composed nearly fifty years after the murder of Strang. A complete reading of the poem first is suggested, skipping the comments, then returning to the first stanza for the review.

> "DARE'S de land — she lay like serpent —
> Twenty mile out in de lake
> She's be name de Isle of Beavair
> 'Cause she's lak de dam dey make.

Ivan Swift is unique when he states that Beaver Island was named "Beaver" because it looked like a dam. Some have said it was named for the beaver found on the island. There were no beaver while Strang was on the island, at least. The island was shaped on early maps like a skinned Beaver laid flat on the ground with legs protruding.

> "I remember Eighteen-Fifty,
>   Den I'm fishing on dat shore;
> Most de people be dose Mormon
>   Who don't stay dare any more.
>
> "What's de reason dey's all scattair?
>   I'm one of de man what know!
> If de fly go, dat is bettair
>   Dan be freeze out by de snow!

If this imaginary French fisherman was "one of de man what know!" he must be considered one of the guilty who drove the Mormons off. Over 2,600 men, women and children were the helpless victims of this exodus.

> "If you lak to know dis story,
>   I can tell you what is true;
> Den you see how some de churchman
>   Be no bettair dan de Jew.

The Jews in the eyes of this Frenchman must have been a pretty low type of human being. Swift considered some of the Saints in the same category. He is merely using this French fisherman as a vehicle for his own message.

> "All de Mormon pay de ten-tax,
>   All de Cat'lic, he refuse;
> So dey steal his net an' fish-boat,
>   Cow an' sleigh an' snow-pack shoes!

There is no evidence anyone outside the Mormon membership was ever forced to contribute to the Church fund. Swift believed what he heard and read, but failed to include justice, compassion and an interview of even one Saint in composing this farce.

> "Many year de Frenchman stand dees —
>   'Cause dat time dare be no law —
> Den de French and Injin contrac'
>   An' de Cat'lic show de claw!

Just how many French were there on Beaver Island? There were a few, but not many. It is more than likely Ivan Swift used this nationality to emphasize the degradation by his effective manner of speaking English! Most of the Gentiles were Irish, and there were many more good ones than poor ones. Like today, those who instigated great problems in the Kingdom were a very small minority.

> "I can stick de stake in san' dare,
> Hundaird of dem, where dey's thieve
> Shoot down lak de dog, an' bury
> Wid no time for pray an' grieve!

This stanza is ridiculous and completely false. Only a naive historian would believe such a condition existed on Beaver Island. Ivan Swift may have, but it is doubtful.

> "Ol' De Strang be king dat Islan' —
> She's de smart man in de worl'!
> He's be lawyer, pries' an' doctair,
> An' de black fox wid de girl!

Strang did not consider himself "King" of Beaver Island. Strang thought of himself as "King" only of his followers. Most of the Saints loved him and believed his religious teachings to the letter. There was no reason for them to be on this island if they didn't believe in his teachings, except for the few fraudulent Saints.

One of the early and most respected believers in Strang was sincere and dignified Wingfield Watson. Following is an excerpt from a letter to the writer, dated October 11, 1965, from Barbara Drew, a granddaughter. In speaking of her grandfather, Mrs. Drew wrote from Burlington, Wisconsin:

> "He was strictly honest and honourable in every dealing and faithfully upheld anyone he thought was right. He was a staunch follower of James J. Strang and spent every minute that he could spare reading, studying, and writing, regarding the church. He was only 24 years old when he went to Beaver Island and 28 years old when they were driven off,

but he said that while he lived on the Island he walked five or six miles every Sabbath to hear Mr. Strang preach as he did not want to miss a single sermon."

No one but Swift ever called Strang "doctair." Historical fact has suffered a bit because this word seemed to "fit" the stanza, a poor reason, to say the least. The last line, "An' de black fox wid de girl!" is properly dismissed in the Epilogue, "The Five Wives and Fourteen Children of James Strang."

> "Fine blue eye an' yellow whisker!
> Straight lak tree, wid voice lak win!
> Sing de song an' play de fiddle,
> Pray de Lord an' mak de "tin!"

What a misleading characterization these lines are! Strang had a reddish beard, was slightly stooped and may never have had enough money to buy a fiddle.

When Swift says "an' mak de "tin!" he means money. Strang cared little for money, except to help his cause. He thought of his own personal needs last and must be considered to have been a very generous man. He once gave his last coat to a complete stranger.

> "Strang have only t'irteen woman,
> So hunt for nodair wife! —
> Lak de Frenchman set he's pon'-net,
> Dey's some white-fish lose her life!

No stanza in "Assassination of the King" can beat this one for utter nonsense. If Swift was trying to capture a reading public, he could have used his talents more dramatically recording the truth.

> "Madame Bedfort be de beauty
> On de Island in dose day —
> So dees King sen' off de husban;
> Den he steal hees dame away!

Strang would have considered this kind of reporting too complimentary to deny! He was not a ladies' man. Nor was

Assassination of the King

"Madame Bedfort" (Mrs. Thomas Bedford) a beauty. Her husband, one of Strang's assassins, was not even a Mormon. The incident Swift had in mind was twisted to suit his own dramatics. Bedford was a fisherman. His fishing partner, Brown, returned home one day and found him in the act of adultery with Mrs. Brown, as narrated previously.

Swift continues in the same mood when he writes:

> "When de news have reach to Guillam,
>   Where he's trapping in de Nord,
> He's go mad an' swear de vengeance
>   By de French an' by de Lord!

The true story about Bedford is more exciting than the less factual poem by Swift. It is obvious this Michigan poet had little respect for Prophet Strang when he continued:

> "In de spring de gov'ment cuttair
>   She's be lan' to Ol' St. Jame'.
> Den de captain send for Strang dare,
>   See'f he know some smugglair' name.
>
> "When de King come to de gang-plank,
>   Hol' hees head high in de air —
> Dare's two pistol-shot from fish-house!
>   Den dey's blood - spot in hees hair!

There were five pistol shots and none came from the fish house. Thomas Bedford and his partner in crime, Alexander Wentworth, shot Strang from behind rows of firewood. Strang was then hit with the butt of a horse pistol as an added precaution against survival.

> "I don't swear who kill de great man,
>   But de cuttair sail away —
> Wid one Frenchman for de deck-han'
>   When de sun go down dat day.

Ivan Swift is hinting that the murderer, after all, was the Frenchman! He is toying with words when he writes, "wid one

Frenchman for de deck-han'." Since the ship was part of the U. S. Navy, it is safe to say that a deck hand was not hired from Beaver Island! The ship was the *"U.S.S. Michigan,"* known later as the *"Wolverine."* It was the first iron ship built for the Navy and was launched as a "steamer" not a "cutter."

This poem, like most of the writing for a century since the assassination, is fictional. It clearly shows how careless authors and poets can be with historical material. When a reader is not familiar with facts, he becomes a victim of the author, many believing what is written is the truth.

Strang suffered, and his memory is still suffering, unfair public ridicule from this kind of reporting.

"A Child of the Sea; and Life Among the Mormons"

By: Elizabeth Whitney Williams

It may conceivably be said there is no such thing as a bad novel. It is either liked or disliked, entirely an individual preference. A chronicle based on personal experiences is something else again. The demand for utmost honesty and common sense evaluation of memories is necessarily great.

In this category falls the narrative, "A Child of the Sea; and Life Among the Mormons," written by Elizabeth Whitney Williams. The chronicle fails historically as trustworthy reporting. It is strictly a Gentile account of the James Strang Kingdom of God on Beaver Island.

Childhood memories suffer an enormous lack of accurate separation. Childhood facts seldom bear resemblance to adult

A Child of the Sea; and Life Among the Mormons

understanding of them, especially after half a century, as in the Williams' narrative.

American history books are filled with beautifully written stories about those who made our country great. Many of these are inaccurate figments of human wishful thinking, grown out of proportion to true down-to-earth beginnings.

Before reviewing "A Child of the Sea; and Life Among the Mormons," examine the following several pages revealing typical "historical" nonsense.

How about the story of Betsy Ross who probably never saw an American flag? How about Barbara Fritchie, the origin of corn and the origin of patriotic Yankee Doodle? There are endless shameful misrepresentations of our history's past. Does the recording of history need to be nine-tenths lying and exaggeration?

According to the Encyclopedia Americana, corn is of American origin, possibly Central American. The authors do not say that corn was developed here and taken to Greece before the time of Christ. Yet, if their information is correct, this would need to be a fact. There is conclusive evidence that Indian corn was known to the Greeks in 450 B.C. This fact "throws much light upon the origin of the aborigines in America" according to the February, 1839, Democratic Review. Most American school-boys still believe corn was first grown by the Indians of North America.

Yankee Doodle? The same encyclopedia places the date of our national air at about 1750. This may sound romantic, but credit again belongs to classic Greece. It was then called "Iankhe Doule" and may be interpreted as "Rejoice, O Slave." The spirit and language is well preserved, incidentally.

A list of fraudulent tales depicting progress of American history would be shocking. America has recorded a long line of questionable folklore. The freedom-loving Pilgrims, simply known as "First Comers" for nearly 200 years, may be considered a starting point for this long line. Nearly two centuries elapsed before serious perpetuation of Pilgrim folklore began.

When it did, we were well on our way toward becoming an ancestral conscious society.

Beaver Island is now only a small fragment of the total Michigan folklore. It was, however, a major part of Northern Michigan history before 1900, and it was very important in a national sense for several years.

It may be interesting to dig into a few facts about the Pilgrims. As stated earlier, they came to the American shore possibly a few years after the first civilization at Beaver Island. The difference, of course, is the planting of a permanent colony at Plymouth.

Not until 1820 did the old Plymouth Colony become a symbol to behold outside its own awareness. Public attention was assured the Colony at the bicentenary by Daniel Webster. Previous to this, in 1802, John Quincy Adams gave a memorial address, expounding the Mayflower Compact as a "unanimous and personal assent" document, which it was not. The Compact was strictly one of minority.

Family records of the writer indicate "clearly" that he is a descendant of Thomas Fuller, "grandson of the Fuller that landed on Plymouth Rock." Personal research, however, disproves this as wishful thinking. A brother of Samuel Fuller did come to these shores about 1640, explaining this undisappointing family "fact." There was also more than one "Mayflower," confusing living descendants of these "First Comers" even further.

Although Daniel Webster may have been the first to symbolize old Plymouth, credit must be given to Henry Wadsworth Longfellow for crystallizing the accepted fanciful folklore. "The Courtship of Miles Standish" in 1858 was a gem of fancy imagination whose main characters were perhaps the least typical of all the Pilgrims.

The Plymouth Colony, shortly after 1847, harbored a Mormon reactionary of the first magnitude, John C. Bennett. He had moved there from Voree. Bennett offered his services to Strang early in 1846, as narrated previously, while residing in

A Child of the Sea; and Life Among the Mormons

Cincinnati. Bennett had served Joseph Smith from September of 1840 to his dismissal 18 months later.

In "The History of the Saints; or an Exposé, of Joe Smith and Mormonism" published in Boston in 1842, Bennett, as author, claimed to have joined the Church merely to expose the leaders. "I never believed them or their doctrines," he wrote. Strang must have known that John C. Bennett was never a true Mormon convert, but, like Smith, he allowed him to join the church.

Like Abraham Lincoln, Strang was a great reader. Both read Volny's "Ruins" thoroughly and both considered it impressive. The library on Beaver Island was of great importance to Strang. Before moving it from Voree to Beaver Island, it may have contained a copy of "Mormonism Exposed." A copy of the first edition, now in the writer's collection, and once owned by William Osgood of Abington, Massachusetts, exposed much more than Mormonism. It exposed John C. Bennett as a man whose main interest in life was his own exaltation.

Why, then, did Strang allow this renegade pseudo-Mormon any breathing space at Voree? The answer can only be expediency in establishing his "Stake" there at any cost. Though the "Story" is primarily confined to the Beaver Island phase of Strangite Mormonism, it should be brought out that John Bennett made overtures from Plymouth as late as 1851 to regain his former position with Strang. His letters were ignored, fortunately, giving emphasis to the original charges of "apostacy, conspiracy to establish a stake by falsehood, deception, etc., and various immoralities" when he was cut off from the Church during October, 1847. Bennett was most enthusiastic about Beaver Island, but was never allowed to go there or to rejoin the Church.

As previously stated, "The Courtship of Miles Standish" is a gem of fancy imagination. Fitting snugly into this same description is "A Child of the Sea; and Life Among the Mormons." Many impressions of its author, Elizabeth Whitney Williams, have emerged as factual Michigan history. Without a doubt, the narrative is the least factually informative effort in all literature about the Strangite Mormons.

Unwittingly, the author of "A Child of the Sea" condemned her own narrative when she wrote this line into the Introductory:

> "What I have written about the Mormons are my own personal experiences and what I know about them by living constantly near them for four years of my life."

"Four years of my life" represents personal experiences between the ages of four and eight. Furthermore, the "experiences" were recorded 52 years later, when Mrs. Williams was nearly 60 years of age. Author Williams observed with more truth than she would have been willing to admit:

> "In this little history I have only touched lightly upon reality."

"A Child of the Sea," though far from being historically correct, has been used as source material for Sunday supplement writers and many unwary historians since the book was first published in 1905.

Elizabeth Whitney Williams was born on Mackinac Island about 1845, moving to Beaver Island when she was too young to remember. At seven years of age, her family moved to Pine River on the mainland, now the modern city of Charlevoix, Michigan. Her father was an itinerant shipbuilder.

In 1853, Elizabeth Williams, at age eight, was living at Pine River. This was the year when the serious skirmish occurred between the Gentiles and the Beaver Island Mormons. A few years after the 1856 exodus of the Saints, Mrs. Williams returned to the Island, living here for an additional 27 years, the first four as the wife of a fish broker. In 1869, her husband was appointed Lighthouse Keeper. After his death, Mrs. Williams was appointed the keeper, and from 1884 she resided at the Little Traverse Lighthouse on Harbor Point.

It may appear somewhat unkind to tag "A Child of the Sea; and Life Among the Mormons" as of no historic value. It does inform us how far the Gentile mind was poisoned with hatred

A Child of the Sea; and Life Among the Mormons 237

and falsehoods toward their unwelcome industrious neighbors from Wisconsin.

In the main, Mrs. Williams merely recorded a great many legends from Gentiles occupying the island after the Saints were driven off, and from descendants of them. Some bitterness toward the Mormons must have been implanted in her mind by her own father and half-brother. They were actively present at the "Battle of Pine River" and the half-brother was one of the Gentiles on Beaver during the forced exodus in 1856.

The Review that follows covers only Part II of the William's narrative and must encompass only the important Mormon falsehoods. Many James Strang "castles of fancy" have been written by other authors. The more important ones have been thoroughly reviewed.

There were only four Mormon families on Beaver Island during the first winter of occupation. During the winter of 1849-1850, there were about 125 Mormons on Beaver, as Mrs. Williams recorded. There were other whites, to be sure, and also many Indians. The Mormons did "keep their doors locked and barred" on many occasions because of the Indians. The Gentiles often got them drunk. During May, 1851, the Gentiles used Indians as a vicious posse to "hunt down Mormons like animals."

An entire page was devoted to Peter McKinley and his family. That "Mr. McKinley was a very kind and pleasant man" may have been an honest description of him, but as one of the complainants at the Strang trial at Detroit in 1851, he appeared less kind and not quite so pleasant. The six week trial, involving many participants, ended in complete acquittal. One of the eventual assassins of Strang, Thomas Bedford, was an employe of Peter McKinley at one time.

Mrs. Williams recorded her narrative as "personal experiences." Following is her "personal" knowledge of the famous Thomas Bedford whipping. At the time the whipping took place, she was merely seven years old.

"A man by the name of Thomas Bedford was employed by Mr. Peter McKinley. He also gave some information about the stealing of property by the Mormons, and he also received seventy-five of the cruel stripes with the blue beeches. For this awful treatment Mr. Bedford swore revenge. The Mormons never proved that Mr. Bedford had given any information about this stealing goods from Mr. McKinley, but just concluded he had and gave him the awful punishment. So Bedford bided his time for revenge."

An inaccurate, and completely different version of this whipping has been narrated in the review of "A History of the Grand Traverse Region." A third version written by the third polygamous wife of Strang is narrated in that review also, the only accurate one of the three.

The author of "A Child of the Sea" apparently considered dates too difficult or too confusing. It is necessary, even for historians already engrossed in a study of the Strang Kingdom, to be alert to her continual passing from one year to another without guidance, forward and backward.

A good example is the Bedford whipping. On the page following the description of the whipping, she writes:

> "So far the King had preached against polygamy and said that it should not be allowed, although there were a number of Mormons that had a number of wives apiece." (This was not true.) She continued: "Now the King had a new revelation that polygamy must be practiced."

Anyone reading the Williams' narrative should have been informed, for the sake of continuity and understanding, that this claimed revelation preceded the Bedford incident by several years. Any reader can be confused by an author failing to reveal dates if it is of importance.

> "The King now took one of his young wives, had her dressed in man's apparel and travel about with him seeking converts."

In 1849, Strang married only one in polygamy and, therefore, had no so-called "young wives." Elvira was his first. As for remembering seeing the two together on Beaver Island with Elvira dressed as a man, as she did on the eastern mission, this was pure theatrical. She never wore the costume on Beaver.

A Child of the Sea; and Life Among the Mormons 239

Elvira did travel one short season in the East, using the name, "Charlie Douglass."

"Beaver Island—1850" offers a true discussion of polygamy. Those who have read this Chapter understand how ridiculous it was to say "Polygamy must be practiced." Proof of economic support was the first requisite and few Saints had that ability.

It is necessary to pass over a great amount of trivial folksy detail. A review could be written as long as the book, itself. Therefore, comments must be limited to the more glaring misinformation, of which there is a great deal.

Milo Quaife "derived no help whatever" from the Williams' narrative. How could he? Reading the narrative is entertaining and may sound convincing, but to a contemporary few who know the facts, despite the "assurance and pretended first-hand authority," as Quaife clearly states, it is clearly an accumulation of Gentile fabrications.

The Bennett affair is a good example. It has been detailed in the review of "A History of the Grand Traverse Region" and need not be elaborated here. Thomas Bennett, readers may recall, was shot by a posse as an act of self-preservation, although the victim, according to Mrs. Williams, "had been a favorite of us all."

To begin with, she writes this questionable line, indicating she felt the Mormons were pressuring for occupation of all Gentile property on Beaver Island.

> "The Bennett brothers had already left their home at the harbor and gone to the Gentile settlement."

This statement sounds rather unimportant, but examined closely, the simple act of leaving their home because of coercion by the Mormons may best be explained by telling how the Bennetts got this home in the first place. Quaife's account considerably reduces any sympathy felt for Thomas and Samuel Bennett when they moved to the Gentile settlement:

> "In 1848 the public lands were thrown on the market. In accordance with a practice general on the frontier, individuals

> had made squatter claims, and had begun to make improvements before the land was open for entry. The fishermen learned of the approaching land sale in advance of the Mormons and proceeded to take advantage of their knowledge by marking out the most desirable tracts of land. It was then proposed that at the sale all should respect these squatter claims, whether occupied or not, and no one should buy in the land to which another had laid claim. The Mormons respected this agreement; but two of the fishermen, Thomas and Samuel Bennett proceeded to enter several lots on which the Mormons had located and built their homes, and the latter saw themselves deprived of their property. By this initial act of aggression the Bennetts laid the groundwork for a quarrel of large dimensions."

This "quarrel of large dimensions" resulted in the death of Thomas Bennett and severe injury to brother Samuel. The unfortunate death was called "murder" by the Gentiles and resulted in nationwide condemnation of the Beaver Island Kingdom.

To avoid repeating the factual story, return to the Bennett killing in the review of "A History of the Grand Traverse Region." The Williams' version appears to be a completely different incident to protect the guilty, only the names being the same.

Here is the story. Keep in mind Mrs. Williams was only six years old during this "personal experience."

> "The killing of Bennett was a great shock to all our people, as no one believed the Mormons would carry things so far. The Bennetts had gone early on the lake, returning before noon. While attending to their work in their workhouse two Mormon men stepped in, demanding the tax money. Bennett answered, "I want to see the King before I pay it." The men went away. The Bennetts stepped out to go to their dwelling, when seven bullets were fired at once into the body of Thomas Bennett. He dropped dead instantly. The brother ran toward the house with his hand up to his head. Bullets came thick and fast around him. He was shot through the hand, shattering all the fingers on one hand. There were many shots entered the windows. Mrs. Bennett to save her life had to go into the cellar."

A Child of the Sea; and Life Among the Mormons 241

Readers may judge for themselves how factual Mrs. Williams' thoughts were regarding polygamy on Beaver Island. At most, only one family in 25 became plural. This disproves her thoughts about polygamy when she wrote:

> "Many of the Mormons believed Strang would take no notice of the refusal of some of his elders to practice polygamy, while others thought that the man (evidently Adams) who hoped to have Strang's place would influence him to make them suffer the penalty, which the Mormons themselves told us was death, this elder contending severe measures was the only way to enforce obedience to the law."

Earlier in her narrative, Mrs. Williams informed readers that a man with four wives kept a boarding house at the harbor. Had she mentioned his name, a more emphatic rebuttal might be made. Perhaps it is sufficient to again relate the polygamy figures of the Mormon colony. Of the 500 families on the island, only 20 were plural. No family could be plural without a satisfactory means of support. Only James Strang, George Miller and Lorenzo Hickey had more than one plural wife.

About 60 pages further into the narrative, the wife of an Apostle is reputed to have related that the feminine statistics of the plural innkeeper included six wives, two being dead. Evidence is well established that Strang, with one legal and four polygamous wives, had one more than any other during the life of the Kingdom. George Miller may have married one of his plural wives on Beaver Island.

The "Battle of Charlevoix" in Mrs. Williams' narrative is better known as the "Battle of Pine River." They are identical. Her story of the battle is so far from accurate, more space than deserved would be needed for a thorough review.

Again, for better comparison, readers may refer to Part II, Chapter IX, if a reading of the Milo Quaife "Battle of Pine River" has not already been completed. His story is historically factual and very interesting to contemplate when critically examining the preposterous report of Mrs. Williams. The most absurd inclusion in her sketch embraces her clumsy attempt to authenticate the deaths of seven men. For authority, she refers to the *Northern Islander,* Strang's own newspaper. In reality, not a single life was lost during the brisk engagement on the shore, nor in the terrifying chase to the unexpected rescue vessel the Saints boarded half way to Beaver Island, the bark *Morgan.*

Mrs. Williams claims to have been an active participant in the "battle" when she records, "thinking there might not be bullets enough, the lead was melted and father said to me, 'Here Elizabeth, take these molds and run the bullets,' which I did." Elizabeth was eight years old, pouring hot lead like a veteran.

An American Weekly newspaper story about Strang, published in 1940, appropriately illustrates this review. It was purportedly written by 91-year-old Stephen Smith, who conceivably may have been a playmate of Elizabeth, even on the day of the battle. Smith claimed he saw the "whole thing." If he did, he had a frog's eye view from the beach at the tender age of four. Elizabeth and Stephen were in the thick of things, if what each described resembled the truth, Stephen on the beach and Elizabeth who related the following:

> "I stood looking out of a small window from Captain Morrison's house. I could see directly onto both boats (the two from Beaver) and was but a short distance from them. I could hear almost every word spoken by the leader, as he spoke in a loud, deep voice.
>
> "Soon shots were fired, I cannot say how many. All was confusion, women were screaming, some were praying. Men were talking, trying to quiet them. I never took my eyes off the Mormon boats. (This may explain whey she did not see Stephen!) When the smoke cleared away I saw the men hurriedly push their boats off and jump into them, taking their oars and pulling with all their might. Then I saw our men coming towards the house carrying a man who seemed to be dead, as blood was streaming down. The form looked familiar to me. I ran to the door and saw it was my brother Lewis (Whitney) (actually half-brother). They carried him home, laying him down and examined his wound. He was shot in the calf of the leg. It was a flesh wound. The place was small where the bullet went in, but the flesh was badly torn where the bullet came out. Excitement was great; the men wanted to follow the Mormon

American Weekly Sunday Supplement, typical of features about Strang and his Kingdom.

boats. At the river there were but two boats at the time, our own, which was too small, and Captain Morrison's which was a large, heavy boat."

Yes, indeed, excitement was great! In fact, the meeting of 15 unarmed Mormons on the shore, against 60 or 70 armed Gentiles, two of them Mrs. Williams' father and half-brother, must have been thoroughly electrifying to young Lewis Whitney. Since the four Mormon guns were left lying in the bottom of one Mormon boat, a reliable conclusion must be made that Lewis shot himself in the leg!

The Williams' finale of the battle continues dramatically:

> "The men concluded at last to take that boat and give chase to the Mormons, as the delay would be too great in getting a boat from the fishermen's landing. So the boat was manned by a double crew to row. One man was placed in the bow with his rifle to shoot into the Mormon's boats and sink them if possible. Every bullet he shot seemed to take effect. Our men were powerful oarsmen, and in spite of the distance the two boats had made before our men had got started, our boat was gaining on them fast. Soon one of the Mormon boats was sinking, and they made some delay by getting out of the sinking boat into the other. Our men were straining every nerve to overtake them, which they soon would have done had not the Mormons hurried toward a large vessel which lay becalmed just ahead of them. It was getting dusk, but everything could be plainly seen.
>
> The Mormons rowed with all their might to the vessel, telling the captain that they were fishermen and that the Mormons were chasing them and begged to be saved from their enemies. Of course, the captain could do no less than let them get aboard his vessel, which they did. The vessel was the bark Morgan. It was stated in 'The Northern Islander', edited and printed at the Island, that seven were killed and five wounded of the Mormons at the battle of Charlevoix (Pine River). A man who boarded with me several years after this happened told me that this was the correct number, as he was in the boat and one of the wounded, he being shot in the shoulder. He was very young when he was training with these bad men. He also told us that Pierce, the leader, was very angry and had planned to come back and drive us away or murder us all."

A Child of the Sea; and Life Among the Mormons 245

The *Northern Islander,* published at Saint James, recorded the casualties in the "Battle of Pine River." The list obviously would have included the dead had there been any.

The casualties were listed as: Isaac Pierce, A. J. Porter, Andrew J. Hale, J. T. Pierce, Alexander Wentworth and Lewis Briggs. Those who escaped injury were: Joshua L. Miller, Sheriff; Franklin Johnson, Lorenzo Tubbs, Orlando P. Briggs, Lorenzo Dow Hickey, David Finch, Egbert Carpenter, Christopher Scott and F. W. Longfield.

This completes the Williams' narrative about the "Battle of Charlevoix." It all ended the night of the same day when the Mormons arrived back at Galilee near the South end of Beaver Island . . . 15 exhausted souls! One of the six injured, Andrew J. Hale, Mrs. Williams failed to name as the man who "trained with these bad men."

In "A Child of the Sea," there is continual confusion of questionable information. Avoiding the use of dates and names certainly was a great help to Mrs. Williams, but a hodge-podge for historians not well versed in the subject. Dates and personal names add authenticity. Without them, a reader has reason to question, not only accuracy, but whether or not a narrative is reliable. "A Child of the Sea" is definitely the least reliable in all Strangite literature.

Though the father of young Elizabeth Whitney (Williams) was an itinerant shipbuilder, his talents could very well have been used "to frame a house for King Strang." Reference to this fact begins by stating that her father was asked by Strang to do this work. It is somewhat strange "Father was gone about six weeks, coming home often to see how we were at home." This was in 1850. The family lived on the island from 1849 to 1853 and their home was easily accessible during construction.

The house was described as "a story and a half high with a porch across the front," in spite of a full-page illustration showing it as a complete two-story building, which it was.

It is most interesting to read these lines in the narrative:

"When we arrived after the Mormons had left the island the house was in good repair. My father and mother occupied it two years, being the first ones to live in it after Strang's death."

That the "house was in good repair" is quite understandable. It was only six years old and "solidly built!" Perhaps Mrs. Williams meant the Gentiles agreed not to burn it down or harm the building in any way. To whom did the Whitney's pay rent for two years occupancy?

The Whitney's, according to Mrs. Williams, "were obliged to leave or become Mormons."

Forced removal of the Gentiles was never attempted. A population count on Beaver in 1854 showed a total of 2,608 inhabitants, about 10 times what it is today. Of this number, it may be estimated that over 200 were Gentiles. Nearly two years after the census, 2,600 Mormons were driven into exile. The increase in population during the 20 odd months after the census may conservatively be placed at 200. This would then leave at least a hundred Gentiles still on the island when Strang was assassinated.

The "Killing of King Strang," as narrated in "A Child of the Sea," is a gem of misinformation. One statement in particular should have caused wonderment in the mind of the author. Reference is made to the appearance of Strang on the dock at Mackinac Island the very day of his murder, to board the U.S.S. *Michigan,* bound for Beaver Island. According to Mrs. Williams, "King" Strang, who was needed for questioning about a Gentile appeal to the Government for personal protection:

> ". . . took passage on her back to the island, and as soon as landing he immediately went to his home not far distant from the dock. He was soon sent for by the officers, as they wished to consult with him about the affair."

Consultation could very well have taken place en route had this been true, and it is possible the author may have wondered why. The answer is quite simple . . . he wasn't on board. Strang would have had no desire to meet the *Michigan* at Mackinac. He didn't even know it was there. Dr. Hezekiah D. McCulloch

A Child of the Sea; and Life Among the Mormons 247

was on board, however. McCulloch represented the moving force in the assassination of Strang that evening, six hours after the vessel arrived at Beaver.

Strang was shot on June 16, 1856. His death at Voree, Wisconsin, at the home of his parents, occurred on July 9. "He was shot through the back twice, but did not die until eleven days after," wrote Mrs. Williams. Actually Strang was on Beaver Island 12 days before his safe removal to Voree where he survived an additional 11 days, making a total of 23 days.

In the "Kingdom of Saint James," Quaife recorded that Strang lived "for nearly three weeks." This error may be due to his computation of time between the issue of the *"Daily Northern Islander"* of Friday, June 20, and death. Strang, however, was shot the preceding Monday.

The "King" suffered three mortal wounds: one in the back of his head, one under his right eye and finally into his back. He was then beaten on the head and in the face by one of the assassins while several on shore, along with personnel from the U.S. Navy looked on without any interference from a smaller boat launched from the *Michigan*.

The battered body of Strang was carried to the Prindle home nearby. Mrs. Williams assumed that Dr. McCulloch dressed the wounds. Though McCulloch did not pull the triggers, he is the one who planned the murder. The surgeon of the *Michigan* examined Strang and declared recovery hopeless.

At the time of this monstrous crime, Saint James was the county seat of Emmet. Though custody of criminals was legally vested in the Sheriff, at this time Joshua L. Miller, Captain McBlair refused to even discuss it when asked to meet with the Mormons. The criminals were held on board the vessel overnight before removal to Mackinac about 10 o'clock the following morning. At Mackinac, they were imprisoned five minutes and released as heroes, never being imprisoned again and never brought to trial.

Captain McBlair exploited his rightful authority as a United States officer, in this writer's opinion, though he could back his authority with sea power. The *Michigan* was fully armed, including cannon . . . and primed for action if necessary, with a captain apparently eager to pit the might of the U.S. Navy against the "powerful" Kingdom. Shades of Gilbert and Sullivan!

Mrs. Williams presented a touching scene, depicting the Prophet begging to be taken to his wife Mary. "Take me to Mary, my true wife. I cannot die here, doctor. I want to die with my wife and children. Take me to Mary, I know she will forgive me." These, she said, were the words of Strang to Dr. McCulloch. Continuing, she narrates:

> "Dr. McCulloch had him put on a mattress, carried on board a steamboat and taken to his wife's home in Wisconsin. The death of Strang was a terrible blow to most of his people, but a relief to those that were suffering such persecutions from him. One woman at Bower's Harbor expressed great joy when she heard it, but I could not understand why she should be glad of anyone's death. She said, "I will tell you just a little of what the King made me suffer."

Dr. McCulloch, as narrated at the close of "The Saga of Beaver Island" Review, was not a man of sincerity. His removal from the Kingdom of God was warranted. He was addicted to liquor, along with other unsavory habits, including dishonesty. After the shooting of Strang, Dr. McCulloch returned to Mackinac on the *Michigan,* a criminal of sorts, having used the Navy steamer as a haven before and after revenge.

The mortally wounded Strang was removed from Beaver Island for the very simple reason that apostles feared Gentiles would return to finish him off. Though conscious to the very end of his life, except when he was taken to the Prindle home from the dock, it is nonsense that Strang "begged to be taken to his wife Mary." This bit of fiction may have originated in the Dr. Leach "A History of the Grand Traverse Region."

Mrs. Williams, at this point in her narrative, inserted 13 pages entitled "The Story Mrs. H - - - told me." (Undoubtedly Hill) Primarily, the insert is meant to add authenticity to the book by injecting a third party with identical thoughts, namely, that Strang

A Child of the Sea; and Life Among the Mormons 249

was a miserable creature bent on ruling the earth. Three additional personalities were prominently included with their personal stories: Mrs. Campbell, Lewis Whitney and a nurse who happened to be on the island when the shooting of Strang took place.

According to author Williams, Mrs. H - - - left New York state in 1847 after five years of marriage. Others included: her husband; father and mother; a deaf sister, Nellie, and her deaf-and-dumb husband, John; a sister, Sarah; and the twins of Nellie. Strang was accused of being one of the three persuading the family to migrate to the Promised Land, Beaver Island.

Disappointment was a bit overwhelming upon arrival. Near Font Lake homes were built on a "choice of a building spot." Beauty was there, but the unsettled state was disheartening to the H - - - family. They "spent a miserable winter during 1847-48," she narrated.

Only two pages were allotted to their first three years on Beaver. Perhaps it should be said two years. It is highly improbable these families went to the island in 1847. Only four families located on the island that year. In fact, only 12 families were there during the winter of 1848-49, among them the Shaws, Parmeters, Browns and the President of the tiny band of Saints and his family, Aldrich. However, Strang did undertake a summer mission east in 1846 to recruit Saints, allowing some possibility of their appearance that year.

After three years on the Island, Mrs. H - - - experienced the shocking rumors of polygamy. Mrs. Williams goes all out in her description of this tearsome farce. It was "forced" upon Mrs. H - - - because the "King" demanded it. This is not true, of course. Polygamy was a mutually satisfactory decision, and every marriage had to have some assurance it was economically possible.

A series of incidents in this story included these tear jerkers: Mrs. H - - - was threatened with a straight jacket, a bread and water diet, and suffering the cold and hunger of Beaver Island for over three weeks of wandering. During this period Mrs. H - - - experienced an attempt at drowning in Font Lake, only to be rescued at the last moment by her faithful dog, Tiger. After this attempt, Tiger continued his rare faithfulness by supplying his mistress crusts of bread and meat bones! Also during this terrifying experience, the hair of Mrs. H - - - turned from auburn to white.

Mrs. H - - - explained the complete lack of concern for her when she said:

> "by the King's orders no one had dared openly to hunt for me or give me aid in any way, claiming that was the way to subdue an unruly spirit. It was told me that he who once had been my loved husband never made an effort to find me, nor even my own father and mother. Strang called all this 'Divine Revelation.' Oh, he was more cruel than the grave to me."

Not long after this, Mr. H--- shot faithful Tiger dead.

> "Then I was roused. All the demons in me came to the surface. I could not keep quiet any longer. I got well as fast as possible and caused the King and Mr. H - - - all the trouble I could."

One remarkable episode in the life of Mrs. H - - - is, if true, worthy of attention and praise. It may, however, be a complete hoax. She spent a winter with Nellie and children at Charlevoix where they nearly "starved before spring came." The following act of mercy, if factual, covered at least 21 miles on frozen Lake Michigan.

> "The snow was very deep and ice heavy in the lake. The latter part of March teams came over from Beaver Island on the ice, bringing us provisions. This was not done by any of Strang's orders."

Mrs. H - - - concluded her story in these character-revealing words: "Now do you wonder I am glad of Strang's death?"

A brief episode, entitled "The Nurse's Story" has every evidence toward fiction, either from the nurse or from the mind of Mrs. Williams. Much of it leans toward sentimental duplication of her own chronicle in which she recorded, "Take me to Mary, my true wife."

"Four days after he was wounded he was carried on board

A Child of the Sea; and Life Among the Mormons 251

the steamer." If this line were true, Strang would have spent eight days aboard the *Louisville* in the harbor. Obviously, it is not true. This fact alone is enough to brand the story a complete hoax.

According to Mrs. Williams, Alexander Wentworth was "a fine looking and intelligent man, very quiet in his manner." This may have been true, but it does not alter the fact he was one of the assassins of Strang. His return appearance on board the *Michigan* at Saint James 10 days after the assassination created suspicion of trouble ahead, if the mortally wounded Strang was not removed to a place of safety. With young Wentworth were his partners in crime, Thomas Bedford and Dr. McCulloch.

If Wentworth "boarded with us for several weeks," the Williams' boarding house gave aid and comfort to a murderer. This young man acted as a fishing and hunting guide to other boarders. Commenting on the crime he and Bedford were guilty of, and never brought to trial for, Wentworth is supposed to have said:

> "I have never yet regretted what I did. The Mormon life was bad, and there was no good in it as far as I can see and I would not live it over again for anything."

On July 27, 1832, at age 19, Strang penned the following lines in his diary. They are worthy of studied meditation in view of his own violent death.

> "From my infancy I have been taught that mankind was totally depraved, and my own observation and experience have demonstrated that the heart of man is an impure fountain from which bitter waters are perpetually flowing. I have long been persuaded that the depravity of man originated in his unnatural habits and when I first made the discovery I firmly believed that I had also found a cure: that if the depravity of man originated in his unnatural habits, a return to those which are natural would effect a cure; that though the cure might be slow yet it would be certain and invariable. All this I still believe, but what are our natural habits?
>
> "I have searched and searched in vain. The question is yet

unsurmountable, and so far as I know or in all probability ever can know, vice, misery, and wretchedness; gold, monarchy and murder; kings, priests, and parasites are man's perpetual associates. My heart sickens at the thought, and my soul shrinks with horror at the idea, and I wish that I had not been born."

"The Kingdom of Saint James: A Narrative of the Mormons"

By: Dr Milo M. Quaife

When Michigan History Magazine reviewed the Milo Quaife narrative about the Strangite Mormons in the summer number of 1930, they rightfully referred to Dr. Quaife as a combination good story teller and historical scholar.

How right they were! "The Kingdom of Saint James," published by Yale University Press in 1930, while not error free, is certainly the most authoritative and scholarly work yet published about James J. Strang and his Beaver Island Mormon Kingdom of God.

In comparison, "The King Strang Story," while attempting to be completely factual, may be subject to more critical comments by knowledgeable historians and the public in general. However, the writer is convinced that the human side of James Strang can survive every severe critical analysis by any individual who cares to pursue it. His life has been analyzed to the satisfaction of the present writer, obviously.

Dr. Quaife was guilty of one regrettable error in "The Kingdom," pointed out justifiably by a grandson of the Prophet, Mark A. Strang. A discussion of this error may be found in the review of "The Diary of James J. Strang."

Two errors involving names are corrected in their proper place in other reviews. General George Miller was called "Sheriff" in commenting on those at the death bed of Strang. James Phineas Strang, the father of Hazel Strang McCardell, was erroneously recorded as James J. Strang, Jr., when listing him as the son of Sarah Wright and "King" Strang.

A great compliment to Quaife is the brevity of this review. Throughout "The King Strang Story," it has been the intention of the writer to give credit to this great historian by frequent use of his name. The importance of "The Kingdom of Saint James" as a dependable source of factual information cannot be ignored. No serious study can be made of Strang's unique personality without the aid of his monumental documented narrative.

Except for the misapplication of a word clearly called attention to by Mark Strang, "The Kingdom" is a gem of impartial truth and a thorough understanding of the problems faced by James Strang.

"Crown of Glory: The Life of James J. Strang, Moses of the Mormons"

By: O. W. Riegel

Many authors writing story-like versions of previously published historical works lean on earlier historians for benefit of their research. This is clearly true of O. W. Riegel, who narrated "Crown of Glory," published by Yale University Press in 1935.

Riegel relied heavily on Quaife and his scholarly work, "The Kingdom of Saint James." In compiling "The King Strang Story," reference to the work of Dr. Quaife became invaluable, especially when composing the Reviews, a rather unique method of presenting the facts about James Strang.

"The Kingdom" had been published only five years before Yale University Press produced the Riegel narrative. It may be assumed that Quaife was more than mildly surprised at its publication. Still, it is a completely different style and may even be considered the more popular format, as Michigan History Magazine indicated in its review of "Crown of Glory" in the Spring and Summer, 1936 edition.

The very unfortunate error made by Quaife also impressed Riegel. Not realizing Quaife had made the error, Riegel gave great prominence to it by writing the following paragraph immediately preceding the chapter he chose to call "The Mad Diciples:"

> "In a less inspired man the fruit of victory might have turned to dust in his mouth. In Strang, it whetted the appetite. Somewhere ahead in the obscure shadows of his destiny lay a victory that would transcend meanness and poverty. Patience, patience ... "All that I profess to know is that I am *'eager'* and mankind are frail": the discovery of his youth surged into his consciousness with renewed force as he gazed with half-closed eyes upon the congregation. The fire of an indominable will ran through his frame. It seemed to him as though the souls of men lay like frail microcosms in the hollow of his hand."

If "Crown of Glory" enthusiasts judged the motives of Strang as evil from that single paragraph, as indeed Riegel appears to convey, nothing could be further from the truth. The correct word *'ignorant'*, changes the meaning completely.

Author Riegel dwells bombastically on the metallic Voree plates. These were dug from the "hill in the east of Walworth, against the White River in Voree" on September 13, 1845, and were the result of a claimed God-given January revelation

Crown of Glory

promising sacred records to his Saints. Nonsense or not, Strang exhibited the inscribed plates as evidence of his prophetic succession. Quaife and Riegel believed the removal of a second set from Wisconsin soil the "capstone of Strang's prophetic career."

The following quote from "Crown of Glory" invites critical comment. Correction must be considered justified because circumstances of the unearthing demand it, whether the inscriptions are judged genuine or fraudulent.

> "The hieroglyphics presumably were made by one Rajah Manchore of Vorito who indulged in such verbal dissipations as 'I an ensign there will set up,' and 'There bones in the death shade toward the sun's rising are covered.' The sense of the last paragraph, where the Rajah said that 'The forerunner men shall kill, but a mighty prophet there shall dwell.' Joseph Smith and James J. Strang were obviously the heroes of the fable.
>
> "This preposterous Asiatic, the Rajah Manchore of Vorito, was the strangest figure in all Mormon literature. Turbaned, exhaling an exotic perfume of the Orient, the Rajah stalked the rude Wisconsin frontier like an apparition out of the Thousand and One Nights, made his single speech, and departed forever."

Although the figure Riegel chose to call a "preposterous Asiatic" may be considered a hoax in the eyes of unbelievers, his mystical existence should at least be recognized by a correct spelling of his name — Rajah Manchou. Recent church publications spell his name incorrectly also. It is spelled "Manchou" in the pre-Beaver Island church newspapers published by Strang in 1846-1849.

Quaife first used the name incorrectly when he wrote:

> "Whatever this translation may have signified to the faithful, to the unbeliever it presents a strange jumble of unintelligible nonsense. The inscription purports to be the record of 'Rajah Manchore of Vorito.' With this single appearance, 'Rajah Manchore' vanishes from the stage of human history."

There is nothing in Strangite literature indicating Manchou made a speech, or appeared bodily, for that matter. It is true his name made a dramatic appearance as recorder of the Voree plates. Numerous references to him appeared for years in the Gospel Herald.

H. P. Brown inserted this personal observation in the Gospel Herald September 21, 1848:

> "Early in the fall of 1845 (October) I went to Voree to investigate the claims of brother Strang to the First Presidency of the church. It was just after he had found the plates. He showed me the plates, his writings on the subjects, Joseph's letter (of Appointment), and the revelations which he had received, and the translation that he had made of part of the record of Rajah Manchou of Vorito."

A news item appearing in the November 9, 1848, Gospel Herald discloses information capable of sparking a concerted effort on the part of present day Strangites toward an important material acquisition for the church archives, if a search has not already been made:

> "A block from the roots of the tree under which the plates of Rajah Manchou were obtained was laid in the wall of the Tower on the Hill of Promise by J. W. Archer, chief mason and Gilbert Watson, chief stone cutter, the 31st of October. It is placed in a wall of stone masonry three feet thick, and is in the southeastern range between the third window from the eastern approach and the next door, and at the level of the top of the door. Immediately above it is a case of archives."

An editorial comment sent to the Herald from Racine, Wisconsin, by Strang, while on his April, 1849, trip to Beaver Island, not only reveals a personal reference to the plates of Manchou, but an interesting evaluation of truth:

> "Today several gentlemen, both citizens and strangers, called on me to make inquiries concerning the plates of Manchou and Mormonism in general. Some listened with much intent and interest, and appeared to feel that they heard the truth.

"Yes, truth, simply told, is all powerful. It is most eloquent preaching. Embellishments and long arguments are useless. It is the simple truth, adorned with its own native beauties, that works deep, lasting conviction."

These references to the correct spelling of Rajah Manchou brings to mind the large 1861 two-volume English translation of the Jules Remy "Journey to Great-Salt-Lake City," published at London. This massive Mormon work was published primarily to offset overloaded misrepresentations of other published works. Yet, a very inconspicuous error eliminated the name James Strang from the translation entirely by using the name J. STRONG! Any reader accepting Remy as authoritative might never be aware that James Strang was the most vigorous unsuccessful claimant to the prophetic office of Joseph Smith. Even in error, the name appeared only once.

O. W. Riegel's "Crown of Glory" may be considered accurate in a broad sense and essentially follows historical facts. The dramatic embellishments throughout do little for a true historian. For those not objecting to having their history romanticized and less factual, it is more entertaining, perhaps.

"The Diary of James J. Strang"
Deciphered, transcribed, introduced and annotated by Mark A. Strang, a grandson

It is unusual to review a book by first discussing its end papers. However, the end papers in the Mark Strang "Diary of James J. Strang" are very significant and thoughtfully used.

The historic design is one page from the manuscript diary now in the Coe Collection, Yale University Library. Part of this particular page was recorded on March 21, 1832, when Strang was 19 years of age. One word clearly shown in the reproduction was mistranscribed by Milo Quaife in his "Kingdom of Saint James." It has influenced, in the words of Mark Strang, "later writers to arrive at distorted opinions of Strang's character."

This is very true. Quaife transposed the word "ignorant" and wrote the word "eager" in its place. Though a seemingly unimportant transposition by such a remarkably accurate historian, it has caused no end of unwarranted and unfriendly character judging by many writers. The sentence as used by Quaife reads:

> "In the last year I have learned all I profess to know. That is, that I am *eager* and mankind are frail, and I do not half know that: — nevertheless I shall act upon it for time to come for my own benefit."

The correct word "ignorant" changes the meaning completely and enhances a truer image of Strang. Perhaps this knowledge will alter the thinking of many historians who have failed to research Strang thoroughly.

More than anything in life, Strang wanted to serve humanity honorably. Strang did everything in his power to prove himself a worthy citizen, even in polygamy. His life may have been one of non-conformity, but he harmed no one knowingly, and dared to be individualistic.

The published "Diary" is a product of Michigan State University Press. Sixty-two pages of this very pleasing volume are allocated to the diary and notations. The book includes an excellent Foreword by Russel B. Nye, MSU Pulitzer Prize-winning historian. The Bibliography of source material, the notations and the Introduction were all written by Mark A. Strang and comprise one-third of the volume.

Every collection of Strang material should include this "Diary." The value, of course, is in the interpreted private cipher not found in Quaife, nor anywhere else to completeness.

Readers may be curious as to the method used by Mark

[cipher text]

The debating school [...] will given up, but I mean to try to revive it [...] There is one established in [Prescottville?]

March 21st Birthday. I am 19 years old and am yet no more than a common farmer. 'Tis too bad. I ought to have been a member of Assembly or a Brigadier General before this time if I am ever to rival [cipher] which I have [cipher]

In the last year I have learned all that I profess to know, That is, that I am ignorant and mankind are frail, and I do not half know that; nevertheless I shall act upon it for time to come for my own benefit

April 22d Time passes on very agreeably but with but little profit I am at a loss what to do: sometimes I think of going into the

COURTESY OF YALE UNIVERSITY LIBRARY

TYPICAL PAGE FROM THE DIARY OF JAMES STRANG

Much of this is in Strang's cipher. All of it was recorded between his eighteenth and twenty-third birthdays. Mark A. Strang deciphered these pages to complete his book, 'The Diary of James J. Strang.'

Strang in deciphering the code young "Jesse" Strang devised to keep prying eyes from some of his confidential thoughts. His private cipher was first recorded on May 29, 1831, at which time he was in his late teens. The final entry was on May 29, 1836, on the fifth anniversary of its inception. The only reasonable explanation for not having written beyond is because he had filled the book and money was too scarce to buy another.

Mark Strang sent the following note in longhand on January 5, 1964, being admittedly too weak to use a typewriter because of a recent illness:

> "I had large photostats made of the pages of the original Diary now held by Yale University.
>
> "Knowing the letter (e) is the most used in the English language, I carefully picked out the character used most in Strang's Diary and labeled it (e). Then I selected the shortest word containing that character and then selected other characters which together with (e) made a word — like "the." That gave me T and H. Then I found other words in the Diary containing the three known characters and filled the new word in with other characters in the Diary. Each time I was able to make out a word in English I learned other characters. By that method, long and tedious, I found a character corresponding to every letter in the alphabet. Thus I constructed a key to the Strang cypher.
>
> "Later I got a key from Yale University that some person unknown to me had worked out. The two keys helped me with the transcription.
>
> "As you can imagine this entailed a great deal of careful work. I am sure that my translation and transcription in the book is accurate and reliable."

The explanation of his decipher was written four days after his 80th birthday, January 1, 1964. Mr. Strang had just endured a severe six-months illness. On January 28, 1964, his first typed letter in many months commented on his health. Among other things, he said he was improving beyond doctor's expectations.

FROM SNAPSHOT, FEB. 1964

MARK A. STRANG AND WIFE GERTRUDE

Mark Strang was a Long Beach, California banker, before his death in 1965. 'The Diary of James J. Strang,' published by Michigan State University Press, represents one of his efforts in honoring his famous grandfather.

During the years of research on "grandfather Strang," Mark Strang gave much credit to Stanley L. Johnston of Lansing, an influential member of one faction of the existing Strangite Church. The present writer has also accepted the generosity of time and counsel from Mr. Johnston toward the accuracy of historical data and wishes to acknowledge this aid.

In April of 1964, Mark Strang spoke of his great concern for Gertrude, his wife. Her advanced age at 90 was becoming a problem of care in their home. Regarding the necessity of taking her to a convalescent hospital, Mr. Strang wrote:

> "It was quite a blow to me to let her go. We had never been separated for as much as a week in our sixty-one years of marriage."

Mark Strang and his wife concluded their long life within two months of each other during the summer of 1965, having lived, in his own words, "a full and good life."

Exposing this bit of personal family history honors the memory of this fine gentleman who is responsible for giving additional insight into the premanhood development of James Strang. Of the Diary and his famous grandfather, Mark Strang said:

> "The idea of exposing a man's private thoughts poses a complex problem in ethics and propriety. Each reader will condemn or applaud this exposure, according to his own code. ... Some readers will seek and find items upon which to base additional unsavory criticism. Some will read for entertainment alone. Some will take special pleasure in, and perhaps gain wisdom from, the reports of intimate experiences which were never intended for eyes other than his own."

The following letter is a "first reaction" to the manuscript of "The Diary" before publication. It was sent to Mark Strang by his talented sister, Hazel Strang McCardell. This letter is most interesting for two reasons; First, she has always been a serious student of her grandfather Strang; In addition, she typed this immediate reply during an evening she was busy

The Diary of James J. Strang

preparing a motor trip to Banff with her author-husband, William H. McCardell.

"As a labor of love it is probably without parallel. Your prose writing, though unimaginative, is excellent. Your command of English shows wide literary education.

"The Diary", like the Bible, is interpreted to mean whatever the interpreter desires it to mean so your comments must of necessity be discounted to a certain extent.

"I have not so far grasped the necessity or benefit to be derived from deciphering and making public the innermost phases of his experiences. (So far as you are concerned it is a wonderful piece of work and commendable, but does it serve Grandfather any good purpose?) That he benefitted from his experiences "using these as guide posts" is common to us all. What a sorry plight we would be in if we did not use our experiences as "guide posts." Perhaps when I read it again I will understand but at present the reason for deciphering and making public, escapes me.

"What I am trying to say is that you have done a great service in making this diary available to those like myself who really care and yearn for truth. The diary without comment stands for itself — a monument to a man who rose above poverty, prejudice and ignorance. For the public who never did want the truth, your interpretation is no doubt necessary. To me it is marvelous as is, but I must confess, Mark, that it only emphasizes the futility I have encountered in trying to get at the truth in this complex personality.

"One should read the diary first, then turn to the beginning and read straight through. You have done a great service. Whether you have done what you set out to do is something else again.

"I still cannot reconcile this wonderful man with the Mormon polygamist.

"Doesn't it appear to you that in leading his people he was really a dictator? The principle of dictatorship is wrong. None of us want what is good for us crammed down our throats. Gradual eternal individual development is the only path to lasting progress.

"From the beginning, outstanding intellects have endeavored

to hasten our progress. (Our grandfather). Necessary elements seen so clearly by our intellectual giants, elude the ordinary mentally lax individual who none the less resents the simple solutions handed him on a platter. There is no substitute for individual development which, of course, may be hastened to a certain extent by the patient prodding of the mental giant. Unfortunately, the element of time enters so strongly into the calculations of the genius as to cancel out or nearly so, the immense opportunity he holds for the advancement of the multitudes. Antagonism and resentment by the many for the few makes progress almost impossible. Whether we are blessed or cursed by our genius is questionable.

"With the intellectual background and knowledge and understanding your manuscript has brought out, how could he entertain for one moment Mormonism and dictatorship? To me this is and always has been the missing link and I had hoped that you would bridge the gap."

This long letter also revealed Hazel McCardell's personal evaluation of grandfather Strang:

"As I read I am given a tantalizing glimpse of innumerable facets of his character, any one of which seems to me worthy of exploration.

"To me "The Diary," although deep and profound, barely touches the surface of the potentialities of this great man. This is no end in itself, but rather a foundation upon which future writers can build. It is unfortunate that up to now, no writer has chosen any but the sensational side-lights for portrayal. This has been useful, of course, for quick sale, but intelligent people have the right to factual information on the life and character of this great American.

"There are those who do not use their talents; there are those who abuse their talents; there are those who use their talents, but make mistakes.

"My father admonished me thus: 'If you have done no wrong you have done nothing PERIOD.' His code was to live so that knowingly he would harm no human being, and die the same way. 'Just as I am, without one plea.'

"A great son of a great father, I try to emulate these unparalleled fore-bearers."

The Diary of James J. Strang

These personal observations were graciously permitted for publication by Hazel McCardell, as have numerous other statements. Her comments throughout "The King Strang Story" cover the seven years this volume has been in preparation. In 1965, one of her letters included this paragraph:

> "I am proud of my heritage and sensitive of unjustifiable criticism or sensationalism. Grandfather's so-called Mormonism must be related to the times, religious fervor and evangelism. Mentally he was far beyond his time. He was a good man and helped all those who came in contact with him. His sex interlude? How many office wives are there, and always have been? Elvira was lovely and willing. Who are we to criticize him for that? Why dwell upon it? At least he legalized all of his women and children. How many of us do that today? I love and respect him deeply and have always hoped that some of his genius would "rub off" on me, or some one of us."

The footnote on page (x) of "The Diary" reads: "Sarah, Strang's fourth wife, raised her son under another name in fear of retaliation against them by Utah Mormons."

It may be appropriate to elaborate on this factual statement by quoting another letter from Mrs. McCardell, dated October 30, 1965:

> "It is true my father was brought up as James P. Wing, for he was very small when my grandmother married Dr. Wing. It was not until he married my mother (Lydia Houtz) that he took his rightful name of Strang. He courted mother as "Jim Wing." It is true that both he and my grandmother would have been persecuted had any of the Utah Mormons known of their Strang heritage. When my mother and father were married they were BOTH disenchanted with the Mormons and so made no bones of the fact that they were Strangs. In fact I think they were both itching for a fight against Mormonism as it was practiced, for they had both suffered under polygamy."

Note: Grandfather Houtz is honored in Springville, Utah, by a water fountain featuring a bronze plaque, for his industrial contributions throughout the State.

During his short life, James Strang clearly gave evidence that he was not a happy man. Mark Strang dedicated "The Diary" to his grandfather, "who devoted his life to the service of mankind and declared: 'Of all that dwell on earth, God has made me the most happy.'" Though Strang did make this statement, it was far from true, as evidenced by the depressing problems he experienced during his entire career.

It is unfair to question a statement in the following review of "The Saga of Beaver Island", without commenting on an equally wrong impression on the identical subject, written for "The Diary" by Russel Nye. The Foreword has previously been called excellent. However, it is certain Mr. Nye will understand and agree if the following is clarified.

The line in question is the second on page (viii) reading: "He (Strang) possessed a letter from Joseph Smith which, if the wording were properly construed, seemed to name Strang as his successor." As stated in the "Saga" review, if this line were true, then Strang indeed was meant to head the Mormon Church after the unfortunate murder of Smith. Mark Strang also quotes from this purported letter, failing to question authenticity.

This "Letter of Appointment" has never been judged genuine or false. There is nothing the Strangite Church would rather prove, than this letter be accepted as "genuine." At least one member of the Church is still attempting, through modern techniques, to accomplish such proof. Strang displayed this letter first at a Mormon conference at Florence, Michigan.

On page (ix), the "Saga" states: "In 1850 Strang was elected to the Michigan State Legislature . . ." The correct date is 1852. On this same page, it would be more correct to say, "In the spring of 1856 *four* Beaver residents conspired against their leader." This is perhaps an unimportant point, but Mr. Nye failed to include the photographer, "Dr." Atkyn, along with Dr. McCulloch, Thomas Bedford and Alexander Wentworth. "Dr." Atkyn was one of the conspirators.

"After the tragic affair at Nauvoo . . ." should read "Carthage." Joseph Smith and his brother Hyrum, were taken to Carthage from Nauvoo and placed in jail. Although they were promised safety by Governor Ford, it was a promise not kept. Both were murdered by a Gentile mob.

Mark Strang deserves much credit for his effort in deciphering the James Strang diary, a copy of which is in this writer's library inscribed, "For one who respects the name of my grandfather."

"The Saga of Beaver Island"

By: Margaret Cronyn and John Kenny

This small paper-covered volume represents the combined efforts of Margaret Cronyn and John Kenny. They have written "The Saga of Beaver Island" in a style not unlike the Reader's Digest. In it may be found an interesting, briefly-written compilation of 106 small pages gleaned from 40 or more books, magazines and newspapers. "The Saga" was published in 1958 by Braun and Brumfield, Inc., Ann Arbor, Michigan. The authors, while not always accurate and often leaving readers with wrong impressions, have written an interesting "Saga."

In the first chapter of "The Saga," page 17, the authors speak of "19th century" French explorers. This is an unintentional error, obviously, since a difference of 200 years places early explorers and Prophet Strang in the same century.

The civilized history of Beaver Island may conceivably be dated earlier than 1608. This would place it before Quebec was settled by Champlain and earlier than our own Pilgrim

Fathers. The recorded discovery of Lake Michigan was in 1634. At this time, Nicolet was looking for a passageway to the Indies.

Who were the first colonists on Beaver? The rune stone, claimed to have been found near Kensington, Minnesota, might indicate the Vikings went that far. However, since there is no documented proof that the rune stone is genuine, Vikings on Beaver must be considered only a possibility.

There is a good probability that the very famous explorer, Baron Lahontan, born in France about 1667, stopped at Beaver Island. This French soldier went to Canada in 1683 and glorified himself fighting the English and the Iroquois. He eventually was appointed the King's lieutenant in Newfoundland and Acadia. Lahontan was also an influential map maker and author.

More than a century ago, there was evidence of 200-year-old plotted gardens on Beaver Island. When some of the trees were cut down at that time, they were found to be over 200 years old. Having grown on banked areas indicates the soil was previously cleared of trees. This is proof some early civilized explorers settled here. In 1658, a group of French fur traders sailed to the Wisconsin shores, returning two years later with about 60 canoes filled with valuable furs. It is possible they stopped at the Beavers on their way back.

In 1703, Lahontan published his famous "Nouveaux Voyages," in which he described prisoners captured by northern Minnesota Indians. Some of these prisoners did escape, and may have gone to the Beavers. During Lahontan's 1683 voyage to the St. Peters River in Minnesota, the Baron recorded passing this group of islands.

Many major discoveries claimed by Lahontan must be accepted with reservation. Although an experienced explorer, he also was an experienced liar. Passing the Beaver group was no great claim, and is easily believable. However, his claim of discovering a non-existent river to the Pacific reveals much

The Saga of Beaver Island

about his career. In addition, he was a great plagiarist, starting his career an exile from France.

The following comments on "The Saga of Beaver Island" are confined to the three Mormon Chapters.

This page-by-page review will begin by saying Strang was not the "leader of a renegade offshoot." It is inaccurate to say James Strang refused to go West with Brigham Young, settling in Voree, instead. As a Mormon, Strang had never been anywhere but Voree from the start. This means that "his small community's departure from the old Mormon capital of Nauvoo" is incorrect. Nor was this an "old Mormon capital." This city in Illinois was founded only five years before Smith's assassination.

The authors state that Strang and four of his companions made their first trip to Beaver in 1846. While this date is only one year earlier than the actual survey, dates are often of great historic importance.

On page 35, it is unfair to call Strang a "dangerous demagogue, ambitious (he was) and cunning; obviously a man without scruples."

Strang was unjustly maligned, especially by the newspapers. But sensationalism sold papers and this is what publishers were after, of course. Circulation at the expense of fact also had a bed partner, the opposing political party. Newspapers were very biased in early pioneer days. Most of them backed a favorite political party and championed a favorite cause.

The authors narrated: "He started immediately to remove the Gentiles." This statement is untrue. The Mormons lived on Beaver nine years without any attempt whatever to remove the Gentile population. This was not their island exclusively, and they knew it. They would have enjoyed this monopoly, however. The guilt of violence on Beaver Island rests solidly on the shoulders of the Gentiles. The Saints were peace-loving people.

This brings to mind a question once asked the writer by his very good friend, Hazel Strang McCardell: "Could you be a descendant of the Irish who drove the Saints off Beaver Island?" It was a genuine pleasure to answer "no" to this query, asked in jest. Or was it in jest?

This grand woman is in accord on all major controversies pertaining to Strang as a man. Her brother, Mark A. Strang, as previously noted, produced for recorded history "The Diary of James J. Strang," completely deciphered.

Without realizing it, the authors of "The Saga" have written a most important historical conclusion in one of the most ordinary looking sentences in the Mormon Chapters. This line is on page 37 and reads:

> "In a letter dated just a week before his martyrdom Joseph Smith had written Strang that he was seriously considering his suggested spot." (Voree, Wisconsin.)

The remarkable conclusion here is the assertion Joseph Smith actually wrote the letter. Ever since this purported letter was claimed to have been received at the Burlington post office from Nauvoo, Illinois, June 17, 1844, it has remained one of the most disputed communications in Mormon history. If, as the authors state, Smith wrote the letter, then, without question, James Strang was indeed appointed ruler of the church and Brigham Young merely a usurper.

"Strang's wicked forgery," as Young called the "Letter of Appointment," is now in the Coe Collection of Western Americana at the Yale University Library. A few historians have given their opinion of authenticity, but most, like Milo Quaife, have been reluctant to champion either side. All seem to agree the signature bears no resemblance to that of Smith. All agree the letter was handprinted by someone other than the Prophet, a practice not uncommon in pre-typewriter days.

On Page 39 of "The Saga" is found this sentence: "He openly declared he intended to appropriate Beaver Island for the Mormons." The word "appropriate" is argumentative. It sounds very much like taking something forcibly. If the authors intend that, a wrong assumption has been made.

In the Strang "Memorial to the President and to the Congress," it clearly indicated they wished to acquire the islands by honest means.

"The harbor thereafter was known as Paradise Bay." This line appears on Page 41. This harbor, one of the finest on the Great Lakes, was called Paradise Bay many years before the Mormons arrived. In fact, they changed the name to "Saint James Harbor."

It would be an excellent decision if the present name, "Beaver Harbor," reverted back to "Paradise Bay" or to "Saint James Harbor." Not only would it be factual, it would add a bit of lustre to the island in the form of historical correctness. Since tourists are now number one in economic importance to the island, it would be appropriate to glamorize the harbor by using the correct original name.

On this same page, the River Jordan is mentioned. It should be pointed out that State of Michigan maps, the Beaver Island Civic Association map and the historical marker locate the River Jordan incorrectly, flowing into Sand Bay. On county maps, readers may readily note a stream from Lake Gennesareth into Cable's Bay. This is the correct River Jordan. Lake Gennesareth has also been known as Galilee.

Several times, the name Elvira "Fields" appears in "The Saga," and rightfully it should. She was quite a woman and this is meant to be complimentary. Her name, however, was Field. Her impersonation name, "Charlie Douglass", has an interesting family connection. One polygamous son was named after this temporarily assumed name.

The Cronyn and Kenny statement on page 45, "as scheduled on July 8 in the roofless, circular tabernacle," should read, "in the 40' x 80' tabernacle."

Some reporters have said that Saints removed the seats for dancing. The seats were securely fastened to the floor, eliminating such a possibility. This unfinished tabernacle was burned by the Gentile mob during the forced exodus.

"Cold blooded murder" and "no longer clean" are unwarranted conclusions to the Thomas and Samuel Bennett affair. An excellent description of this shooting, written by Milo Quaife, appears in this volume.

Of the many serious charges brought against Strang and his Saints, no major crime of any description was ever proven in a court of law. This includes "systematic robbery" on page 50.

The following paragraph is quoted in full from page 47:

> "Governor Bingham of Michigan and President Fillmore both hesitated to take the political risk of angering Mormon voters. There was much correspondence between Washington and Michigan until finally it was decided that Brigham Young was too far West to bother with, while Strang was closer by and could be checked."

This, indeed, gives the impression Brighamite Mormons were also a serious concern of Governor Bingham and President Fillmore. Such was not the case. In fact, Brigham Young was appointed Governor of Utah in 1850 by President Fillmore, an office he held until 1858.

"Beaver Island—1851" explains this situation clearly. No tie existed between Brighamite Mormons and Strangite Mormons. While Strangites use the Book of Mormon, they also use the Book of the Law of the Lord. Both are supplemental to sacred writings of the Bible. At one time it was suggested that Strang publish a revised edition of the Book of Mormon on Beaver Island!

Page 47 also included this indifferent statement:

> "The main charge (at Detroit), that of his men attacking a mail train in broad daylight, didn't stand up in court due to the lack of witnesses."

This is the type of legal hocus-pocus reporting that gave the Kingdom a bad name. With regret, it is necessary to spoil this mental image of a steam train being boarded by desperate Mormons rifling a mail car. No such rail service existed even on the mainland until 1872. It was installed first at Traverse City, but never on Beaver Island, of course. A small

The Saga of Beaver Island

engine on iron rails operated on the island while virgin timber was available.

The date of this alleged "mail train" robbery was February 18, 1851. The location was in front of the Indian Village on Garden Island, a few miles north and east of Beaver . . . on the ice! At the trial in Detroit, it was brought out that for eight additional months after this date, the Mormons were still entrusted with the mail by the same Assistant Postmaster making the charge. Cross-examination branded his testimony false. The "mail train" was a dog sledge!

One of the early mail carriers in the Grand Traverse Region was William Davenport of Mackinac Island. He made a trip to Grand Traverse every two weeks with a toboggan sledge drawn by four large hound dogs. An overnight stop was always made at Beaver Island. Mail accumulated at Croton, south of Grand Traverse, during the winter of 1851, was taken north by a six-or-eight-harnessed dog sledge. Twenty snow-shoed Indians, each with a dog, first made a single path on which the "mail train" could travel the 120 miles to Grand Traverse with comparative ease.

The title of Chapter 4 is "Gentile Trials and Mormon Errors." There are many false stories in this Chapter, having been researched from earlier prejudicial reports. These stories are typical anti-Mormon fabrications of that period.

Most of the hierarchy and members of the original Mormon Church created their own friction wherever they went. The Strangite Saints have been compared unfairly with the Brighamites. The Brigham Young brand of Mormonism created many of its own violent situations by being continually too possessive. Their religious zeal was carried to extremes. They were an industrious people, to be sure, and commendably thrifty, but these two compliments did not combine favorably with their bombastic energy. Their unlimited boldness caused great resentment everywhere. Persecution was often a blessing in disguise to their leaders, however.

It has been stated that the Strangite Mormons were as different from Brighamite Mormons as Brighamites were from Catholicism. The real reason for resentment toward the Strangites appears to have been a carry-over from the fierce hatred of Mormons in general, escalated during the early years of violence in Ohio, Missouri and Illinois.

All Gentiles on Beaver Island, in fact in all of Michilimackinac, admittedly had a difficult adjustment in welcoming these "strangers." However, most of the burden of dissension rests upon their shoulders in spite of it. It must be noted clearly that constant conflict between Ohio, Missouri and Illinois Gentiles and the Joseph Smith Mormons prior to 1844, was a great burden to the Beaver Mormons who moved to the island in large numbers during 1849 and 1850.

There is no reason why permanent public condemnation of their leader, James Jesse Strang, should go into history books solely because little concerted effort has been made toward the truth about his Kingdom. Fictional stories have been repeated for more than 120 years. Much has been said and written against Strang; not enough has been said and written in his defense.

In the "Saga," at the beginning of Chapter 4, it is unfortunate that kindness on the part of Strang, that of feeding the Indians on Garden Island, was considered an act of selfishness. The authors merely state Indians were needed as cohorts, instead of giving Strang credit for offering food as an act of human mercy. Simply stated, the Book of Mormon is primarily a unique history of the American Indian Tribes.

Strang was genuinely sympathetic toward the Indians on Beaver and the surrounding islands. His was a sincere feeling of mercy . . . but he also had a desire to convert them.

When Strangites, in desperation, protected themselves from assault by fighting back, they were branded aggressors. When performing acts of mercy, they were labeled opportunists. Saints were misjudged constantly.

Defending major actions of Beaver Island Mormons

The Saga of Beaver Island

toward the Gentiles of Michilimackinac, reverses 120 years of misplaced justice. Mormons were not only mistreated and ridiculed by these Gentiles, they were ridiculed unmercifully in the nation's press. Many completely biased, historically inaccurate stories are still being published every year.

The authors of "The Saga" are perhaps victims of previous inaccurate and prejudicial historians. Their description and concern for Indians on Garden Island indicates they are. The authors may not have realized that Mormonism, from its inception, embraced Indians as descendants of the lost tribes of Israel. This makes a great deal of difference in stating, as they did on page 51, "Should there be any hostilities he (Strang) would prefer the Indians to be on his side rather than on that of the Gentiles." Further, one of the first considerations before going to Beaver was "to give the Indians the arts of civilization." Since this was an announced purpose, and a claimed God-given revelation, the authors did Strang an injustice, labeling him an "opportunist."

On page 52, a most unfair statement was made: "Flogging at the whipping post was the penalty for non-payment of these tithes." There were only three Mormon whippings on Beaver Island. The crime for adultery, Mormon justice could not carry out, obviously, since this provided the death penalty. The culprits were whipped publicly, instead. The penalty for delinquent tithing was only a guilty conscience.

Regarding the battle of Pine River (Charlevoix) narrated in "The Saga," it is worthwhile to compare the excellent Quaife account for an accurate version of this struggle for justice. A reading of Quaife will clear up who the guilty were. The authors misjudged who fired the accidental shot. The Quaife version is a moving, sympathetic narration, allowing each reader to judge for himself just who the culprits were. Strang summarized that the time had come when he and his Saints would not be judged fairly regarding any conflict.

When reading about Dr. H. D. McCulloch on page 58, keep in mind he was the major influence behind the murder of "King" Strang. While Thomas Bedford despised the "King" because of the whipping for his act of adultery and, in his own mind, had reason to hate, it is important to understand he was a weak character. He was a Mormon only because his wife was. Some of these traits apply to Alexander Wentworth, another assassin. Strang cannot be said to have been killed by two "disgruntled Mormons."

Dr. McCulloch influenced Bedford and Wentworth to assassinate the Prophet. Dr. McCulloch had been cut off from the Church because of a long series of complaints against him. These included drinking, dishonesty and in many instances, unlawful behavior.

McCulloch was one of many who were given every opportunity by Strang to become a respected Saint. In 1856, however, McCulloch planned the death of "King" Strang, assisted by still another scoundrel, "Dr." Atkyn, the photographer on Beaver Island. What he was doctor of, no one seems to know.

There were very few "disgruntled Mormons" on Beaver Island.

"The City of the Saints"

By: Sir Richard Burton

Sir Richard Francis Burton, English historian, died October 20, 1890, 30 years after completing one of the most noteworthy contributions toward Gentile understanding of the Mormons. His uncanny, oftentimes humorous, insight into early public and family life in Salt Lake City encouraged belief that his observations were totally unbiased.

The City of the Saints

Today, the Joseph Smith-Brigham Young chronicle is valued highly as honest disclosure of a 19th century controversial subject, one rather difficult to be unbiased about prior to the period "The City of the Saints" was compiled and published.

The Richard Burton self-assigned 1860 exploration to the Valley of the Great Salt Lake remains historically important today because it is fully realized how well equipped he was mentally to record such a study without prejudice.

A study of polygamic living was his prime reason for the exploration. Burton had great ability to dissociate himself from any religious influence, not being concerned that the world must accept his atheistic leanings. Seventeen years after "The City of the Saints" was published, Burton still ignored the existence of a soul and spirit.

A mania for comparing multiple marriages throughout the world prompted the journey to the Mecca of the Mormons. In Africa and the Near East, where some native chiefs had as many as 300 wives, Burton had already studied plural customs, always at close range accomplished by devious means. In Arabia, he disguised himself as a doctor. Literary friends thought it impossible to study harem life. The disguise, though inviting danger, satisfied his curiosity, and he succeeded in his great desire to record their plural customs.

According to Burton, monogamous matrimony in mid-19th century English homes brewed far more domestic troubles than polygamy in the Utah Territory. Feminine attitude in Utah never suffered his description of English women. Comparison of educated English women with improved female Mormons revealed the former considered themselves "Creation's Cream."

Early Mormon teachings forbid sensuality in marriage, except for insuring progeny. "Strictly forbidden" is a more exact description. In males, at least, Burton thought "positive necessity" created the need for polygamy. This was not contrary to God's will, however, since, according to Mormon beliefs, the Omnipotent recognized the need and relieved the situation by revelation to insure numbers of progeny.

It is fascinating to note that the polygamic revelation received by Joseph Smith on July 13, 1843, was revealed on that date to only three followers. Brigham Young did not announce the celestial law until August 29, 1852. Polygamy was practiced secretly at Nauvoo prior to the announcement, however, and Strang supported it secretly as early as 1849, advocating it openly in July, 1850.

A rather humorous observation, described by Burton after his long stage coach trip to Salt Lake City, is worthy of mention. One woman on the coach wore Amelia Bloomer "Bloomers," the costume "King" Strang advised for his female members. Burton described this woman as "an uncouth being." In a short time, she was simply called "The Bloomer." His humorous observation revealed a woman "whose only expression was sullen insolence . . . with haunches which would be admired only in venison."

When quite young and in the service of the Crown, Burton was one to create situations appearing serious but often to mystify friends. On one occasion, associated subject-wise to Mormon history involved him as author of a fake grammar. It is known that American Indians were thought by Joseph Smith to be descendants of the Lost Ten Tribes of Israel. The fake grammar, compiled by Burton during his seven-year service in the Indian Army, was humorously compiled to prove that members of an obscure tribe in the north were actually the Lost Ten Tribes. Historian Fawn M. Brodie states that Burton very nearly published the grammar as authentic!

Although Burton was a distinguished author and considered eccentric, he oftentimes was a prevaricator, especially in his younger days. His genuine mania for getting at the truth of man's thoughts and behavior brought him the respect of 19th century scholars around the world.

Nevertheless, the woman Sir Richard loved for many years and finally married when he was 39, deceived his

The City of the Saints

memory by insisting to the world that Burton had become a Catholic before he died. Perhaps she proved it untrue when she destroyed great quantities of his manuscripts after his death. Burton, at 69, was still ignoring the existence of soul and spirit, in spite of the effort his wife expended to the contrary in "The Life of Captain Sir Richard F. Burton."

Had the manuscripts survived, Isabel Arundell Burton would have been unable to mould the memory of her husband to her own wished-for image. While giving the world a false religious image of Burton, destruction of the unpublished manuscripts also deprived the literary world of many great works, according to those who were allowed to examine them.

Had Isabel Burton continued her passionate devotion to husband Richard, as evidenced in her Diary before marriage, the world would have benefitted further from his unique talents . . .

> "Whatever the world may condemn in him of lawless actions or strong opinions, whatever he is to the world, he is perfect to me; and I would not have him otherwise than he is — except in spiritual matters. This point troubles me."

As previously stated, this point troubled Isabel Burton enough to announce, falsely, he had been converted to Catholicism. In this, she partially failed, fortunately. Much of Burton's value and charm was his intense desire to be Richard Burton.

"The City of the Saints, and Across the Rocky Mountains to California" is an engrossing book. Not only is it considered by many historians the best book about the Mormons published in the 19th century, including biographer Fawn Brodie, no 20th century author has equalled its importance as a monumental detailed description of their Utah formative history.

An excellent edition of "The City of the Saints" edited by Mrs. Brodie was published by Alfred A. Knof in 1963. As one of their Classic Commentaries on America's Past, this edition is highly recommended to those interested in the phenomena of the Mormon movement in the United States.

Index

Acadians, expulsion of Mormons from Beaver Island compared to, 3

A Child of the Sea; and Life Among the Mormons (Williams), characterized, 232-252

A History of the Grand Traverse Region (Leach), Mormon chapters characterized, 202-214

Alden, John, compared to George Adams, 137

A Moses of the Mormons (Legler), characterized, 222-226

Adams, George J., pre-Babylonian record revealed to, 38; on Smith's problems, 75; as unruly Strangite, 86-87; meets widow, after Gentile blood, cut off from Strangites, 87, 158; as lecherous charlatan, after Beaver Island, launches new career, 138-142; plans American colony at Jaffa, establishes Palestine Emigration Association, 139; failure at Jaffa, 141-142; fails in England, establishes "Church of the Messiah" in Philadelphia, 142; career at Nauvoo and Voree, 142-151; meets Heber Kimball, becomes a Mormon, 142-143; joins Strang from Cincinnati, accompanied Orson Hyde to Jerusalem, 147; denounced in England by *Millenial Star*, 149-150; as counselor to Smith and Strang, 151, 152; Strang-pampered, 155; concubine on Beaver, crowns Strang 'King' of Saints, 156; has Strang arrested, as witness in Detroit trial, 157

Adams, Mrs. George, on Beaver, 87; quarrels with husband, 140; third party to deeds at Jaffa, 141

Aldrich, Marvin, spirits among the Beaver Island Saints revealed, as President of first settlement on Beaver, 66

Amann, Peter, aid acknowledged, XVIII; as author of *Prophet in Zion: The Saga of George J. Adams*, XVIII; exposes George Adams, 137, 138

Ancient and Modern Michilimackinac, (see illustration and evaluation of on 103)

Assassination of the King (Swift), characterized, 227-232

Astor, John Jacob, as fur trader in Michilimackinac, buys North-West Co., 45, 47

Atkyn, Dr. ——, as conspirator to murder Strang, 110; as Beaver Island photographer, Quaife describes, 111, 224, 225

Baker, John, Elvira Field marries, 121, 122

Bates, George C., prosecutes Saints, 89; as author of *The Beaver Island Prophet*, as U.S. District Attorney prosecuting Strang, 203

Beaver Island, explorers and Indians at, 4; description of, 43, 44, 49; Strang investigates, first named, surveyed by Farmer, 44; as trading post, 45; Strang describes, 52-57; first Mormon migration to, 65; Aldrich comments on spirits, 66; opened for entry, Kings Highway built on, 68; crime on, *Destroying Angels,* 206; population of in 1854, 246; Lahontan may have passed near, 268

Beaver Island and its Mormon Kingdom (Charles Strang), characterized, 215-222

Bedford, Thomas, assassin of Strang, 110, 211, 217, 218; adulterer, 205, 206, 210; whipping, 208, 210; Williams narrates story of, 238

Bennett, Dr. John C., Mormon career at Nauvoo, 143-146; suggests moving bodies of Joseph and Hyrum to Voree, 143; career at Voree, 143-151; medical career, suggests a University of Wisconsin to Strang, birth, 145; writes exposé of Smith, 145, 146; expelled by Nauvoo Church, 146; joins Strang from Cincinnati, 146, 147; denounced by *Millenial Star*, 149; accuses Saints, expelled from Voree Church, 151; at Plymouth, 234; at Cincinnati, 235

Bennett, Samuel, defies authority, 212; wounded, 213

Bennett, Thomas, defies authority, 212; killed, Quaife narrates, Saints innocent, 213; Williams' version of killing, 239, 240

Bevan, Anna Strang, writes vignette on rescue of Strang portrait, 189-190

Bibliography of the Church of Jesus Christ of Latter-day Saints (Strangite), characterized, Morgan publisher of, 185

Blakeslee, James, describes Beaver conditions and needs, 60-63

Bonner, John, removes door from Strang *Castle*, 82

Bonner, Patrick, aid acknowledged, XVIII, 82

Bonner, Rose, aid acknowledged, XVIII

Book of the Law of the Lord, characterized by Quaife, 70; as Strangite bible, 99, 272

Book of Mormon, characterized, XIX; birth of, XXII, 205; Smith as author of, 39; Strang asked to publish on Beaver Island, 272

Briggs, Jason W., share in founding Reorganized Church, 81

Brodie, Fawn M., *The City of the Saints* characterized, 279

Brooks, Lester, debates Orson Hyde, 149

Brown, David, relations with Thomas Bedford, 205, 206, 210

Brown, Gurdon, as disturbed Saint, 66

Burlington, (Wis.), as center of Mormonism, 24

Burton, Sir Richard, Mormons of Great Salt Lake researched to explore polygamy, 277; Utah and English women compared, 277; wife's opinion of, 279

Carthage, Miller vision of Smith assassination, 160; city in Illinois Joseph and Hyrum Smith jailed and murdered, 267

Castle, Strang's home on Beaver Island, destruction of, remains of, 225 (see illustration on 83)

Chambers, William, leads posse against Bennetts, 212, 213

Cheboygan County, Strang leader in organizing, 100

Chicago, Mormon refugees at, 184, 185

Charlevoix (see Pine River)

Chidester, Edward, marked for murder, 92; at death of Strang, 200; last person spoken to by Strang, 200

Churchill, Winston, letter from Franklin Roosevelt to, XIX

City of James (Saint James), first conference of Saints on Beaver Island, 68

Clarke Historical Library, has Strang collection, 203

Communism, abandoned on Beaver, 66, 67

Counterfeiting, Saints accused of, 89

Crown of Glory (Riegel), characterized, 253-257

Daily Northern Islander, as second northern Michigan newspaper, 208; assassination issue, 209

Davenport, William, mail taken to Beaver Island in 1851 by, 273

Deam, Henry H., share in founding

Index 283

Reorganized Church, 81
Destroying Angels, Saints accused as, 206; Martin-Scott story, 207, 208
Detroit, trial of Strang at, 89, 90, 157
Douglas, Stephen A., favors prosecution of Saints, 89
"Douglass, Charlie J.," pseudonym for Elvira Field, 78, 79, 215, 271
Dress, styles prescribed by Strang, 200, 201
Drew, Mrs. Barbara, eulogy to George Miller, 175; aid acknowledged, 178
Drummond Township, Strang leader in organizing, 100

Edison, Thomas, admires C. Latham Sholes, 36
Edwards, Thomas, with Miller in Kentucky when Smith was murdered, 160
Ellison, Chester, aid acknowledged, XVIII
Emmett County, Beaver Island attached to, 99; Strang leader in organizing, 100; census of 1854, 246
Everitt, Charles P., finds Book of Mormon sections published before 1830, 204

Farmer, John, surveys Beaver, 44
Field, Elvira, union with Strang, 76; masquerades as "Charlie J. Douglass," 78, 79; career, 118-122; children, 121, 215, 220, 221
Fillmore, Millard, seeks nomination at Baltimore, needs Beaver Island votes, 88, 89; appoints Brigham Young as Governor of Utah, 272
Foster, Nathan, appeals to Saints to gather at Beaver Island, 63, 64

Galille, biblical name in 1852 for largest lake on Beaver Island, later called Gennesareth, 271
Garden of Peace, translation of Voree, 160
Graham, L. D., as Voree visitor, describes Voree plates, Strang's environment, 34-37
Graham, Samuel, marked for murder, 92; assaulted, 212
Grand Traverse County, Strang leader in completing organization of, 100
Granger, Sheriff ———, aids in forming posse to hunt Mormons, 93, 94; refuses warrant in Graham assault, 212
Green, John P., as City Marshall of Nauvoo, dies mysteriously, 153
Greig, James M., Jr., as draftsman at Troy, Beaver Island, 44 (see end papers)
Greig, Judge James M., as minister and judge, 44, 45; marked for murder, 92
Gurley, Zenas H., share in founding Reorganized Church, 81

Hale, Emma, marries Joseph Smith, XXIII; leaves Church, marries a Gentile, XXIII
Hanna, Archibald, aid acknowledged, XVII, XVIII
Harris, Martin, as witness of Mormon plates, as follower of Strang, debates Orson Hyde and John Taylor in England, 149
Hickey, Lorenzo Dow, opposes polygamy, accuses Strang, 79, 80; embraces polygamy, 80; as presiding high priest, 179; in battle of Pine River, 245; at deathbed of Strang, 200
Hickey, Mrs. Lorenzo, as gossiper on Beaver Island, creates disturbance, 79
Hill, Ludlow P., in Strang's *Ancient and Modern Michilimackinac* as member of a disaffected family
Holy Bible, characterized by Quaife, 70; as used by Mormons, 272
Holy Island, Church conference on, 110
Houtz, Lydia, marries James Phineas Strang, as mother of Hazel Strang McCardell, children listed, 128

Hyde, Orson, accompanies George Adams to Palestine, 147; warns Mormons against Strang, 148; refuses to debate Strang, 149; debates less able Brooks and Harris in England, 149

Indians, in Beaver Island archipelago, 4, 47, 56, 65, 274; as Lost Ten Tribes of Israel, 278
"Indian whiskey," defined, 47; Strang presses for liquor law enforcement, 102
Irvine, Hon. J. P., as member of state legislature, 95

Jefferson, Thomas, George Miller talks with, a possibility, 170
Johnson, Andrew, receives George Adams, 140
Johnston, Mrs. Stanley L., aid acknowledged, 178
Johnston, Stanley L., aid acknowledged, XVIII, 262
Judicial, Strang leader in completing organization in Michigan, 100

Kingdom of God on Earth, feared annihilation of in 1851, 96, 97; Dr. Leach summarizes, 214
Kirtland stake, becomes Strangite possession, 149

Laban, plates of, compared to Voree Plates, 34; as basis for *Book of the Law of the Lord*, description of, Strang publishes translation, 38; revelation announced, 69, 70; Quaife evaluates, 70; Sarah comments on, 71
Lamanites, Mormon name for Indians
Lansing *State Journal*, compliments Strang, 102
Legler, Henry E., writes first serious study of Strangite movement, 222
LeMaistre, Charlotte, as wife of Daniel Streing, flees France, 4, 7-9 (see *The Strang Ancestry*, 3-22)
Letter of Appointment, claimed by Strang, 28; at Yale University Library, 28; characterized, 148, 166, 266, 270 (see illustration on XXV)
Lincoln, Abraham, Strang compared to, Volney influences, 26, 235
Liverpool *Millenial Star*, organ of the Twelve in England, denounces Strang, 149, 150
Louis XIV, Edict of Nantes revoked by, Streings flee France, 4, 8, 9
Louisville, removes Strang from Beaver after assassination, 125, 174, 251
Luther, Martin, polygamy permitted by, 79

Mackinac, center of fur trade, 45; attempted arrest of Strang as legislator, 101; authorities arrest Strang, display legal ignorance, 88; defies liquor law enforcement, Quaife summarizes defiance, 102, 103; Strang arrested, burlesque trial, 157; haven for assassins, 211; farce in Bennett killing, 213
Marks, William, as Strang advocate, XXIII; distrusts Brigham Young, as president of Nauvoo stake, signer of Strang memorial to U.S. government, joins Strangites, 153
McCardell, Hazel Strang, aid acknowledged, XVIII; Strang's wives evaluated, XXVII; career, 127-131; wearing of bloomers evaluated, 201; evaluates *The Diary of James Strang*, 263, 264; grandfather Strang characterized, 264, 265; father and mother characterized, polygamy and mormonism, 265; author kidded by, 269, 270
McCulloch, Dr. Hezekia D., on murder list, 92; assassin of Strang, characterized, 110, 111, 247, 248, 275, 276
McKenzie, A. K., George Adams' financial angel, joins Palestine emigration, 139-141; launches *Nellie Chapin*, 140

Index

McKinley, Peter, owns trading post on Beaver Island, cousin of William McKinley, in Michigan Legislature, 48; description of by Williams, 237

McNutt, Betsy, marries Strang, 85; career, 122-125; children, 124, 125

Memorial to U.S. government, requests Beaver archipelago, 68, 69

Michigan, State of, legal authorities fail to prosecute Gentiles, 96; fail to prosecute assassins of Strang, 251

Michigan, Steamer, role in assassination of Strang, 113, 210, 211, 246; returns to Beaver Island with assassins, 251

Michigan Legislature, Strang record in, 100

Miller, Bishop George, as Bishop of Mormon Church, starts for Beaver Island, 159, 163; vision and dreams about Smith and Strang, 160-162; belief in Strang, 159, 162, 163; arrives at Voree, as author of *Letters of George Miller,* 163; appointed Bishop, forms Masonic Lodge at Nauvoo, 164; Brigham Young and, 164-167; expected Joseph Jr. to succeed father, 167; diary of, 167-171; diary of rescued by Dr. Mills, 172; describes trip to Beaver Island, 173, 174; at deathbed of Strang, 200

Miller, George, Jr., eulogized, 163, 164; in California, 175

Miller, Sheriff Joshua L., (Mormon Sheriff at Beaver Island) shown evidence of father's murder, 94; with father on journey from Texas, 159; refused jurisdiction of assassins, 211

Milliken, Governor William G., aid acknowledged, XVIII

Mills, Dr. H. W., eulogizes George Miller, Jr. in *De Tal Palo Tal Astilla,* 163, 164

Moore, E. J., Strang arrives at Beaver Island at dock of, 57; attempted arrest of, 95, 96

Morgan, Dale L., as publisher of Strangite Bibliography, 185

Morgan, bark, rescues Mormons in battle of Pine River, 106, 242

Mormon Church (Reorganized), legal original body of, organizers of, XXVI, 201

Mormon Church (Smith), origin, XIX, XX; Masonic members, XX; swore "eternal enmity" toward United States, 39; persecution of members, 86; name-calling by members, 150; gentiles at conflict with members of, 274

Mormon Church (Strang), abandons communal policy, 66; present status of, dissension in, 187

Mount Pisgah, characterized, 43 (claimed location of counterfeiting)

Mummies and papyrus, one of Smith's amusing impostures, 143

Murder, Joseph Smith, XXII; James Strang, 113, 183; Young Joseph a possible victim, 167; Saints accused of, 207, 213

Nauvoo, Mormon capital in Illinois, 267, 269

New Rochelle, ancestors of Strang promote settlement of, 4 (see *The Strang Ancestry)*

New York Genealogical and Biographical Record, Strang genealogy currently being researched and compiled by Charles A. Strange being published in, 3

Newspapers, American, persecution of Strang in, 90, 242 (see illustration on 243)

Northern Islander, opinion of State in prosecuting Mormon murder, 90, 91; reveals Mormons hunted like wild beasts, 93, 96; reports Strang courageous, 97; calls Pine River settlement band of vagabonds, 104; suggests prison terms for guilty at Battle of Pine River, 106; defies gentile position in Cheboygan and Grand Traverse counties, 109; plot to murder Strang public knowledge, 113; as first northern Michigan newspaper, 208

Nye, Russel B., writes Foreword for *The Diary of James J. Strang,* 258, 266

O'Donnell, Richard, assaults Graham, 212; attempts escape, arrested, 213

O'Malley, Judge Charles M., orders arrest of Strang, 93, 94

O'Neal, William B., interest in George Miller as University of Virginia carpenter, 169

Page, Ebenezer, leads first Mormons to settle on Beaver, opinion of Indians sent to Voree, 65

Page, John E., advocate of Strang, XXIII; comments on Polygamy, edits Voree Herald, 74; denounced in England by *Millenial Star,* 149; distrusts Brigham Young, 153

Palestine Emigration Association, characterized, 139-141

Parmeter, Levi, heads religious outbreak on Beaver Island with Samuel Shaw and Gurdon Brown, 66

Partridge, Bishop Edward, replaced by Bishop Miller in Nauvoo, 164

Perce, Benjamin C., Mormon brother-in-law of Strang, migrates to Wisconsin, 24; journey to Nauvoo with Strang, 27

Perce, Mary, marries Strang, 24; opposes church policies, 82; career, 117, 118

Pine River, battle of, narrated by Quaife, 104-107; narrated by Williams, 241-245; Williams claims seven killed, 244; participants in, 245

Pine River (Charlevoix), fishermen resist law enforcement and tax assessment at, 104; Mormon expansion at, 108

Polygamy, characterized, as Brigham Young cornerstone, 73; Joseph Smith practices, Strang opposes, 74; as source of conflict, 78, 79; on Beaver Island, 81, 84, 85, 205, 218, 219; Williams assesses, 241

Post, Warren, plates of Laban characterized by, 38

Quaife, Milo M., aid acknowledged, XVIII; Voree plates evaluated, 37; *Book of the Law of the Lord* characterized, 70; opinion of Strang marriage to Elvira Field, 76, 77; battle of Pine River narrated, 104-107; theorizes United States agency assisted in plot to assassinate Strang, 113; reveals amusing imposture of Joseph Smith, 143; reveals curious reflection on James Strang, 150; Saints innocent in Bennett killing, 213; evaluates Legler, 222, 224; misquotes word from Strang diary, 253; author compliments, 252, 253

Riegel, O. W., battle of Pine River narrated, 106, 107; error by Quaife influences, 254; author compliments, 257

Rigdon, Sidney, at baptismal of Strang at Nauvoo, 118

River Jordan, on Beaver Island, 43, 44; location of in error, 44, 271

Roosevelt, Franklin, appraises and credits Mormons, XIX

Seward, Sec. of State, assists George Adams, 139

Shaw, Samuel, as disturbed Saint, 66

Sholes, C. Latham, characterizes Voree plates, Edison admires, 34

Smith, Aaron, journey to Nauvoo with brother Moses and Strang, 118

Smith, Joseph, had visions, XX; as projector of Mormonism, XXII, 205; opinion of as a youth, Harper editor judges murder of, XXIII; as author of Book of Mor-

Index

mon, admires Strang, authorizes Mormon Stake at Voree, 39; seeks Presidency of United States, 88; murdered, 148; Jesus answers first prayer of, 205

Smith, Lucy, reveals murder attempt on son Joseph as a youth, XX; advocates Strang as successor, 153

Smith, Joseph, Jr. ("Young Joseph"), Brigham Young and Heber Kimball hint killing of, implied as successor to father, 167

Smith, Moses, as brother-in-law of Mary Perce, as Mormon, at Burlington, 24; journey to Nauvoo with brother Aaron and Strang, 27

Smith, William, (brother of Joseph) advocate of Strang, XXIII, 153

Somers, Rev. A. N., as author of *An American King,* eulogizes Eugenia Strang, 132

Southern California Historical Society, as publisher of *The Letters of George Miller,* 163, 164; honors George Miller, Jr., 164; hears Dr. H. W. Mills' dissertation on George Miller, Jr., 172

Spalding, Rev. Solomon, as author of *Manuscript Found,* XXII

Spiritual Wifery, *see* Polygamy

State Archives, Michigan Historical Commission, aid acknowledged, XVIII; (end papers)

Strang, Eugenia, describes polygamy on Beaver Island, 84; as child of Phoebe Wright, as "Princess Eugenia," 132

Strang, James Jesse, advises love of husband, XXVII; as infant, 23; recalls babyhood, early life, in Burlington, 24; compared to Volney, 26; baptized by Joseph Smith, 27; affirms presence of God, 29-33; eulogy to Smith, 40; urges Saints to gather at Beaver, 58-60; opposes Polygamy, 74, 75; reverses opposition to Polygamy, 75; marries Elvira Field, 76; persecuted in nation's press, 85; marked for murder, 92; on old governments, 92; on new governments, 93; as member of state legislature, 99-102; record in legislature, 100; presses for liquor law enforcement, 102; earns right to enforce laws, 109, 110; plot to assassinate, 113; (see Wingfield Watson assassination story on 183), claims omnipotent appointment and *Letter of Appointment* to head Mormon church, 148; denounced in England by *Millenial Star,* 149, 150; memorial to U.S. government, 153; marital career, 117-134; assassination 177, 183, 211; death, burial, reburial, 199, 200, 211; writes of the depravity of man, 251, 252; public condemnation of unwarranted, 274

Strang, John, writes early genealogy, 4; statements challenged, 4

Strang, Mark A., Strang's religion defined by, 29; method of deciphering Strang diary revealed, 260; private thoughts of Strang disclosed by deciphering, 262

Strange, Charles A., aid acknowledged, XVIII; challenges John Strang manuscript, 4; documents *The Strangs of Westchester,* 5

Streing, Daniel, flees France, 4, 7-9; as promoter of New Rochelle, 11, 12 (see *The Strang Ancestry,* 3-22)

Tabernacle, house of worship in Beaver Island Kingdom, 271

The City of the Saints (Sir Richard Burton), characterized, 276-280; recommended reading on Mormon phenomena in United States, 279, 280

The Diary of James J. Strang (Mark Strang), characterized, 257-267

The King of Beaver Island (Backus), characterized, 199-201

The Kingdom of Saint James (Quaife), characterized, 252, 253

The Saga of Beaver Island (Cronyn and Kenny), characterized, 267-276

The Star in the East, Baltimore organ of Strangites, 154, 155 (see illustration on 154)

Throe, Mrs. Guy, aid acknowledged, 178

Tithing, prescribed at Beaver Island, 66, 67

Treason, Saints accused of, 89, 90, 157

Trial at Detroit, great concern to Beaver Island kingdom, 96

Turkey, government of, refuses transfer of Jaffa acreage to Adams, 140, 141

United States, in theory, supports private plot to assassinate Strang, 113; State Department assists repatriation of Adams' Saints from Palestine, 141, 142

University of Virginia, George Miller carpenter at, 169, 170

Urim and Thummin, Strang claims miraculous use of, 34; characterized, first bible reference to, 39

Utah Mormon Whiskey, defined, 47

Volney, Constatine, influences Strang with *Ruins,* projects virtues needing elevation, 26; career, 26, 27

Voree, Strang's *Garden of Peace,* 28, 34, 37, 51, 57, 65, 67, 269

Voree *Herald,* Official organ of Voree stake (see illustration on 31)

Voree Plates, unearthed, described, compared to plates of Laban, 34; (see illustration on 35)

Watson, Wingfield, on Strang virility, 75; on polygamy, 85; autobiography, 178-186; at assassination of Strang, 177, 183, 211; describes exodus after assassination, 183-186; location between 1856-1866, as publisher of the *Wingfield Watson Pamphlets,* 185; as presiding high priest of Strangite Church, 185-187; with Milo Quaife on Beaver, death, 187; Thomas Bennett killing, 212, 213

Webster, Daniel, shuns decision about arrest of Strang, 89

Wentworth, Alexander, assassin of Strang, 110, 211; in battle of Pine River, 245

Wessen, Ernest J., *The Star in the East* characterized, 155

Whig Party, concerned about Beaver Island voting in Presidential election, 88

Whiskey Point, as rendezvous of fisherman, 86

Whitney, Clark, with George Miller on journey from Austin, Texas, 159

Whitney, Newell, as trustee-in-trust for Mormon property, 159

Wight, Lyman, Texas colony, 161; trouble with Bishop Miller, 161

Williams, Elizabeth Whitney, as author of popular, but highly unreliable, *A Child of the Sea; and Life Among the Mormons,* 232-252

Wisconsin, University of, suggested by John C. Bennett, 145

Wright, Phoebe, marries Strang, 131, career, 131, 132; children, 132

Wing, Dr. ——, marries Sarah Wright (see career, 125-131)

Wright, Sarah, marries Strang, 84, 125; career, 84, 125-131; children, 127; grandchildren, 128

Yale University Library, aid acknowledged, XVIII, 191, 224; end papers of *The Diary* from Strang collection at, 257; Letter of Appointment at, 270

Young, Brigham, importance of isolation, XXIV; claims Strang a fraud, 28; boasts about naming a future U.S. President, 39; accused of false interpretation of scripture, as usurper of Smith regime,

145; opposes Strang, 147, 148; purges church leaders, 150, 151; Bishop Miller and, 164-167; wives, 219; Legler evaluates, 226; *Letter of Appointment* evaluated by, 270; appointed Governor of Utah, 272; resentment of, 273

Photocomposition on Mergenthaler Super-Quick by *Central Trade Plant of Grand Rapids,* Grand Rapids, Michigan.

Lithographed by *Lansing Lithographers,* Lansing, Michigan.

Paper used 70*-Laid finish Creme Blanc manufactured by *French Paper Company,* Niles, Michigan.

Bookbinding by *John H. Dekker & Sons,* Grand Rapids, Michigan.

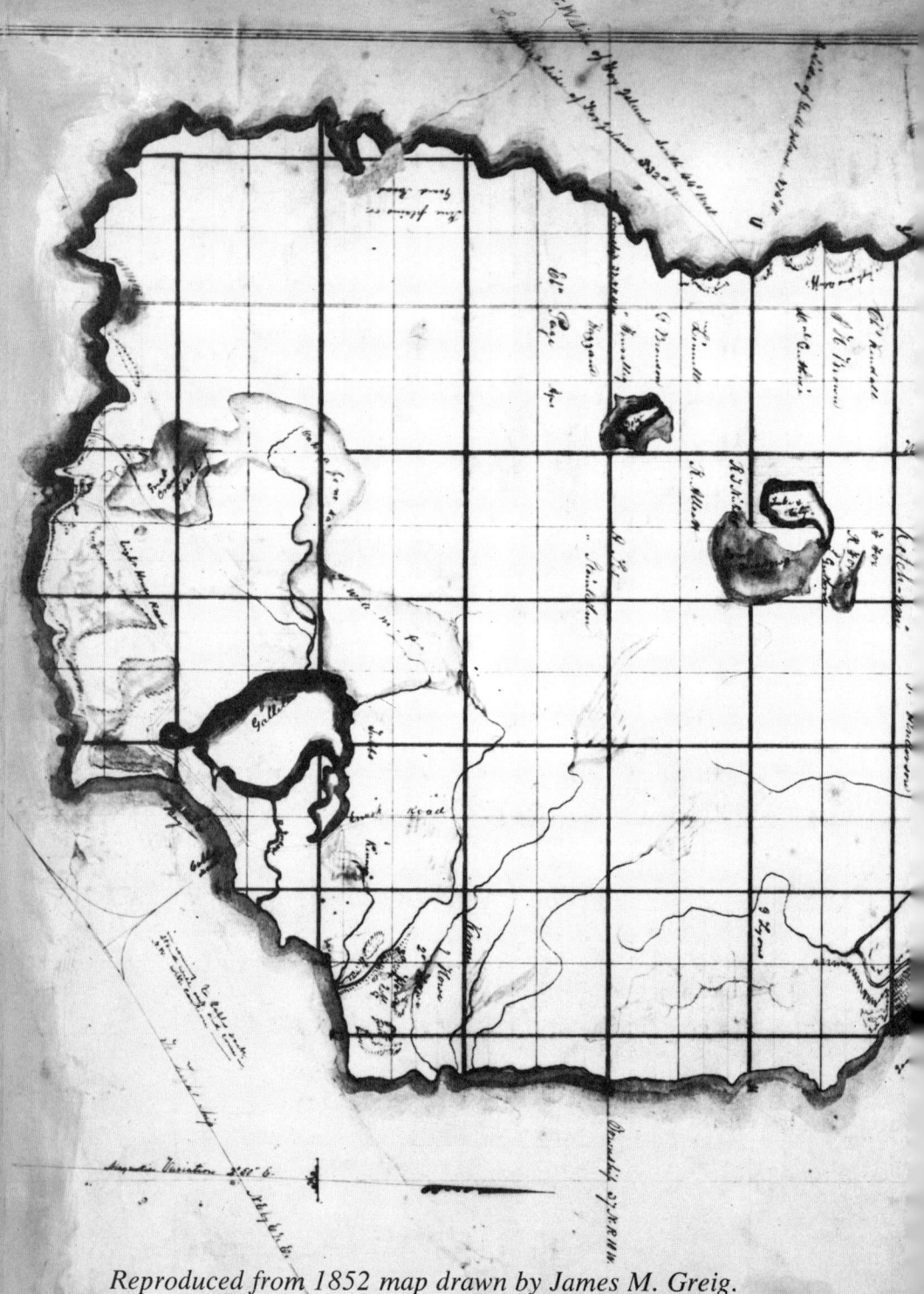

Reproduced from 1852 map drawn by James M. Greig.
Courtesy of the State Archives, Michigan Historical Commission.